THE
COMPUTER
IN THE
LANGUAGE ARTS
CURRICULUM

THE
COMPUTER
IN THE
LANGUAGE ARTS
CURRICULUM

Rebecca E. King
National Center for Family Literacy

Edward L. Vockell
Purdue University Calumet

McGRAW-HILL PUBLISHING COMPANY

New York St. Louis San Francisco Auckland Bogotá
Caracas Hamburg Lisbon London Madrid Mexico
Milan Montreal New Delhi Oklahoma City Paris
San Juan São Paulo Singapore Sydney Tokyo Toronto

Mitchell Publishing, Inc.
INNOVATORS IN COMPUTER EDUCATION

55 PENNY LANE, SUITE 103   WATSONVILLE, CA 95076
(800)435-2665   IN CALIFORNIA (408)724-0195

Mitchell **McGraw-Hill**
55 Penny Lane
Watsonville, CA 95076

The Computer in the Language Arts Curriculum

1 2 3 4 5 6 7 8 9 0 DOH DOH 9 0 9 8 7 6 5 4 3 2 1

ISBN 0-07-557460-8

The sponsoring editor was James Hill.
The production supervisor was Pat Moran.
The cover design was by Juan Vargas.
The production management was by Bookman Productions.
R. R. Donnelley & Sons Company was the printer and binder.

Library of Congress Catalog Card No. 89-062067

CONTENTS

CHAPTER 10   KEYBOARDING SKILLS   205

CHAPTER 11   WHAT THE FUTURE OFFERS   225

CHAPTER 12   SOFTWARE REVIEWS   233

APPENDIX A   Glossary of Important Terms   255

APPENDIX B   Software Summaries   266

APPENDIX C   Annotated Bibliography   297

APPENDIX D   Sources for Software   303

PREFACE

This book presents an introduction to using the microcomputer in language arts instruction. It assumes no initial knowledge of computers. And although it assumes some knowledge of language arts theories, it also summarizes those theories when necessary for the readers' understanding. This book will be useful to language arts teachers, to curriculum supervisors, and to others who are interested in integrating the computer into the language arts curriculum in order to make instruction more effective.

THE SERIES

The Computer in the Language Arts Curriculum is a companion volume to *The Computer in the Classroom* by Edward Vockell and Eileen Schwartz (1988). That book can be considered Module 1 in a series on integrating the computer into the curriculum. Designed for educators in general, it contains a discussion of educational theory applied to the computer across all areas of the curriculum. It also discusses guidelines for software and hardware selection and some programs (such as test generators and gradebooks) that are of interest to teachers in the various curricula.

The present volume is designed for language arts teachers and for curriculum directors and others interested in applying the computer to their language arts programs. While it can be regarded as Module 2 in the series, it is also designed to stand alone or to be used as a supplement to other textbooks. For example, many readers will probably use this book as a supplement in a language arts methods course.

In many cases, information that is presented in greater detail in *The Computer in the Classroom* is summarized in this book at appropriate places, and—when deemed helpful—a citation is given to the chapter in the former book where readers can find more information. In addition, some basic information (such as general guidelines for evaluating drills and a discussion of major brands of computers) is not repeated in the present book. Readers can decide for themselves whether they wish to pursue more detailed information in *The Computer in the Classroom* or in some similar book on instructional applications of microcomputers.

Other titles that serve as Module 2 in this series include the following:

- *The Computer and Higher-Order Thinking Skills*
- *The Computer in the English Curriculum*
- *The Computer in the Foreign Language Curriculum*
- *The Computer in the Mathematics Curriculum*
- *The Computer in the Reading Curriculum*
- *The Computer in the Science Curriculum*
- *The Computer in the Social Science Curriculum*

Although each of these books is designed as a companion volume to *The Computer in the Classroom*, it is not essential that you read the entire series in order to benefit from any one of them. Each book presents a complete and useful set of information to introduce educators to instructional applications of microcomputers in a particular curriculum.

THE STRUCTURE OF THIS BOOK

Chapter 1 presents a description of three models for language arts instruction in the elementary classroom and the role of the computer in each of these models. It shows that the computer can improve language arts instruction primarily by enhancing academic learning time. Chapter 2 examines a few of the general principles important in language arts instruction and shows how the computer can be integrated with these principles to teach language arts skills more effectively. The chapters that follow describe more specific applications of these principles.

Chapter 3 describes how to use the computer to create a language-rich learning environment, emphasizing classroom arrangement, lesson planning, and models for large-group, small-group, and individual instruction. Chapter 4 describes basic strategies for developing reading skills. While focusing on reading comprehension as the major goal, the chapter also discusses using the computer to promote phonics and letter and word recognition skills. Chapter 5 provides suggestions for improving speaking and listening skills with computer-related activities, including those involving computerized speech, making picture books, giving and following directions, oral reports, and collaborative projects (games, choral reading, drama, and the like). Chapter 6 discusses simulations, tutorials, and drills that support the development of vocabulary, spelling strategies, and grammar awareness. It includes activities using word processing to enhance these skills. Chapter 7 describes how to use word processing programs effectively in prewriting, writing, rewriting, and publishing. It also covers writing across the curriculum and discusses the importance of writing to the development of thinking skills.

Chapter 8 focuses on the computer in the library or media center, examining strategies for teaching basic research skills, dictionary proficiency, card catalog use, and on-line database searches. The chapter also discusses how the computer helps students select books, improve their comprehension skills, and augment their reports, at the same time that it provides instructional support to the teacher of language arts. Chapter 9 discusses tools for teachers, including using the computer to create materials for original units of instruction. It also provides a discussion of electronic gradebooks and the uses of word processors and databases for teacher tasks. Although this chapter is not presented first, it deserves special priority: our experience is that teachers who use the computer as a tool to solve their own problems are the ones who are most likely to integrate the computer effectively into their classrooms.

Chapter 10 discusses the teaching of keyboarding skills to elementary students and emphasizes the need for such skills for effective word processing. It includes a comparison of available keyboard software programs and additional activities to motivate students to practice proper methods. Chapter 11 suggests ways in which future developments in technology and its application are likely to influence the language arts curriculum.

Chapter 12 provides detailed reviews of software that illustrate effective computer applications in the language arts curriculum. In addition, the appendices supply useful supplementary material. The glossary in Appendix A defines important terms used in language arts and in instructional computing. Appendix B provides brief summaries of a large number of programs. Although these summaries are not nearly as detailed as the reviews in Chapter 12, they will enable readers to search more efficiently for good software to enrich their language arts curriculum. Appendix C contains an annotated bibliography of related readings to help educators find additional sources of information about the effective use of computers in the language arts curriculum. Finally, Appendix D lists the vendors from whom computerized language arts materials or information about them can be obtained.

In order to use computers in the language arts classroom effectively, teachers need active, hands-on experience with computers. This text cannot replace such experience. Instead, it is our hope that this book will provide an introduction and theoretical background that will render more productive the reader's personal experience with the computer in the language arts curriculum.

THE
COMPUTER
IN THE
LANGUAGE ARTS
CURRICULUM

C H A P T E R 1

THE COMPUTER IN THE LANGUAGE ARTS CURRICULUM

WHAT DO THE FOLLOWING have in common: a telephone conversation, a TV advertisement, a Garfield comic strip, and a word processing program? Answer: all four hold the interest of young people and could be used to teach language arts in a K–8 classroom. By far the most versatile of these four examples is the word processing program. For instance, by providing editing and information processing capabilities, the word processor could enhance the other three examples. This is only one of the many ways in which the computer can help students master language arts. But let's look behind the word processing program to the machine that gives it life and opens the language arts classroom to a wealth of activities.

Our grandmothers often spoke of a "machine." They would say, "Let's take the machine to the ice cream parlor." Or, "Would you like to go for a ride in the machine?" The machine of their generation drastically changed the boundaries of personal transportation. They witnessed a shift from the horse and buggy to gasoline-powered vehicles. Transportation emerged as an industry in their lifetime, creating jobs that were not even imagined previously. The industrial age prospered and much of its profits eventually depended upon Grandma's machine—the car.

We are now witnessing the emergence of another machine. This one enables us to store, retrieve, and process the vast amount of information that pours into our world daily. This new machine is becoming a necessity for the information age in which we teach and live. It is as vital a tool for our students, the young adults of the twenty-first century as was the car for the twentieth century. Grandma used the car to transport her own granddaughter to the ice cream parlor. But we as educators have only begun to see where our new machine can transport us intellectually. Our students will no doubt share stories with their grandchildren about the old days when classrooms were just beginning to realize the capabilities of the computer.

This is not a computer book, however. It is a book about teaching and learning. The computer serves a dual role in the language arts classroom: it is both an instructional tool and a medium of expression for listening, speaking, writing, and reading. Although reading is an extremely important topic, note that it is addressed only briefly in this book. Because reading is such an important topic, a separate module in this series is devoted entirely to it (see *The Computer in the Reading Curriculum* by Whitaker, Schwartz, and Vockell, 1989). This book, then, is a guide to teaching and learning language arts with the assistance of the computer. It will suggest strategies, based on sound instructional principles, for making the computer an effective part of the language arts curriculum.

LANGUAGE ARTS GOALS AND OBJECTIVES

Our communication skills—speaking, listening, writing, and reading—allow us to share the human experience. We do not wait until we enter the classroom to begin learning these skills. On the contrary, children begin to develop the ability to communicate in a passive sense perhaps even before birth, by hearing and feeling things in the womb and responding to them. By the time children attend school for the first time, their language experiences are broad. They can speak and listen, and some can read and write, without a formal curriculum bound by textbook objectives and study guides. To continue growing in language skills, children must be exposed to a continued variety of learning experiences that motivate them to explore the nature of language and its use.

To better define the term *language arts*, two experts in the field (Moffett and Wagner, 1976) have framed goal statements dealing with composition and comprehension at levels K–13. Each can branch into numerous separate statements of student goals in language arts:

1. Make language choices wisely, choosing how to express things and how to understand them (composition and comprehension).
2. Expand to the maximum the repertory of language resources to employ and to respond to—from vocabulary and punctuation, phrasing and sentence structure, to style and dialect, points of view and compositional form.
3. Extend to the maximum the fluency, facility, pleasure, and depth of speaking, listening, reading, and writing (the target activities of language learning).
4. Expand to the maximum the range, depth, and refinement of the inborn operations—classifying, generalizing, inferring, and problem solving.

The goals stated above have been and could continue to be met in varying degrees without using the computer to guide or support them. When there are materials, methods, or activities that develop particular skills more appropriately than the computer, teachers should use them. However, if a computer and a good software package can enhance the mastery of a language arts skill or concept, the computer should be used for optimum learning.

MODELS OF TEACHING LANGUAGE ARTS

Defining *language arts* within the framework of the preceding goals is not enough to satisfy the need for direction in curriculum. To present the skills, concepts, attitudes, and abilities that comprise the language arts curriculum, elementary and middle-school teachers have used multiple approaches. It is neither possible nor desirable to dictate one "correct" model that would incorporate the specific needs of all students, teachers, and classrooms. It is more useful to examine a variety of models and use each as appropriate to address the individuality of a student's learning process; to adapt to the unique presentation style of the teacher; and to incorporate the local curricular objectives.

The National Council of Teachers of English responded to the need for national direction in the language arts curriculum with *three* models (Mandel, 1980). The three paradigms—the new heritage model, the competencies model, and the process model—are each considered powerful by their advocates. The models are not mutually exclusive, and none has been proven definitively superior to the others. Each offers an approach that has been used effectively in the elementary classroom either as a pure model or in combination with aspects of the other two paradigms. Although the computer was not actively used as a tool for language arts instruction at the time these models were developed, it can easily support the philosophy of each as an instructional tool or a vehicle for expression.

The *new heritage* model is an updated version of the traditional approach that works toward the goal of using standard, edited American English. It is based on the history, values, and skills that have made it possible for our generation to learn about our culture and to continue to share that knowledge with our descendants. Evertts (1980) describes the new heritage approach as a blend of the communication skills—listening, speaking, writing, and reading—with the content of language, or more precisely, literature. It incorporates the social, personal, intellectual, and creative experiences of the learner in this process. Literature is the central focus, providing a variety of experiences through large-group discussion, small-group projects, and individual study.

Learning centers, an integral component of this first model, are a perfect setting for using the computer. The learning center may be geared to provide short-term practice dealing with a specific skill or story. Or it may be designed to provide a setting for ongoing exploration in creative writing. In either case, the computer affords a wide variety of possible activities to support the learning process and to provide motivation for the student. Examples of software especially suited to the new heritage model are shown in Figure 1.1.

The second paradigm, the *competencies* model (Mason, Lundsteen, and Martinez, 1980), is based on the behavioral studies that have found children

(a)

I WENT FOR A WALK IN THE JUNGLE. I SAW
A LION. IT DID NOT SEE ME! I WAS GLAD.

PRESS <ESC> WHEN DONE WRITING

Language Experience Recorder

Do an experience story.
Look at a story
Show story analysis.
Show cumulative word list.
Analyze a text file.
Teacher utilities menu.
Exit the program.

Use ARROW KEYS, then RETURN.

(b)

    Today we did finger
painting
next to my desk   .
First, I soaked the paper
with ████████████   .
Then, I took some globs of
paint and rubbed them
_____. My
picture looked like
_____.

        WHAT
my old shoes
a smelly skunk
a garbage truck
seventy snails
-- Type your own. --

(c)

---

1. AT THE BEGINNING OF THE STORY MRS.

WHATSIT UPSETS MRS. MURRY WHEN SHE

SAYS THE WORD _____.

     A. IT

     B. CAMAZOTZ

     C. TESSERACT

WHICH ANSWER IS CORRECT? C

            EXCELLENT!

        PRESS SPACE BAR TO CONTINUE.

(d)

Figure 1.1 The programs shown in this figure support the new heritage model ONCE UPON A TIME (Compu-Teach) (screen a), LANGUAGE EXPERIENCE RECORDER (Teacher Support Software) (screen b), and WRITER RABBIT (The Learning Company) (screen c) allow students to create their own "literature" or respond to stories they have read. Programs such as Sunburst's NEWBERY ADVENTURES: A WRINKLE IN TIME (screen d) offer a way to review main ideas and vocabulary in a private setting.

to mature in predictable, recognizable stages. Taking that concept further, the competencies model assumes that language arts skills can be broken down into components that lead to the defined skill or concept. The teacher's role is to present new concepts and skills to students at the appropriate time and in sequential increments so that they can be easily mastered. *Mastery* is a key term in the competencies model. In order to achieve mastery, a student's skill level must be properly diagnosed, activities prescribed, and learning evaluated.

Preparing materials to support this model is time-consuming for teachers. In this setting, the computer can be an effective instructional tool. New programs that diagnose, prescribe, and evaluate student performance can support the task of the classroom teacher using this model. Educators also must identify the need of slower students to "overlearn" skills toward their goal of mastery. Again, the computer can be a patient, nonjudgmental tool for repeated drill and practice, providing as much repetition as necessary. Figure 1.2 shows an example of a program especially suited for this model.

In the third design, the *process* model, the purpose is to guide learners to use language for effective communication. However, rather than a teacher-directed approach, this paradigm is a learner-generated process (Stauffer, 1980). Interaction with persons, places, and things is the basis for the child's learning. In this model, the teacher must be sensitive to each individual, aware of the cognitive level of each, and possess a high degree of patience. Modes of instruction capitalize on immediate opportunities and therefore do not fabricate a purpose for the activity. Because students are central in the initiation and direction each activity takes, they are highly motivated. This is not to say that the teacher's role is unimportant. The teacher is responsible for acknowledging the students' interest and for promoting skill development by responding with appropriate projects and activities.

The flexibility of the computer as a tool for instruction and, even more, as a medium for expression, makes it very useful in the process model. The computer is first and foremost a machine used to "process" information. Its word processing and graphics capabilities enhance the strengths of the process model. Students who without computers would be restricted by time or lack of artistic talent can use the computer as a tool to create original projects. Figure 1.3 shows an example of software especially suited to the process model.

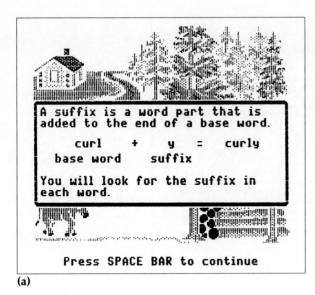

(a)

(b)

Figure 1.2 WORDS AT WORK: SUFFIX SENSE by MECC leads students through a step-by-step practice on the use of suffixes.

(c)

A fourth model for teaching language arts has appeared in classrooms since the National Council of Teachers of English first described the three original paradigms in 1980. The *whole language* model is a natural outcome of the process model in its purest form. According to Goodman, the whole language approach to language arts incorporates the following traits:

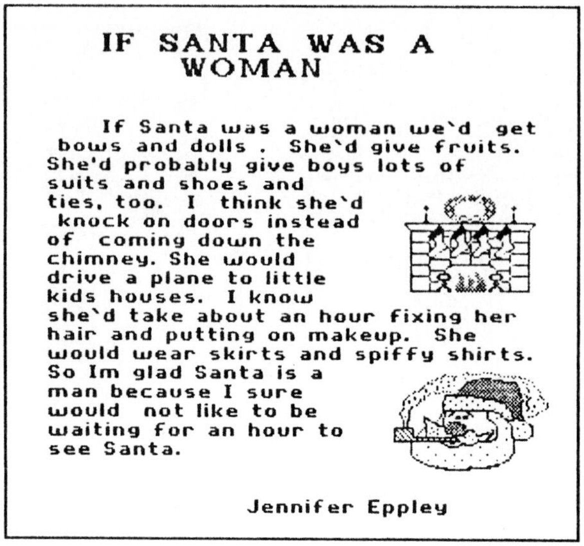

Figure 1.3 An easy-to-use program like THE CHILDREN'S WRITING AND PUBLISHING CENTER (The Learning Company) encourages students to write and illustrate their experiences.

IF SANTA WAS A WOMAN

If Santa was a woman we'd get bows and dolls . She'd give fruits. She'd probably give boys lots of suits and shoes and ties, too. I think she'd knock on doors instead of coming down the chimney. She would drive a plane to little kids houses. I know she'd take about an hour fixing her hair and putting on makeup. She would wear skirts and spiffy shirts. So Im glad Santa is a man because I sure would not like to be waiting for an hour to see Santa.

Jennifer Eppley

- Whole language learning builds around whole learners learning whole language in whole situations.

- Whole language learning assumes respect for language, for the learner, and for the teacher.

- The focus is on meaning and not on language itself, in authentic speech and literacy events.

- Learners are encouraged to take risks and invited to use language, in all its varieties, for their own purposes.

- In a whole language classroom, all the varied functions of oral and written language are appropriate and encouraged. (Goodman, 1986, p. 40)

The whole language approach is best implemented in a language-rich learning environment, like that described in Chapter 3 of this book. A teacher using the whole language approach will find the computer to be a useful tool for student expression. Literacy events mentioned in the description of the model might take the form of journals written by the students with a word processing program. Figure 1.4 illustrates journal entries on MAGIC SLATE (Sunburst).

No matter which model is used as a foundation for teaching and learning language arts skills, the computer can be employed to enhance academic learning time, as the next section of this chapter will describe.

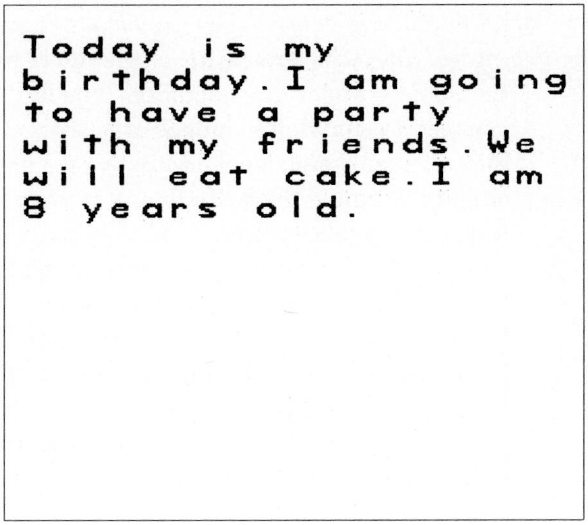

Figure 1.4 Even young children can relate their experiences through journal entries on a program such as MAGIC SLATE by Sunburst. Notice the large type available with the twenty-column version.

```
Today is my
birthday.I am going
to have a party
with my friends.We
will eat cake.I am
8 years old.
```

ACADEMIC LEARNING TIME

Academic learning time (ALT) is defined as the amount of time a student spends attending to relevant academic tasks while performing those tasks with a high rate of success (Caldwell, Huitt, and Graeber, 1982; Berliner, 1984). In any designated subject area, ALT is likely to be more strongly related to academic success than any other variable over which the teacher can exercise control. The concept of academic learning time and its relation to instructional computing is discussed in detail in Chapter 1 of *The Computer in the Classroom* (Vockell and Schwartz, 1988). Here, ALT will be discussed as it relates to language arts education.

Even without research to prove it, it would seem fairly obvious that we learn more about any given topic or skill when we spend more time on it. Research has proven that this relationship exists for many academic activities, including language arts instruction. However, simply assigning more study time to language arts will not automatically increase the student's learning of it—the relationship is a bit more complicated than that. For example, not *all* the time officially scheduled for studying language arts is likely to be allocated to that activity. If an hour is assigned to working on a language activity but the teacher devotes five minutes at the beginning of the session to returning papers and five minutes at the end collecting milk money or reading announcements, then only fifty minutes have actually been allocated for study. *Scheduled time* merely sets an upper limit on *allocated time*. Likewise, *allocated time* merely sets the upper limit to *engaged time*, which refers to the amount of time students actively attend to the subject under consideration. Finally, even when they are actively engaged in studying language arts, students learn effectively only when they are performing mental activities at a high rate of success. This smaller amount of time is the factor that is most strongly related to the amount of learning that takes place.

In the language arts classroom, students learn efficiently to the extent that they turn their class and study time into academic learning time. Neither "class time" nor "study time" automatically qualifies as ALT, but both may become ALT to the extent that the learner actively attends to relevant tasks with a high rate of success. A student who devotes 100 hours to academic learning time to a topic will learn more than an equally capable student who devotes only 50 hours. However, a person allocating only 50 hours to study but spending 90 percent of it in active academic learning will learn more than an equally capable student who allocates 100 hours but spends only 30 percent of it in active academic learning.

ALT can be increased not only by lengthening the school year, but also (and more importantly) by enabling the teacher to manage a classroom more efficiently and by enabling students to study more efficiently and at a higher rate of success. Although computers cannot lengthen the school year, they *can* help teachers and students improve the quality of the ALT. Although it is not <u>necessary</u> for language arts students to have access to computers to make effective use of academic learning time—good teachers are good teachers precisely because they help students do this; it is obvious that the computer *can* make an important contribution to ALT. Simply stated, in most situations in which computers enhance learning, they do so because they increase effective academic learning time. When computers fail to improve learning, very often it is because they do not increase ALT. In looking for areas in which computers can enhance language arts instruction, therefore, we should look for ways in which they can increase the academic learning time available for effective use by students and teachers.

The computer can enhance ALT in the area of language arts in several ways. First, it permits learners to acquire specific information and practice specific skills at the proper pace, providing the opportunity to repeatedly practice skills until the learner is confident. Second, the computer helps the student develop basic tools for learning that can apply in a variety of settings. In a narrow sense, the computer as a word processor can help students complete language arts lessons. In a larger sense, it can guide the learner in the development of problem-solving strategies and thinking skills that apply beyond the language arts classroom. These strategies prepare the student to be a lifelong learner and effective communicator.

BENEFITS OF COMPUTERS

Other significant benefits of using the computer in the classroom were highlighted in a study of eight thousand educators (Becker, 1987). According to the teachers and principals surveyed, the benefits of using the computer for instruction were:

1. Student motivation
2. Student cooperation and independence
3. Opportunities for high-ability students to engage in programming activities and in other higher-order thinking skills
4. Opportunities for low-ability students to master mathematics and language arts skills

In addition to providing benefits directly to the student in the learning environment, the computer can also be an effective tool for language arts teachers. By using the computer to handle management tasks such as recording and calculating grades or creating printer-generated materials based on individual student needs, the teacher has more time to spend in people-oriented tasks. Creating study guides, tests, and home-school communications with a word processor lends a more professional appearance to the final product and eases the burden of editing. Computer-generated graphics enhance bulletin boards, learning centers, and other displays. Authoring systems allow the teacher to individualize materials in a way that was impossible in the past, so that teachers are no longer entirely at the mercy of distant publishing houses to provide instructional materials.

Letting the computer do what machines do well frees the educator to do what machines cannot do: communicate human-to-human with students and respond to their needs. Giving teachers more time, not to talk but to listen, is one advantage that is seldom stated in literature on computer effectiveness. Yet using the computer, especially in the language arts classroom, focuses on just that—communicating! By interacting with or observing students working at computers, teachers can better understand the needs of their learners and therefore communicate with them more effectively.

What does all this mean to you as a current teacher or future practitioner? As such, you are challenged to meet the individual needs of your students in a way that entices them to grow in their language skill development. Your job is to integrate a variety of activities, materials, and approaches to make the most efficient use of academic learning time. The computer can be a welcome resource to accomplish these ambitious goals.

Although many language arts experts agree that the skills we use to speak, write, read, and listen cannot be separated into neat categories, the chapters in this book *do* address these as individual topics, for ease of presentation and reference. The examples of computer-related lessons, projects, materials, methods, and approaches presented herein are just that—examples. Use them as a framework to create a learning environment in which your students' language arts skills can blossom!

SUMMARY

This chapter has described four approaches to language arts in the elementary classroom and has discussed the role the computer can play in each model. We have seen how the computer can improve language arts instruction primarily by enhancing academic learning time. Subsequent chapters will discuss strategies for integrating the computer into the language arts curriculum and will describe software and hardware to help accomplish this integration.

REFERENCES

Becker, H. J. *The Impact of Computer Use on Children's Learning*. Baltimore, Md.: Center for Research on Elementary and Middle Schools, 1987.

Berliner, D. "The Half-full Glass: A Review of Research on Teaching." In P. Hosford (Ed.). *Using What We Know About Teaching*. Alexandria, Va.: Association for Supervision and Curriculum Development, 1984.

Caldwell, J. H., W. G. Huitt, and A. O. Graeber. "Time Spent in Learning: Implications from Research." *Elementary School Journal* 82 (1982): 471–480.

Evertts, E. L. "A New Heritage Approach for Teaching the Language Arts." In B. J. Mandel (Ed.). *Three Language Arts Curriculum Models: Pre-Kindergarten Through College*. Urbana, Ill.: National Council of Teachers of English, 1980.

Goodman, K. *What's Whole in Whole Language?* Portsmouth, N.H.: Heinemann Educational Books, 1986.

Mandel, B. J. (Ed.). *Three Language Arts Curriculum Models: Pre-Kindergarten Through College*. Urbana, Ill.: National Council of Teachers of English, 1980.

Mason, B. O., S. W. Lundsteen, and P. S. Martinez. "Competency-Based Approach to Language Arts: Pre-Kindergarten Through Grade Five." In B. J. Mandel (Ed.). *Three Language Arts Curriculum Models: Pre-Kindergarten Through College*. Urbana, Ill.: National Council of Teachers of English, 1980.

Moffett, J., and B. J. Wagner. *Student-Centered Language Arts and Reading, K–13*. Boston: Houghton Mifflin, 1976.

Stauffer, R. G. "Process-Oriented Instructional Activities: Pre-Kindergarten Through Grade Five." In B. J. Mandel (Ed.). *Three Language Arts Curriculum Models: Pre-Kindergarten Through College*. Urbana, Ill.: National Council of Teachers of English, 1980.

Vockell, E. L., and E. Schwartz. *The Computer in the Classroom*. Watsonville, Calif.: Mitchell, 1988.

Whitaker, B., E. Schwartz, and E. L. Vockell. *The Computer in the Reading Curriculum*. Watsonville, Calif.: Mitchell, 1989.

CHAPTER 2

HOW THE COMPUTER CAN ENHANCE LANGUAGE ARTS SKILLS

ACADEMIC LEARNING TIME

THIS CHAPTER EXPANDS UPON the introduction in Chapter 1 of academic learning time (ALT) by describing specific instructional strategies that can enhance it. These strategies are based on principles that have been validated by careful educational research during the past twenty years. Even without computers, these principles are important elements of language arts instruction. A major premise of this book is that the computer should serve as a useful tool to help apply these and other effective instructional strategies in the language arts curriculum.

The Computer in the Classroom (Vockell and Schwartz, 1988) discusses several instructional principles that can be integrated with computerized instruction, which are summarized in Table 2.1. The following sections of this chapter discuss in detail a few of the principles especially relevant to using the computer to teach language arts skills.

Table 2.1 Summary of major instructional principles and guidelines for using the computer.*

Principle: Mastery Learning

Summary: Given enough time, nearly all learners can master objectives.

Guidelines:
1. Use programs that provide extra help and practice toward reaching objectives.
2. Use programs to stimulate and enrich students who reach objectives early.
3. Use record-keeping programs to keep track of student performance.

Principle: Direct Instruction

Summary: If teachers describe objectives and demonstrate exact steps, students can master specific skills more efficiently.

Guidelines:
1. Use programs that specify exact steps and teach them clearly and specifically.
2. Show the relationship of computer programs to steps in the direct teaching process.

Principle: Overlearning

Summary: To become automatic, skills must be practiced and reinforced beyond the point of initial mastery.

Guidelines:
1. Use computer programs to provide self-paced, individualized practice.
2. Use computer programs that provide gamelike practice for skills that require much repeated practice.
3. Use computer programs that provide varied approaches to practicing the same activity.

Principle: Memorization Skills

Summary: Recall of factual information is a useful skill that enhances learning at all levels.

Guidelines:
1. Use computer programs to provide repeated practice and facilitate memorization.
2. Use programs designed to develop memory skills.

Table 2.1 (continued)

Principle: Peer Tutoring
Summary: Both tutor and pupil can benefit from properly structured peer tutoring.
Guidelines: 1. Have students work in groups at computers.
             2. Use programs that are structured to help tutors provide instruction, prompts, and feedback.
             3. Teach students to give feedback, prompts, and instruction at computers.

Principle: Cooperative Learning
Summary: Helping one another is often more productive than competing for scarce rewards.
Guidelines: 1. Have students work in groups at computers.
             2. Use programs that promote cooperation.
             3. Provide guidelines for cooperative roles at computers.

Principle: Monitor Student Progress
Summary: Close monitoring of student progress enables students, teachers, and parents to identify strengths and weaknesses of learners.
Guidelines: 1. Use programs that have management systems to monitor student progress.
             2. Use record-keeping programs.
             3. Use computer to communicate feedback.

Principle: Student Misconceptions
Summary: Identifying misconceptions helps develop an understanding of topics.
Guidelines: 1. Use programs to diagnose misconceptions.
             2. Use programs to teach correct understanding of misunderstood concepts.

Principle: Prerequisite Knowledge and Skills
Summary: Knowledge is usually hierarchical, and low-level skills must be learned before higher-level skills can be mastered.
Guidelines: 1. Use programs to assess prerequisite knowledge and skills.
             2. Use programs to teach missing prerequisite skills.

Principle: Immediate Feedback
Summary: Feedback usually works best if it comes quickly after a response.
Guidelines: 1. Use programs that provide immediate feedback.
             2. Use programs that provide clear corrective feedback.

Principle: Parental Involvement
Summary: Parents should be informed about their children's progress and assist in helping them learn.
Guidelines: 1. Use computers to communicate with parents about educational activities and progress.
             2. Exploit home computers.

Principle: Learning Styles
Summary: Learners vary in preference for modes and styles of learning.
Guidelines: 1. Use programs that appeal to students' preferred learning styles.
             2. Use programs that supplement your weak teaching styles.
             3. Use programs that employ a variety of learning styles.

(continued)

Table 2.1 (continued)

Principle: Classroom Management
Summary: Effective classroom management provides more time for instruction.
Guidelines: 1. Use the computer as a tool to improve classroom management.
              2. Use programs that have a management component.

Principle: Teacher Questions
Summary: If teachers ask higher-order questions and wait for students to answer, higher-level learning is likely to occur.
Guidelines: 1. Select programs that ask higher-level questions.
              2. Use programs that individualize pace of instruction, since wait time is likely to be better than with traditional instruction.

Principle: Study Skills
Summary: Effective study skills can be taught, and these almost always enhance learning.
Guidelines: 1. Teach students to use the computer as a tool to manage and assist learning.
              2. Use programs that teach thinking skills.
              3. Teach generalization of thinking and study skills across subject areas.

Principle: Homework
Summary: When homework is well planned by teachers, completed by students, and related to class, learning improves.
Guidelines: 1. Assign homework for home computers.
              2. Have students do preparatory work off the computer as homework.

Principle: Writing Instruction
Summary: Writing should be taught as a recursive process of brainstorming, composing, revising, and editing.
Guidelines: 1. Use word processors for composition.
              2. Use programs that prompt writing skills.
              3. Teach students to use grammar and spelling checkers effectively.

Principle: Early Writing
Summary: Encourage even very young children to write "stories."
Guidelines: 1. Use simple word processing programs.
              2. Use programs that combine graphics with writing.
              3. Use graphics programs to stimulate creativity.

Principle: Learning Mathematics
Summary: Concrete experience helps students understand and master abstract principles.
Guidelines: 1. Match programs to children's level of cognitive development.
              2. Use programs that provide concrete demonstrations with clear graphics.

Principle: Phonics
Summary: Instruction in phonics helps students to "break the code" and develop generalized word attack skills.
Guideline: 1. Use programs that combine sound with visual graphics to teach the sight/sound relationships of reading.

Table 2.1 (continued)

Principle: Reading Comprehension
Summary: Students often learn better if reading lessons are preceded by preparatory
             materials and followed by questions and activities.
Guidelines: 1. Use programs that have pre and post activities to accompany them.
             2. Use computer programs before or after traditional reading materials.

Principle: Science Experiments
Summary: Students learn science best if they can do concrete experiments to see science
             in action.
Guidelines: 1. Use computer simulations.
             2. Use tutorial and drill programs with concrete graphics.
             3. Use database and word processing programs to manage and report
                noncomputerized science experiments.
             4. Use science interface equipment to manage and analyze science
                experiments.

* From *The Computer in the Classroom*, Vockell and Schwartz, 1988, pp. 87–90.

MASTERY LEARNING

Mastery learning holds that given enough time and help, about 95 percent of the learners in any group can come to a complete mastery of designated instructional objectives. Traditional instruction holds time constant and allows achievement to vary within a group. For example, a punctuation unit may last nine weeks; at the end of that time, students mastering the subject thoroughly receive grades of *A*, those who have mastered it slightly less get grades of *B*, and so on. Mastery learning reverses this relationship by holding achievement constant and letting the time students spend in pursuit of the objectives vary. In the same punctuation unit, a few students might meet the standards in three weeks; most in nine; but several might take fifteen or twenty weeks.

Mastery learning is not synonymous with pass/fail grading nor does it imply that standards should be lowered. When mastery learning is successful, high standards are articulated, and students receive ample time and help to meet them. Additional information about mastery learning can be found in Guskey and Gates (1986), Slavin (1987), and Levine (1987).

Although mastery learning has received formal emphasis only in the past twenty years, students and teachers have known about this principle for a long time. For example, students having trouble in any subject usually believe they can master it if they are given enough time.

Two problems often arise with mastery learning. First, grouping and scheduling may become difficult. It is easier to force people to work at a constant pace and to complete tasks at a predictable rate than to permit wide variations in activities within a class. Second, while slower learners spend extra time on minimum standards, faster learners may be forced to wait, when they could be progressing to higher levels of achievement. However, these problems are not insurmountable. They can be overcome by providing individualized attention, setting high but attainable standards, and making additional materials available for those students who master objectives more quickly than others.

Computers can aid mastery learning in three ways:

1. Many students need additional time and individualized practice with feedback to meet objectives. Computer programs can often provide opportunities to study at times and at a pace suited to the individual's needs.
2. Additional programs can be made available for students who master objectives quickly. These additional programs can either provide more intense study of the same objectives, move on to higher objectives, or integrate the objectives covered in the unit with other objectives.
3. Gradebook and other record-keeping programs can help teachers keep track of student performance.

Mastery learning overlaps considerably with other principles discussed in this chapter. For this reason, the three contributions listed above will be mentioned in conjunction with several of these other principles. Keep in mind that although mastery learning has worked quite well for many years without the aid of computers, using computers wisely can often make mastery learning work more effectively.

DIRECT INSTRUCTION

The term *direct instruction* refers to academically focused, teacher-directed classrooms using logically sequenced instructional materials or teacher guidance to see that students stay on task effectively. Further characteristics include goals that are clear to students; sufficient and continuous time allocated for instruction; monitoring of student performance; questions at an appropriate cognitive level so that students can produce numerous

---

Mastery Learning by Computer

Mr. Jordan's third graders were studying antonyms. The children went to the computer at the back of the room at assigned times, where they ran OPPOSITES by Hartley. This program permitted Mr. Jordan to change lesson content or create new lessons to meet the needs of his students. He was easily able to change topics and level of mastery for each student and to monitor progress by occasionally running the management program after school. When a student met the designated mastery level (which could be different for each learner), that student was permitted to engage in some other enjoyable activity at the computer, such as WORD BLASTER by Davidson. All students were eventually required to reach a score of 80 percent, but they did this at their own pace.

Mr. Jordan was, among other things, using the computer to effectively monitor his students' progress while they engaged in mastery learning.

---

correct responses; and immediate and academically oriented feedback. The teacher controls instructional goals, chooses materials appropriate for the students' abilities, and paces instruction. Interaction is structured but not authoritarian. Learning takes place in a convivial atmosphere. For basic skills in such areas as reading, language arts, and mathematics in the elementary school, direct instruction has consistently proven to be more effective than informal or nondirective strategies to accomplish the same goals (Rosenshine, 1986).

Direct instruction is most obviously compatible with the new heritage and competencies models, since these focus largely on specific skills. However, effective implementation of the process and whole language models also requires direct instruction at important points during the learning sequence. The difference is that in the latter model the teacher introduces direct instruction only when necessary to help students meet needs that arise during self-initiated activities.

Although it is possible to design computerized units that employ all the principles of direct instruction, this is by no means necessary. A good teacher can use almost any good program in conjunction with the principles of direct instruction. For example, a student might be having a problem with word usage in her writing assignments. The computer-using teacher might see to it that the student understands the problem and that the goal of solving it is clear to the student, then introduce her to a good program that asks questions at an appropriate cognitive level so that the student can produce numerous correct responses and receive immediate and academically oriented feedback. The teacher would also see to it that the student has sufficient and continuous time allocated for instruction at the computer, monitor her performance, and offer guidance as necessary to see that the student is able to transfer the skill to her own writing on later assignments. This is only one example of the many ways in which a teacher can combine computerized and noncomputerized strategies to deliver direct instruction to help solve specific problems.

OVERLEARNING AND AUTOMATICITY

It is important to continue studying and applying many of the skills and concepts in language arts well beyond the point of initial mastery. Teachers working with large groups of students are often forced to violate this principle. In most classes, some students master objectives quickly, a large number learn at a medium rate, and others learn very slowly. Because of the way class time must be structured, the teacher is practically forced to move on to the next objective as soon as the middle group of students demonstrate an initial understanding of the topic. Therefore, the students who get the most overlearning are the brightest students, who mastered the objectives quickly and then may have continued to practice beyond the point of initial mastery. Paradoxically, the students who *need* overlearning the most are the slowest students—who probably get none at all. This is especially unfortunate with regard to basic skills, which must be mastered to a point where they become automatic; such automaticity allows these skills to be incorporated into subsequent higher-level objectives.

Computers can help solve this problem. Just as computers can help learners achieve mastery learning by allowing students to study at times and a pace suited to the individual, computers can help students practice skills well beyond the point of initial mastery until they become overlearned or automatic. The interest, variety, and gamelike atmosphere provided by computers offer a considerable advantage when students practice an activity beyond initial mastery. The simple fact is that there are numerous skills that must be practiced in spite of the fact that students "already know them." By selecting computer software that provides repeated practice in different contexts and through different formats, students can achieve the necessary repetition without the stultifying monotony that might otherwise occur.

GROUPING, COOPERATIVE LEARNING, AND PEER TUTORING

When students work alone at computers, the following disadvantages are likely to occur: (1) the social isolation can create mood states (such as loneliness, boredom, and frustration) that interfere with sustained effort to complete learning tasks; (2) students are denied the opportunity to summarize orally and explain what they are learning; and (3) computers cannot provide social models to be imitated and used for social comparisons (Johnson and Johnson, 1987). Working as a whole class with the teacher can solve these problems, but the cooperative learning and peer tutoring literature suggests that small groups can also overcome these difficulties.

Students can work in groups in many different ways at the computer. For example, they can work individually, taking turns; they can compete to see who is best; or they can cooperate. Current research suggests that the cooperative approach is usually best. The key components of effective cooperative learning are positive interdependence, individual accountability, and shared responsibility for one another. This means that the success of the group requires that each person have a role and be accountable for that role and that the individual members be interested in helping one another attain important goals. Closely related to the concept of cooperative learning is that of peer tutoring. Research on this topic indicates that when students tutor their peers, both the tutor and the tutee benefit. The research on cooperative learning and peer tutoring is discussed in greater detail in Cohen, Kulik, and Kulik (1982); Slavin (1983, 1986); Slavin, et al. (1985); Vockell and Schwartz (1988); and Wang and Walberg (1985).

What all this amounts to is that small groups at the computer are very often preferable to individual students working at the computer—especially when working on communications or higher-order thinking skills. In addition, large-group (whole-class) presentations are often preferred over introducing a computer skill to one student at a time. But once important skills have been thoroughly learned by some members of the class and at least partially mastered by everyone, small groups may provide a better use of academic learning time than a continued large-group session. Individual work at the computer will be most useful when a student needs practice on a skill that other students have already mastered or in which the others have no interest.

Small-group activities at the computer will support the learning of language arts skills only if the group sessions are specifically structured to promote learning of the skill. Usually, this means incorporating the direct instruction approach described in this chapter; assigning group activities only after the unit has been appropriately introduced to a large group; ascertaining that group members have actual roles that they understand and objectives that they can meet; and teaching students to interact properly with the program and with one another.

There is an important distinction between the *learning phase* and the *practice phase* of instruction. During the learning phase, students who have not yet mastered knowledge or skills need feedback to focus attention correctly, to detect and clarify misconceptions, and to come to a relatively clear understanding of concepts or principles under consideration. During the practice phase, external feedback from a skilled teacher is less important, since the student is practicing skills previously learned; feedback will arise automatically from the situation or from the student's own insights. Because students naturally are more active when communicating with their

---

Miss Clark's Students Master Spelling

Each student in Miss Clark's fourth-grade class was assigned to a study group for spelling. There would eventually be a spelling test based on a list designated by the school district as valuable words for fourth graders. Each student would take the test individually, but the group whose members averaged highest on the test would receive the highly prestigious Superintendent's Spelling Award, an interview (with photograph) in the local newspaper, and a pizza party.

The students fed their own word lists into MECC's MASTER SPELL, Gamco's SPIDER HUNT SPELLING, and Hartley's CREATE SPELL IT. Students chose the program with which they were most comfortable. Then they ran the program as a group. Since the eventual prize would be based on the performance of all the individual members of the group, the faster students had incentives to help the slower students. In fact, the winning group was successful largely because its members hit upon the idea of entering into each of the computer programs lists of "spelling demons" tailored to each student in the group. The students enjoyed the challenge of these individualized games and easily mastered the words. Of course, many of the students also studied the words in noncomputerized settings—for example, by asking each other to spell the words, by trying to use the words correctly in their own writing, and by going over them with their parents at home.

This example shows an interesting way to apply the computer to cooperative learning strategies for mastery learning.

peers than with their teacher, they can greatly benefit from *practicing* language arts skills in small groups with other students.

Our belief is that many teachers make the mistake of sending students off without supervision or guidance to practice skills that they have not yet learned. Students can (and should) practice together; and sometimes students can help other students understand and master complex skills—but this is comparatively rare. Peer tutoring of *factual* information and peer *modeling* of process skills are extremely effective. But peer teaching of process skills is not likely to be effective; the teacher should maintain responsibility for monitoring progress in language arts skills and prompting their development through effective interaction and discourse.

We are not suggesting that if you find a group of children deeply engrossed in vivacious discourse you should tell them to stop thinking until you have time to teach them how to do it. Many students can and do learn by making discoveries on their own. What we *are* suggesting is that teachers should assign students to small-group or individual work on language arts software—especially when it deals with fairly complex objectives—only when the teachers have good reason to believe that their students are in the practice phase and therefore likely to benefit from the software.

Finally, we need to say a few words about competition. It has almost become a platitude among American teachers that students should compete against their own past performance rather than against one another. While there is considerable wisdom in this belief, there is also some error. In the world of sports, for example, there is ample evidence to suggest that top athletes rise to the peak of their performance only when challenged by other athletes. Outstanding runners, for instance, usually run their fastest races only in direct competition with other runners; competing solely against a time clock simply does not lead to equally fast times. In the same way, the very best students in a class actually benefit from competing with one another. The problem, however, is that such competition is often a huge turn-off to those students who know they cannot win. In fact, students who lose competitions with others often lose more than the winners gain; and the winners can often be almost equally well motivated by competing with their own scores.

If teachers *must* make a choice, they should probably foster self-competition rather than competition against others. However, teachers can sometimes combine competition with others and competition with self in such a way as to gain the benefits of both. For example, one cooperative learning strategy is to have teams of students compete for prizes or honors. These teams can be assigned in a way to ensure that comparable numbers of strong and weak students are on each team. In this way, the slowest member of any team can still make a valid contribution, even if he cannot compete with the brightest members of the class. For example, if each team in a group competition is originally assigned a member who can spell only 50 percent of the words correctly, another team member who brings her score up to 80 percent is actually helping her team more than a person who starts at 90 percent and moves up to 100 percent. In addition, the other team members have incentives to help the weaker student. Furthermore, even the "losers" can often take pride in the fact that they have improved their own performance.

Some computerized learning programs make excellent use of competition. For example, WORD MUNCHERS by MECC (Figure 2.1) provides a "Hall of Fame," which lists the top players and their scores. These lists are similar to those that often accompany arcade games. We have seen children work for hours to get their names onto such a list; and the learning that goes into this activity is certainly beneficial. However, the obvious disadvantage is that after one player has achieved a score of 20,000, then another player whose current high is only 500 has little incentive to try to win. One solution is to employ team rather than individual competition, as was suggested in the previous paragraph. A second strategy is for the teacher simply to erase some of the names from time to time. A third strategy is to

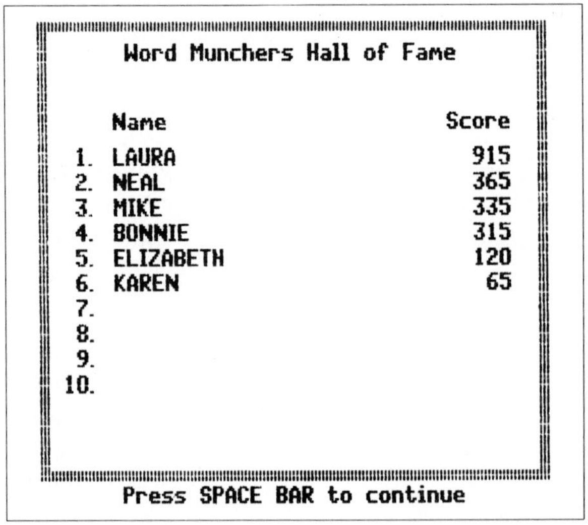

Figure 2.1 WORD MUNCHERS "Hall of Fame" can be a good motivator if the teacher incorporates the strategies described in this chapter.

```
          Word Munchers Hall of Fame


          Name                    Score
       1. LAURA                     915
       2. NEAL                      365
       3. MIKE                      335
       4. BONNIE                    315
       5. ELIZABETH                 120
       6. KAREN                      65
       7.
       8.
       9.
      10.


          Press SPACE BAR to continue
```

make up more than one disk. Since MECC disks can be copied as necessary within a licensed school, a teacher could unobtrusively make available one disk for the strongest students and another set of individual disks for other students. Another useful strategy is to encourage students to use pseudonyms rather than their real names, thereby reducing direct competition and possible hurt feelings.

The fact is that in American schools competition is likely to continue to be a factor—with or without computers. Students implicitly compare themselves to other students, which in turn contributes to their own self-concepts. Even when a student is competing against his own past performance, there is nothing to stop another student from looking over his shoulder and saying, "I can do better than that!" Teachers cannot eliminate competition; they can only be aware of it and channel it into positive directions. The proper way to control undesirable competition is for the teacher to foster a friendlier, more mature atmosphere, in which students try to be the best that they can be without hurting other students. Research shows that cooperative learning environments can help provide such an atmosphere while actually enhancing academic performance—and computers can play an important role in cooperative learning.

FEEDBACK

In order for learners to receive maximum benefit from feedback, it should be supplied as soon as possible after performance. Actually, mature learners can often wait a few days or even weeks to find out whether their response was a good one. In addition, there is research to indicate that sometimes learners make their own assessments when teacher feedback is lacking; and these self-assessments are useful. But, in general, the best time to tell learners whether they were right or wrong is when they are most interested in this information—usually right after they have given their answer. For various reasons, classroom feedback is often delayed for several minutes, hours, days, or even weeks. Positive feedback (knowledge that you are right) is obviously important; but negative feedback (knowledge that you are wrong) is sometimes even more crucial, since a blissfully ignorant student may spend several minutes, hours, days, or weeks mispronouncing a word or misapplying a concept before discovering the error.

The computer has the capacity to give almost instantaneous feedback. Rapid positive or corrective feedback and branching based upon student responses are important components of drill and tutorial software. Another feature that computerized feedback can add is objectivity. If a student gives a disastrously inappropriate answer, the computer neither attacks the personality of the learner nor helps out with inappropriate hints: a wrong answer or bad decision simply leads to its logically programmed consequences. Since they are warm, compassionate human beings, teachers often sympathize with students who are making errors (for example, by following blind leads) and inadvertently supply hints that prevent the students from learning through their mistakes. The impersonal objectivity of the computer sometimes offers the advantage of taking teachers out of the evaluative process and letting them join the learning team on the side of the students. Without jeopardizing the instructional setting, teachers can supply the personal touch missing in the computer program.

INDIVIDUALIZATION

One major, obvious advantage offered by the computer is individualization. In the typical classroom, students vary widely in their instructional needs with regard to language arts skills. As this chapter has indicated, students effectively learn communication skills if they spend useful instructional time on tasks suited to their own needs. However, in a class of thirty students, teachers are faced with major difficulties. Some students will have mastered all the prerequisite skills to begin working toward mastery of a more advanced skill, while others will have mastered none of them. In between are students with a tentative mastery of some and a solid mastery of others. If all the students have mastered the prerequisite skills, helping them master the new strategies is fairly straightforward. However, this is rarely the case, and teachers are often overwhelmed by the need to give attention to individual weaknesses while simultaneously trying to "enrich" the curriculum for the stronger students.

Moreover, since basic communication skills need to become automatic to provide the foundation for more advanced skills, it is important to provide repeated practice. But such repetition can be boring, painful, and frustrating; and this is why many students turn off to academic subjects. A computer can help reduce repetition for those who do not need additional practice. But for those students who do, creative teachers can use the computer to help overcome this difficulty by making the practice interesting (even gamelike), by supplying informative feedback, and by making the repeated practice relevant to the students' present or future needs. A microcomputer can surely be helpful in making the practice more interesting or in changing the repetitive drill into a challenging game.

The principle of individualization does not contradict the principle of cooperative learning. When students are focusing on objectives of unique interest to themselves alone, working alone at the computer is the most effective strategy. However, such solitary objectives are indeed rare in the language arts curriculum. It is the contention of this book that very often the best strategy is to have the students work in small groups or even to have the entire class work at a single computer. The computer can become the focal point for class activity, thinking, and discussion.

The key point is that individualization is *not* synonymous with individualistic learning. Research supports the concept of individualization, which suggests that students learn best when instruction is suited to their individual needs. Individualization does not by any means require that students work alone. The key requirement of individualized instruction is that each student works at his or her maximum level of performance on tasks related to his or her needs. Students experiencing individualized instruction can definitely benefit from interacting with peers; for example, they may profit from modeling, from motivating social interactions, or from feedback. They can also benefit from interacting with a knowledgeable teacher, who can keep them on task, model useful strategies, and provide feedback and insights as needed. On the other hand, research does *not* support the concept of individualistic instruction, which suggests that students should pursue their own instructional objectives without concern for the needs or interests of their classmates. As an earlier section of this chapter indicates, research suggests that a cooperative approach is likely to be more effective for most educational topics in most classrooms.

Several companies (e.g., Tom Snyder Productions, the makers of DECISIONS, DECISIONS) have begun to introduce software designed to stimulate normal classroom discussion and activities. This approach should appeal to good language arts teachers who have resisted using computers. Having already created effective strategies to develop communication skills, some teachers feel that the incorporation of computer software would require them to abandon tried-and-true techniques in favor of an unknown novelty. This fear is overcome if teachers emphasize using the computer as an effective tool within existing sound instructional frameworks.

TEACHER-GENERATED QUESTIONS

Student achievement rises when teachers ask questions that require students to apply, analyze, synthesize, and evaluate information in addition to simply recalling facts; and when teachers give students time to think in order to answer these questions. Two factors that seriously inhibit learning are when teachers tend to ask questions that only require rote memorization and when teachers expect answers immediately. Research shows that when teachers ask higher-order questions and give appropriate feedback for answers, students learn higher-order skills more effectively. In addition, research indicates that if teachers pause a few seconds longer and provide appropriate prompts, students can often answer higher-order questions and benefit accordingly. Excellent summaries of research on teacher questioning and wait time can be found in Barell (1985) and Tobin (1987).

Computers are not automatically superior to teachers at asking higher-order questions that involve nonrote skills. In fact, a very large number of drills require nothing more than rote responses. Note, however, that even if all computer-assisted instruction programs required merely rote responses, they could still enhance higher-order thinking by performing this rote function and freeing teachers to engage in higher-order thinking with students. Of course, it is also possible to use computer software to ask higher-order questions, as Figure 2.2 indicates. If teachers are interested in promoting nonrote skills, they should carefully examine various computer programs and select software that requires higher-order performance.

Figure 2.2 A word processing program such as APPLEWORKS (Claris) gives the teacher the freedom to frame questions that promote the use of higher-order skills, as shown in this example (a review of the book *A Wrinkle in Time*).

1. List the problems Meg was having in school. (knowledge)

2. What evidence verifies that Mrs. Who, Mrs. Which and Mrs. Whatsit were not human? (comprehension)

3. What other reasons could the Mrs. Ws have for wanting Meg and Charles to save their father? (application)

4. Compare and contrast the personalities of Mrs. Who, Mrs. Which, and Mrs. Whatsit. (analysis)

5. Create a new ending for the story. (synthesis)

6. Evaluate the effect of the "tesseract" on modern transportation. (evaluation)

Computers do have an inherent advantage over teachers in terms of how long they are willing to wait for a student to respond. When a teacher asks a question, a lengthy silence may signal a coming disruption in the teaching process; and many teachers feel compelled to indicate that the student is "wrong" or to call on another student almost immediately. This is unfortunate because the most sensible approach to answering a difficult question aloud is to pause; analyze the problem; bring to mind relevant information; develop a tentative answer; check the validity of this tentative answer; and then give the answer out loud. It's difficult to do this within the short time provided by most teachers; and so students (at best) "think on their feet." If they understand the question, they either give a memorized (or previously thought out) response or start talking and develop their answer while giving it. This may be a useful strategy for winning prizes on a game show, but it hardly enhances effective thinking. (In fact, the students who benefit are probably the ones who go through the appropriate steps while the teacher is calling on the first student.) The computer solves this problem simply by waiting as long as necessary for the student to respond. There is no ominous silence after the computer presents a question and no pressure to move on to another student. When asked a higher-order question, the student can pause, go through the appropriate steps, and then respond.

WRITING INSTRUCTION

The principle for the most effective way to teach writing is to teach it as a process of prewriting, writing, rewriting, and publishing. Students at whatever age or grade level develop their writing skills through frequent practice of these skills. Ideally, this practice includes writing across the curriculum, not only in English or language arts classes. Feedback is important—and it should come from teachers, peers, and the writers themselves. A good summary of current research on the teaching of writing skills can be found in Hillocks (1984).

It is obvious that the word processor can play a significant role in teaching writing as delineated in this principle. Writers who use word processors are easily able to generate ideas and create rough drafts without fear of wasting time. Rough drafts can be shared with peers and teachers and modified in response to feedback. Mechanical correctness no longer inhibits the composing process and falls into place as a part of the editing process: the student who realizes he has made a grammatical error can finish his thought first and return later to correct the mistake.

Word processing programs are available for students at all age and ability levels. MAGIC SLATE by Sunburst (Figure 2.3) can be used by students from the early elementary grades through graduate school. It comes in three versions. The simplest uses large letters and provides only a few word processing options (such as insert, find, and replace). The most complex version includes all the options that adults would want to use in writing complex term papers.

Grammar and spelling checkers can also help students with editing. These tools can become extremely useful aids in the learning process, not crutches that teach students to rely on the computer to correct their mistakes rather than they themselves learning to spell or use grammar correctly. Students can learn that editing is only one aspect of the writing process, that the computer can help them more effectively if they learn to spell and understand the rules of grammar themselves, and that the ultimate decision regarding editing is still up to them. These programs merely flag possible errors and enable the writer to exercise appropriate judgment.

In addition, there are numerous programs that help students with various steps in the writing process as it is described in this principle. For example, the printed materials that accompany Sunburst's MAGIC SLATE and Scholastic's BANK STREET WRITER stimulate students at all four stages. In addition, various programs are designed to help students with specific types of writing. For example, WRITING A NARRATIVE helps students write about a specific series of events, whereas STORY TREE helps them generate stories that branch to provide almost endless variety for the reader. COMPUPOEM helps students write poems. CHILDREN'S WRITING AND PUBLISHING CENTER helps integrate a wide variety of writing activities by introducing desktop publishing to young learners.

EARLY WRITING

Children who are encouraged to draw and scribble "stories" at an early age will later learn to compose more easily, more effectively, and with greater confidence than children who do not have this encouragement. When their parents encourage or permit them to do so, young children attempt to "write" things long before they are in kindergarten. Research suggests that these scrawls have meaning to the children and that the best way to help

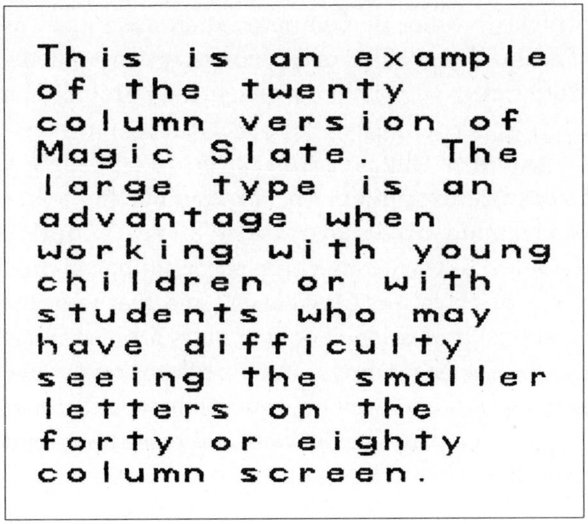

This is an example of the twenty column version of Magic Slate. The large type is an advantage when working with young children or with students who may have difficulty seeing the smaller letters on the forty or eighty column screen.

(a)

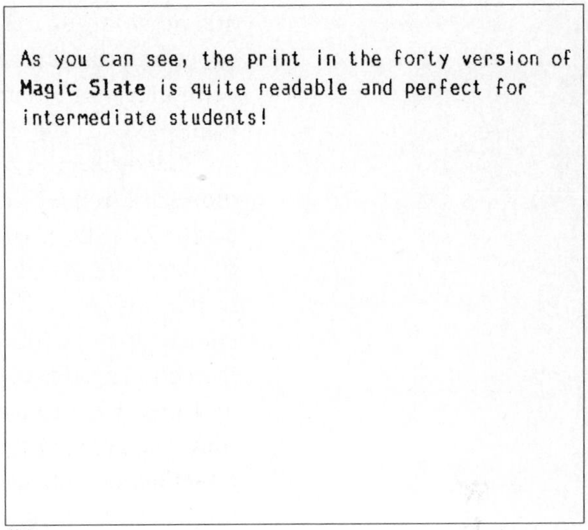

As you can see, the print in the forty version of Magic Slate is quite readable and perfect for intermediate students!

(b)

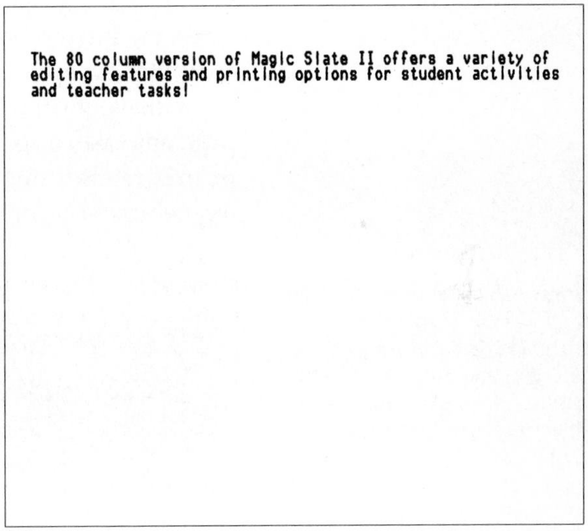

Figure 2.3 The three versions of MAGIC SLATE by Sunburst give all students and their teachers the opportunity to utilize the same program at different levels of sophistication.

The 80 column version of Magic Slate II offers a variety of editing features and printing options for student activities and teacher tasks!

(c)

children is to respond to the ideas they are trying to express rather than to the correctness of the letters or grammar.

Obviously, many young children will continue to write without approaching the computer. However, it is equally obvious that many youngsters are enticed by the computer's keyboard, especially if parents and other family members clearly value the computer. There are numerous programs that are specifically designed to help youngsters write at the computer and to combine writing with drawings. Figure 2.4 provides an example.

In addition, simple word processing programs can be used by slightly older children to write stories, letters, and plays. For example, the son of one of the authors of this book suddenly discovered MAGIC SLATE during the spring of the second grade. His teacher had been encouraging children in the class to write their own plays, and Steve had found that with the computer he could write almost professional-looking plays for his friends to read. His plays increased in length from fifty words to nearly five hundred within a single week. As time went on, his friends would corner him at recess to discuss a plot for a play, then Steve would come home and type the play into the computer. Although he noticed occasional errors, he got bored with making all the corrections. His father compromised by sitting next to him during the editing process and making the corrections that Steve suggested. It is unlikely that Steve and his friends would have taken an interest in writing or felt pride in their output without the computer's help.

Finally, if drawing and scribbling are useful activities, then graphics programs may also be good tools. LOGOWRITER is specifically designed to integrate writing with student-designed graphics; but students and teachers must become fairly familiar with the Logo programming language

Figure 2.4 Primary children can write a story with pictures taken from programs like the one illustrated in this figure. Young authors can use programs such as KIDWRITER by Gessler to choose illustrations before they begin writing.

to use this program effectively. Even fairly complex graphics programs (such as PAINTWORKS PLUS and FANTAVISION) can be used by students at every grade level. By following instructions, children can use these programs to draw pictures, which can eventually be printed out, to provide the basis for oral or written stories. The pictures can even be transferred to a VCR and spoken or graphic lines added to make "television programs." As graphics capabilities improve on the newest computers, the potential becomes even greater.

Mrs. Robinson Uses Computers

Mrs. Robinson was a fifth-grade teacher who taught twenty-two students in a self-contained classroom. She had one Apple computer in the learning center at the back of the room. She also had access, for one hour on Tuesday and Thursday afternoons, to a computer lab containing twenty-four Apple computers. In addition, each of her students was allowed to go to the school's media center for one hour each week to work independently at the Apple computers located there. When her students went to the computer lab, Mrs. Robinson accompanied them and was solely responsible for supervising their behavior. However, when they went to the media center, the media specialist supervised them, while Mrs. Robinson stayed in her classroom with the rest of the class.

Mrs. Robinson decided to use the entire Tuesday session each week to teach writing skills through word processing activities. Her students had already developed reasonable keyboarding, so she could count on them to type at a moderate rate. She now wanted them to learn how to brainstorm an idea, write a rough draft of a paragraph on a chosen topic, revise the draft as often as necessary, and edit it to eliminate errors in grammar, word usage, and spelling. On Friday, she set up an LCD (liquid crystal display) projection system and brainstormed for fifteen minutes with her pupils on a topic of interest to them. Responding to input from the students, she then moved from brainstorming to drafting by typing their ideas into paragraph form as they gave them. If either she or they made mistakes, she simply left the errors on the screen. Once a student said, "Wait. That's spelled wrong." But Mrs. Robinson just commented, "We'll get that later," and continued with the composition. When they had finished producing ideas, she suggested that they go back and look for ways to improve the essay. The students suggested several insertions, alterations, and deletions. At one point, one block of students wanted to go one way, while the others wanted to go another. Mrs. Robinson simply

(continued)

duplicated the file and did it *both* ways! Finally, the students and teacher jointly edited the composition. After school, Mrs. Robinson had the computer generate copies for everyone while she corrected papers.

On Monday, Mrs. Robinson again set up the LCD projection system, and she and the students again brainstormed another topic of interest to the class. This time, however, they went no further; Mrs. Robinson told the students that they would have time to work on their compositions in the computer lab the next day. She printed out a hardcopy of the brainstorming list for each student.

On Tuesday, the class went to the computer lab for an hour, where the students used APPLEWORKS to write their compositions. Mrs. Robinson had a "computer mom" who helped the students with technical problems, leaving Mrs. Robinson free to focus on helping students with composition skills. Individually, the students followed the same steps that they had followed as a group on Friday—drafting, revising, and editing. They were permitted to share their essays with other students to obtain peer feedback. The session was moderately noisy but very productive. As she moved about the room, Mrs. Robinson talked to students about their ideas and made mental notes of areas in which they were encountering difficulties.

Mrs. Robinson never found it necessary to teach grammar to her class. Instead, she gave the students assignments on topics related to punctuation, word usage, and spelling as they encountered the need for these in their own writing. Although her students were allowed only one hour a week at the computer in the media center, Mrs. Robinson arranged to double this work time by having her students work there together in pairs. During one session, the students worked on writing-related activities. Sometimes these media center assignments consisted of drills related to the needs of the students; the drills might focus on mistakes the students made in their writing, or they might focus on "challenges" that Mrs. Robinson thought could expand the students' horizons. At other times the students worked together with the word processor proofreading and editing text files that Mrs. Robinson had devised on specific topics. In addition, Mrs. Robinson referred her students as necessary to appropriate chapters in their language arts textbook to help them with their personal needs. She also gave them worksheets to complete as "seatwork" or homework. Some of these she designed herself on the word processor, but others she took from the textbook or workbook. Mrs. Robinson kept track of her students' performance on her APPLEWORKS database, and she talked to them personally about their progress.

The students did some writing almost every day. On days when they did not have access to computers, they simply used pen and paper.

Note that the Thursday lab session, the second media center session, and the computer located in the classroom have not been accounted for in the preceding paragraphs. Although these were occasionally used for writing activities, they were mostly employed for other subjects, such as reading, mathematics, and social studies. Mrs. Robinson was fairly sure that if she were able to double her access to computers, her students would make good use of the time.

In this example, Mrs. Robinson enhanced the academic learning time of her students by applying several of the principles discussed in this chapter. The students easily moved back and forth between computerized and noncomputerized activities. The overall atmosphere was designed to keep the students actively involved in highly individualized, useful, academic activities related to developing communication skills. Mrs. Robinson used principles of direct instruction to promote mastery learning and automaticity by assigning students specific study packages as they saw the need for them. She saw to it that her students received feedback for their work—either from her, from their peers, or from the computer. She moved among large-group, small-group, and individual applications of the computer as need demanded. She supervised and guided her students during the learning phase of instruction, and gave them much more freedom during the practice phase.

Five years earlier, Mrs. Robinson did many of these same things without the computer; but now she could do them more effectively.

SUMMARY

This chapter has examined a few of the important principles in language arts instruction and has shown how the computer can be integrated with these principles. In addition to the principles discussed in this chapter, many of the other principles briefly summarized in Table 2.1 can also be applied to language arts instruction. For example, the principles related to learning styles, classroom management, and prerequisite knowledge are obviously applicable to language arts instruction. More detailed discussions of these other principles can be found in *The Computer in the Classroom*.

The key point made here is that computers will help students improve their language arts skills if—and only if—computer activity leads to more effective use of academic learning time. This chapter has also shown how procedures for promoting mastery learning, direct instruction, overlearning, automaticity, peer tutoring, cooperative learning, feedback, individualization, and effective questioning by teachers can be integrated with the computer to facilitate language arts instruction. Subsequent chapters will apply these strategies to more specific instances of integration.

REFERENCES

Barell, J. "You Ask the Wrong Questions." *Educational Leadership* 42 (May 1985): 18–23.

Cohen, P. A., J. A. Kulik, and C. C. Kulik. "Educational Outcomes of Tutoring: A Meta-Analysis of Findings." *American Educational Research Journal* 19 (1982): 237–248.

Guskey, T. R., and S. L. Gates. "Synthesis of Research on the Effects of Mastery Learning in Elementary and Secondary Schools." *Educational Leadership* 43 (May 1986): 73–80.

Hillocks, G. "What Works in Teaching Composition: A Meta-Analysis of Experimental Treatment Studies." *American Journal of Education* 93 (1984): 133–170.

Johnson, D. W., and R. T. Johnson. *Learning Together and Alone: Cooperative, Competitive, and Individualistic Learning.* Englewood Cliffs, N.J.: Prentice-Hall, 1987.

Levine, D. U. *Improving Student Learning Through Mastery Learning Programs.* San Francisco: Jossey-Bass, 1987.

Rosenshine, B. V. "Synthesis of Research on Explicit Teaching." *Educational Leadership* 43(7) (1986): 60–69.

Slavin, R. E. *Cooperative Learning.* New York: Longman, 1983.

Slavin, R. E. *Educational Psychology: Theory into Practice.* Englewood Cliffs, N.J.: Prentice-Hall, 1986.

Slavin, R. E. "Mastery Learning Reconsidered." *Review of Educational Research* 57 (Summer 1987): 175–213.

Slavin, R. E., S. Sharan, S. Kagan, R. Hertz-Lazarowitz, C. Webb, and R. Schmuck (Eds.). *Learning to Cooperate, Cooperating to Learn.* New York: Plenum, 1985.

Tobin, K. "The Role of Wait Time in Higher-Level Cognitive Learning." *Review of Educational Research* 57 (March 1987): 69–95.

Vockell, E. L., and E. Schwartz. *The Computer in the Classroom.* Watsonville, Calif.: Mitchell, 1988.

Wang, M., and H. Walberg (Eds.). *Adapting Instruction to Individual Difference.* Berkeley, Calif.: McCutcham, 1985.

CHAPTER 3

CREATING A LANGUAGE-RICH LEARNING ENVIRONMENT

ACCEPTING THE PREMISE THAT the computer is an effective tool in the language arts classroom is one thing; taking steps to assure its beneficial use is quite another. Effective implementation of this tool does not happen automatically. Where do you begin? By considering learning environment, software choice, and lesson planning. This chapter offers suggestions in each area to create the foundation needed for teaching and learning language arts skills with the help of the computer.

A LANGUAGE-RICH LEARNING ENVIRONMENT

All children are best able to develop communication skills in an environment that is language rich. In such an environment, students are encouraged to interact not only with the teacher and materials provided but also with one another. The physical setting, the characteristics of the students, and the teacher's style of communication combine to establish the learning environment. The computer and appropriate software influence the physical setting while providing numerous opportunities for student-to-teacher and student-to-student communication.

The physical setting of a language-rich environment is a warm, cheerful place in which the student feels comfortable. The classroom is filled with books, newspapers, magazines, and other reading material. Listening tapes and filmstrip previewers add a different perspective to the language experiences offered. This setting respects the student's need for individual space while also promoting group interaction. Providing a suitable furniture arrangement (and "something to talk about") promotes student thought and talk. Often a teacher inadvertently discourages student interaction by arranging desks in rows facing the front of the room. While this arrangement is sometimes convenient, it may encourage a passive, individualistic style of learning. Yet research tells us (Mayer and Brause, 1986) that in language arts, students benefit most from talking with each other in guided activities. It is possible to arrange desks and other furniture—including computers—in a way that promotes orderly activity and minimizes distractions without introducing obstacles to communication.

Many teachers find that they can facilitate communication by arranging desks in groups or having students sit at tables, an arrangement that frequently encourages student interaction and cooperative learning. Proper placement of the computer in this setting is important, too. The computer's capacity to promote communication skills in the classroom expands or diminishes depending on where the computer is placed, as addressed below.

Bulletin Boards and Displays

Besides the arrangement of desks, the physical setting can enhance a language-rich environment by providing "things to talk about." Bulletin boards can invite discussion. Displays that focus on current events, hobbies, or other favorite topics can initiate conversation. A bulletin board that requires interaction is a perfect spot for study partners to discuss a subject and learn together with or without assistance from the computer. Placing the computer adjacent to the bulletin board can enhance that learning experience. Figure 3.1 shows a screen from MECC's OREGON TRAIL. This program could be an effective part of a bulletin board display about pioneers. By discussing responses to various questions in this program, study partners gain verbal experience while sharing their simulated pioneer journey. This example shows how the computer and bulletin board can mutually supplement each other: the bulletin board draws attention to and motivates students to use the computer; and the computer augments information introduced on the bulletin board.

The language-rich classroom values each individual and provides opportunities for classmates to know each other while expanding their written and spoken language skills. Displays that highlight a "student of the week" (a student brings pictures and personal "treasures" to share) can provide an opportunity for children to get to know one another through questions suggested by the objects in the display. To enhance this effort, students can use the computer to write a book or create a poster (see Figure 3.2).

Figure 3.1 This screen from OREGON TRAIL (MECC) can be the basis for a bulletin board in a social studies learning center.

Learning Centers

Many elementary classrooms feature learning centers—nooks, corners, or tables in the classroom where related materials are collected for individual or group exploration. A center may include an assortment of reading materials, manipulatives, artists' tools, or whatever is appropriate for the given topic. The inclusion of a computer in the center creates exciting possibilities. Depending on the software, a learning center can become a writing center, providing word processing programs such as KIDWRITER or MAGIC SLATE to create journals or short stories; desktop publishing programs like CHILDREN'S WRITING AND PUBLISHING CENTER to publish newsletters; a spelling center providing additional practice on assigned word lists using WORD WIZARD or MAGIC SPELLS; or a vocabulary development center with a database package to create classroom glossaries or personal dictionaries of new words. Obviously, a major advantage of the computer is its flexibility. The computerized learning center is not restricted to any *one* of these applications. The insertion of a different disk and the press of a button can instantly change a spelling or mathematics center into a desktop publishing center.

The learning center opens up a wealth of language experiences whether or not the topic addressed is actually language arts. While using a software package called ZANDER from SVE, social studies students can create an imaginary society. In this program, students use language arts skills to voice opinions on everything from the structure of the government

Figure 3.2 Students create personalized books with I CAN WRITE (Sunburst).

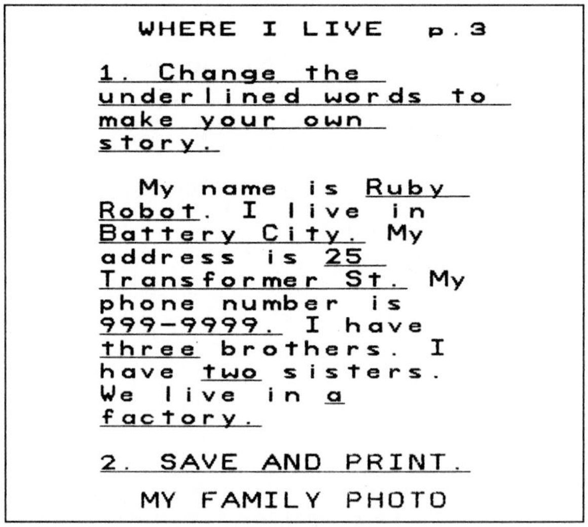

```
     WHERE  I  LIVE    p.3

  1. Change  the
  underlined words to
  make your own
  story.

     My  name   is  Ruby
  Robot.  I  live  in
  Battery City.  My
  address  is  25
  Transformer St.  My
  phone  number  is
  999-9999.  I  have
  three  brothers.  I
  have  two  sisters.
  We  live  in  a
  factory.

  2.  SAVE  AND  PRINT.
     MY  FAMILY  PHOTO
```

to conservation of resources. With Broderbund's SCIENCE TOOL KIT, where the computer becomes a lab instrument and the students become scientists, students use written and oral language skills to form and test hypotheses and to explain their rationale to peers.

Figure 3.3 shows an example of a physical setting that promotes a language-rich environment. Note that this floor plan includes a simple but revolutionary "technological" innovation that vastly enhances the impact of the computer in the classroom: a second chair at the computer station! It is amazing how often schools will spend several thousand dollars on computer hardware and software but not the extra ten dollars that would allow a second student to share the computer. Making it easy for students to work together at the computer can greatly increase the opportunities for cooperative learning and peer tutoring discussed in Chapter 2 and later in this chapter. Of course, a floor plan alone cannot support a language-rich

Figure 3.3 Floor plan of an elementary classroom containing a computer.

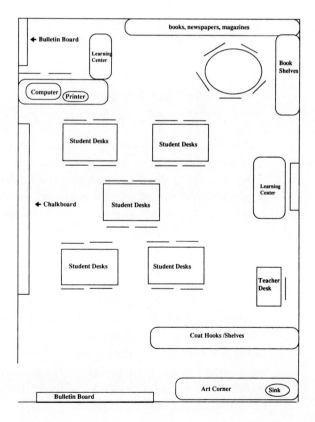

Interactions at the Computer

One of the early predictions of the demise of computer use in the classroom centered around its supposed lack of encouragement for inter-action among students. Many educators feared that students who were glued to the computer screen would miss out on the conversational give-and-take in a classroom of peers. They predicted computer-using students would be isolated learners. Actually the computer has accomplished the opposite! In Mr. Thompson's classroom, for example, Lauren quietly observes the daily routines. She seldom volunteers answers, nor does she interact with other students. But her behavior changes dramatically when she and another student sit at the computer. Lauren discusses not only the software on-screen but frequently shares personal stories that relate to the program's topic. Why the change of behavior? Perhaps the computer provides a nonjudgmental backdrop for conversation. Or perhaps she simply feels more confident working in tandem. Whatever the reason, Lauren's time at the computer is filled with language experiences that are difficult to replicate at any other time of her school day. Far from isolating her, the computer connects Lauren to her peers.

---

environment—it must be complemented by effective teacher guidance in communication experiences.

The Teacher's Role

The physical environment alone does little to assure effective development of language arts skills—even if it includes a computer and good course-ware. It is up to the teacher to provide guidance so that discussions are channeled and meaningful to participants (Dudley-Marling and Searle, 1988). Working at the computer can certainly encourage students to use language and share experiences with their peers or their teacher. Skillful teachers will maximize this use, integrating such opportunities for learning with the background skills of their students and thereby increasing the power that knowledge and language can give them.

When promoting computer use, teachers should apply the principles of large and small groups (discussed in Chapter 2 and later in this chapter), remembering that, when developing language arts skills, students move through a learning and then a practice phase. The learning phase requires more direct teacher supervision. An effective classroom environment enables students to move easily and freely from large-group to small-group to individual use of the computer.

In a language-rich environment, the teacher capitalizes on each opportunity for students to broaden their language skills. Interviewing family members for historical data, debating school issues, tutoring younger students, taking responsibility for room tours at open house, and quizzing guest speakers for details of their topics are samples of such opportunities. And teachers should be alert to ways in which the computer could enhance such activities.

One of the best opportunities for students to broaden language arts skills is by talking with each other. Therefore, teachers must stimulate effective interaction and communication not only by students by *among* them—being sure to monitor such communication. Listening, thinking, and expressive skills are nurtured in a language-rich environment when the teacher not only allows such "continued talk" but truly encourages it (Dudley-Marling and Searle, 1988).

Sometimes teachers unintentionally eliminate opportunities for language development. In a discussion or conversation, they may anticipate a student's comment, lead the student to a response, or talk *for* the student. However, students improve their language-related skills by taking the lead in conversations, and teachers must be careful to allow this to happen.

Such assertiveness can be fostered in computer use as well. For example, one way to promote communication skills is to allow students to be the first to examine a new software package and then introduce it to the teacher or the class. Another is to show an interest in the programs students are running and to ask them pertinent questions about what they have been doing. Having a group of students run several programs and then discuss them with one another is another good way to promote communication skills. The point is that the computer should not serve as a barrier but rather as a stimulus to thinking, listening, and expression.

SOFTWARE SELECTION

The physical setting and the teacher's style of communication in a language-rich learning environment merely set the stage for teaching language arts skills. To make the computer an effective tool in this environment, the teacher must select suitable software and have a plan for implementing it. Since many elementary schools possess an extensive software library, teachers may find good software already available. Or teachers may have a lesson plan in which the computer would be a natural teaching tool but suitable software is not available. In either scenario, the teacher needs to become familiar with evaluating and choosing appropriate software to meet classroom objectives.

The seven steps that follow can serve as guidelines for selecting software. It is important to note that these guidelines should be applied in a complete instructional context. This means that the teacher should *first* think about effective instructional strategies such as those described in Chapter 2 and *then* select software for situations in which these strategies can appropriately be integrated with the computer to enhance academic learning time. In other words, teachers should first see a need for computerized assistance and then select software to fill this need.

Teachers sometimes view the task of finding, evaluating, and choosing software as a time-consuming, overwhelming burden. It need not be! Assistance is available from many sources. Professional journals, such as *Classroom Computer Learning*, *Electronic Learning*, and *The Computing Teacher* publish frequent reviews of instructional software. Nearly all software companies offer a thirty-day preview period so that educators can try out the software in a true classroom environment. Local colleges, state departments of education, educational service centers, or intermediate school districts may provide a software preview center or clearinghouse so that teachers have the opportunity to preview before purchasing programs.

An annual publication, *TESS: The Educational Software Selector*, includes brief descriptions of software for all curriculum areas. The book's author, EPIE Institute, suggests the seven-step process that follows to achieve responsible software selection, purchase, and integration into the curriculum (TESS, 1986).

Step 1: Analyze Needs

Before looking at software, carefully examine curricular objectives and/or competencies to decide whether or not software logically fits into the curriculum. The questions posed in Figure 3.4 serve as a guide to assessing needs that might be met by the use of the computer. Questions may be modified to address any subject area or grade level. This step establishes the vital connection between the software and curriculum.

Step 2: Specify Requirements

Results of the needs assessment serve as a basis for creating a formal (usually written) specification of software requirements. This step provides specific criteria for selection.

Figure 3.4 Questions to address: needs assessment.

1. What curricular objectives/competencies present problems in student achievement/understanding?
2. What methods and materials are currently being used to address these objectives/competencies? Analyze each in relation to student achievement/understanding.
3. Would the use of software be an appropriate choice to address any of the objectives/competencies above? List and describe.
4. Identify the type of software most appropriate in meeting each objective/competency above. (drill-and-practice, tutorial, application, simulation)

Step 3: Identify Promising Software First

This step could be time-consuming without the help of a resource such as The Educator's Software Selector (TESS) from EPIE Institute. TESS provides thousands of descriptions of educational software packages. The most recent edition has fifty pages of language arts programs alone! In TESS, teachers will find a complete description of the program and, if a national service has evaluated the package, a rating as well as other pertinent information. In addition, TESS provides suggestions for use of the programs described. We have also supplied concise descriptions of a large number of courseware products related to language arts instruction (see Appendix B).

Step 4: Read Relevant Reviews

Reviews of chosen programs are readily accessible through a variety of resources. *Micro-Courseware PRO/FILE* from EPIE Institute is available by subscription. Computer magazines such as *The Computing Teacher*, *Classroom Computer Learning*, and *Electronic Learning* print evaluations and reviews monthly. The latter two compile a "top programs" list yearly. In addition, subject matter journals often provide reviews and demonstrations of programs specifically related to language arts. In Chapter 12 of this book, we provide detailed reviews of forty programs worth considering. By reading reviews in any of these sources, teachers can narrow the list of possibilities.

Step 5: Preview

Neither compiling a list of promising software that meets curricular objectives nor reading reviews guarantees that the software listed will be appropriate for the classroom. Hands-on preview continues to be the best way to guarantee that a software program meets classroom needs. As we stated earlier, nearly all publishers provide a free thirty- to sixty-day preview period, although they may require a purchase order to initiate it. A preview period gives the educator ample time to look at the program and judge its adaptability. If possible, both students and teachers should use the software during this time. When time constraints prevent students from preview, the teacher must preview with two perspectives in mind: that of the student, who will respond correctly and incorrectly to the screen; and that of the educator, who will implement the software. The following points can be used to guide the teacher in hands-on evaluation of software:

- *Match with curricular objectives:* Although the previous steps should have insured this, a hands-on approach will confirm a match.
- *Documentation:* The manual should contain a full description of the program objectives, directions for loading, and sample screens.
- *Instructions:* On-screen instructions for using the program should be clear. It is *not* safe to assume that learners will read the manual. The simple fact is that almost no learners ever read the manual to find out how to run a program!
- *Accuracy of content:* Facts should be accurate and the reading level appropriate.
- *Modifiability:* Programs that contain teacher authoring features allow the addition of text and can add to the usefulness of the program.
- *Reinforcement:* The program's response to correct and incorrect answers should offer variety and should be appropriate. Sometimes problems arise when the feedback to an incorrect answer is more "fun" for the student than the feedback for a correct answer.
- *Corrective feedback:* The student should receive help in determining the precise nature of mistakes. If appropriate, the student should have an opportunity to try again, based on this corrective feedback.
- *Pacing:* Usually, the more control the user has over the pace, the better. But there are some instances when the computer should at least partially control the pace (for example, by forcing the student to slow down and read the information on the screen).
- *Interaction:* The program should require student responses and react to this input. Otherwise the software is simply a textbook on the screen.
- *Incorrect response limit:* An announced limit on the allowed number of responses avoids frustration.

- *On-screen help:* Directions and prompts should be available for the student. When asked for a response, the student should always have access to all the information needed to provide it.
- *Graphics:* These should provide appropriate motivation without overwhelming the student.
- *Sound:* Being able to control the sound can be an asset in a classroom situation.
- *Escape option:* The user should be allowed to get out of the program without turning off the computer. A student who exits early should receive appropriate feedback, and proper records should be kept.
- *Report/record keeping:* Although this area is optional, a student appreciates feedback at the end of a session that reports both success and need for improvement. Many programs offer a recording system that the teacher can access later.

This rather lengthy list can be organized into an evaluation form such as that in Figure 3.5. A form helps to focus thinking and can be supportive in requesting funds to purchase selected software.

Step 6: Make Recommendations

At this point in the process, the teacher decides whether to recommend purchase based on the outcome of preview. Reasons for the decision can be included in the preview form.

Step 7: Get Postuse Feedback

Collecting student and teacher comments on actual software use can provide valuable information that, one hopes, will affirm the purchase of the program and assist teachers in planning for its use. If possible, teachers should collect valid, concrete data to verify that anticipated instructional outcomes have occurred.

LESSON PLANNING

The seven-step process suggested by EPIE Institute helps assure success in selecting and purchasing software. However, effective use requires that the software be a part of a well-designed instructional sequence. The categories addressed in Figure 3.6 assist the teacher in focusing on the elements necessary for software implementation.

Title _____

Publisher _____

Hardware required _____ Cost _____

Subject area _____ Topic _____

Type:
　　Drill　　　　　Tutorial　　　Utility　　　Management
　　Simulation　　Game　　　　Application

Grade Level　P　K　1　2　3　4　5　6　7　8　9　10　11　12

Objectives _____

_____

_____

Please evaluate software on the criteria listed below. Circle a rating of 1,
2, 3, or 4 with 1 indicating a very low level of compliance and 4 indicating a very high level of compliance.

Matches curricular objectives?	1　2　3　4　NA
Well documented?	1　2　3　4　NA
Includes clear on-screen instructions?	1　2　3　4　NA
Provides accurate content?	1　2　3　4　NA
Can be modified according to student need?	1　2　3　4　NA
Offers positive reinforcement?	1　2　3　4　NA
Provides corrective feedback?	1　2　3　4　NA
Allows user to control pace?	1　2　3　4　NA
Promotes interaction?	1　2　3　4　NA
Limits incorrect responses?	1　2　3　4　NA
Contains easily accessible help screen?	1　2　3　4　NA
Uses color, graphics, and sound effectively?	1　2　3　4　NA
Provides a report or record keeping option?	1　2　3　4　NA

As you can see in Figure 3.6, the first category is the objective, which
stresses once again the importance of basing computer use on classroom
instructional objectives. After supplying the software title, publisher, and
type, the teacher is directed to decide how the software fits in a particular
lesson. There are actually nine events of instruction in any well-designed
instructional sequence (Gagne and Briggs, 1979), as summarized in Figure
3.7. Software can be used to support any one of these nine phases. For
example, it may be part of the lead-in, in which the software is used to grab

Figure 3.6 Software
implementation plan.

Objective: _____

_____

_____

Title _____

Publisher _____ Grade _____

Type:
    Drill   Tutorial   Utility   Management
    Simulation   Game   Application

Software will be incorporated in the following lesson structure:
    ___ Gaining student attention
    ___ Sharing objectives
    ___ Recalling prerequisite knowledge
    ___ Presenting content
    ___ Providing guidance
    ___ Eliciting performance
    ___ Providing feedback
    ___ Evaluating performance
    ___ Enhancing retention and transfer

Interaction: Individual   Small-Group   Large-Group

Other peripherals required _____

_____

Student involvement time _____

Precomputer activities _____

_____

_____

Computer activity _____

_____

_____

Follow-up activities _____

_____

_____

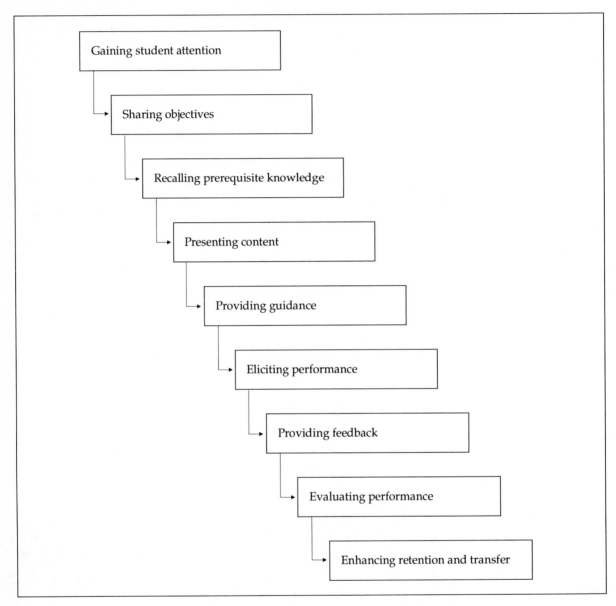

Figure 3.7 Events of instruction (Gagne and Briggs, 1979).

interest. It may be used in an instructional phase to present knowledge or to develop skills. Or it may be used in a follow-up phase to enhance retention and transfer.

A TASK ANALYSIS APPROACH TO SOFTWARE SELECTION

It is impossible to select appropriate software without considering the situation in which it will be used. A program that is "good" for one teacher or in one situation may be "terrible" for another or in another setting. One of the best ways to evaluate the potential usefulness of a piece of software is to perform a task analysis of the instructional activity for which it will be used and then check to see how well the computerized material fits this instructional unit. For example, imagine that a teacher is planning to teach a unit on punctuation, in which the major goal is that the student will understand the basic concept of punctuation at the end of a sentence. Before selecting a software package, the teacher should ask, "What do I actually want to *do* with the program? Why do I need a computer program at all?" Let's assume that the answer to this question is that the teacher wants to give a good introduction to the concept, encourage discussion, and then have students interact with the computer program to verify that they have understood the concept before applying it or going on to more advanced topics.

With these objectives, the teacher is actually using the computer as a "surrogate tutor." In selecting software, therefore, it is appropriate to list the tasks that the teacher would ask the tutor to perform and then see how well the computer performs these same tasks. See Figure 3.8 for a list of tasks that a good tutor would perform for individual students being tutored on a concept in language arts, if an individual tutor were available.

Figure 3.9 shows several screens from PUNCTUATION RULES (Weekly Reader Software). If our teacher examined this program, she would discover that it performs Steps 1 through 3 fairly well. The computer does not perform Step 4, unless the student requests "help," and if the student asks for help more than once, the program simply gives the same explanation with no increase in clarity and no improved focus on the concept under consideration. The computer does not perform Steps 5 through 8 at all. It performs Step 9; but because of some weak questions and a lack of branching, it is actually fairly easy for a student who knows very little about end punctuation to be "certified" as understanding the concept.

Is this a good program? The answer is that for students who have already attained a reasonable understanding of the concept, this program may work as well as a good individualized tutor. This is because these students would need only Steps 1, 2, 3, and 9; they would not need Steps 5 through 8. However, for students in need of remediation and refocusing, the program would be far less effective. Some students needing help would

1. Give a verbal summary (if necessary) of the concept. Or have the student give a verbal summary of the concept. (Often this step can be skipped, and the tutorial sequence begun at Step 2.)

2. Ask a question about the concept (or part of the concept). A correct answer to this question should demonstrate an understanding of the concept.

3. If the student answers the question correctly, give positive feedback; ask additional questions if more are necessary to verify understanding.

4. If the student answers the question incorrectly, provide a verbal restatement of the concept. This should paraphrase the original statement, focusing as specifically as possible on the misunderstanding that led to the incorrect answer.

5. Instead of Step 4, the tutor could offer prompts to stimulate the student to think more carefully and thereby generate the correct answer. This is often a better idea than Step 4, especially if the tutor is able to focus on the student's misconception.

6. If the student continues to make errors, repeat Steps 4 and 5. If the student seems to be getting closer to the right answer, it may be appropriate to repeat these steps even more often. If the student is making no progress, move on to Step 8.

7. If the student gives the correct answer after Step 4 or 5, ask another question to verify that the student really understands the answer to the question. Eventually ask questions that will apply the concept in settings that require generalization of the concept. Repeat Steps 4 through 6 as necessary.

8. If the student shows a persistent misunderstanding of the concept, cycle the student back to an earlier phase of instruction, prior to this tutorial sequence, providing concrete experience for the concept under consideration. When the student is ready, return to Step 1.

9. When the student has answered sufficient questions to demonstrate mastery of the concept, verify that he or she is ready for the next step in the learning sequence.

Figure 3.8 Nine steps typically peformed by a good human tutor during individualized instruction to verify that a student understands the concept under consideration. (Note that this task analysis is offered purely as an *example*. We are by no means suggesting that all language arts units should follow these steps.)

get it in Step 4; but the program provides no prompting (Step 5), and many students would not benefit from the rephrasing of concepts supplied by the program. The decision regarding whether to use this program would depend on the abilities and understandings of the students and on the

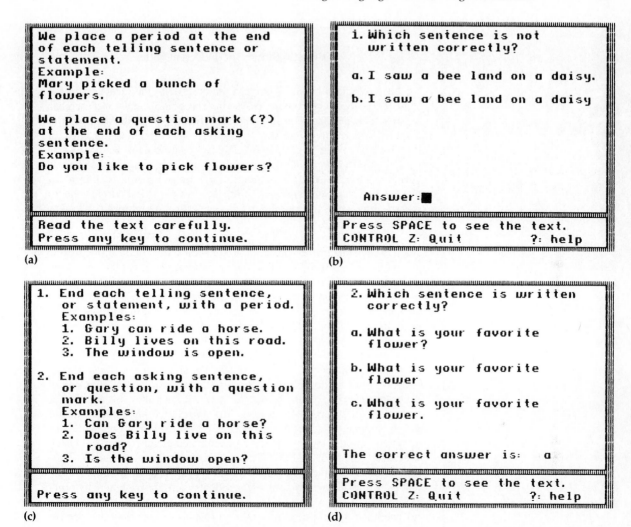

Figure 3.9 Screens from PUNCTUATION RULES (Weekly Reader Software) showing (a) the presentation of a concept, (b) a question about the concept, (c) a help screen, and (d) feedback for an incorrect response.

teacher's capacity and willingness to supply the remediation not supplied by the program.

In addition to the steps that appear in a task analysis, there are other considerations in effective software selection. For example, if students are likely to let their minds wander because they are not particularly interested in the concept under consideration, it would be extremely important for

Different Strokes for Different Folks

Mrs. Wright and Mrs. Hartigan are both first-grade teachers in the same school. Both are teaching basic letter recognition skills, and each has a computer in her classroom. Mrs. Wright is using STICKYBEAR ABC from Weekly Reader Family Software to introduce her children to the letters of the alphabet. When a child presses a letter key on the keyboard, the computer provides an animated picture involving a word that begins with that letter. The major advantage of the computer is that children can feel that they themselves are generating the examples. Mrs. Wright believes that the interaction and animation will hold children's interest and lead to increased learning.

Mrs. Hartigan uses "ABC Discovery" from DR. PEET'S TALK/WRITER by Hartley. The program presents the letters of the alphabet one at a time on the screen in both upper and lowercase and at the same time says the name of the letter. In another program on the same disk, children merely type any letter they wish on the keyboard and it is shown and spoken. When they press the Return key, the letters are repeated in the order in which they were typed.

The same programs are available to both teachers; but Mrs. Wright never uses DR. PEET and Mrs. Hartigan never uses STICKYBEAR ABC. Is one program better than the other? Perhaps in some sense one is superior, but that doesn't really matter. It is not really useful to think of programs as being either "good" or "bad." Rather, they are effective or ineffective for a particular purpose. Mrs. Wright felt her children would benefit immensely from generating their own examples and would be attracted by abundant interaction with animated pictures. Because she felt she herself could not offer this combination of activities, she used STICKYBEAR ABC to supplement her own endeavors. She already had an excellent peer tutoring system, in which students were shown letters by other students, recited the letters out loud, and obtained feedback. Since she had no need for a computer program to duplicate her already effective strategies, she chose one that would give her help where it was needed. STICKYBEAR ABC was the program for her.

Mrs. Hartigan had opposite needs. She was a creative genius at providing vivid examples of words beginning with various letters, and her students were already adept at this. Since her students were already motivated to learn the letters, they did not need animated graphics for inspiration. However, Mrs. Hartigan's students had problems with simple letter recognition. Several students were unable to recognize and relate the upper and lowercase versions of the same letter. This skill really had to become automatic in order for the students to move on to higher-level skills. Mrs. Hartigan herself found it boring to spend time on this activity. To help her students with this skill, Mrs. Hartigan chose the repeated practice that DR. PEET offered. DR. PEET was the program for her.

the computer to provide motivational features to keep their interest. On the other hand, if students are already highly motivated to master a concept, then a no-frills approach (without a gamelike atmosphere) might be more effective. In addition, as we shall discuss later in this chapter, if software is to be used for group instruction, the "friendliness" of the user interface must be considered.

Language arts software continues to proliferate rapidly, and many teachers acquire software simply by looking for titles that sound like they fit their needs. This is not wise. Shelves and file cabinets in schools are filled with programs that "sounded good" but have never been used at all. The task analysis strategy suggested in this section may take more time, but it is much more likely to lead to the selection of good software. It will help you to choose software that meets your *real* needs.

CLASSROOM MANAGEMENT

Classroom management refers to the way in which the students interact with the computer and each other. Many teachers still view the computer as a tool for one-to-one instruction only. Although individual use represents a valuable model, as we've already pointed out, this narrow view eliminates many learning experiences that can take place in small-group as well as large-group instruction. Let's take a look at the three management techniques.

The Computer as a Tool for Individual Instruction

One way to use the computer for instruction is to have a student work alone at the computer. As a tool for individual instruction, the computer provides a patient, self-pacing, nonjudgmental approach. It allows the teacher to assign software that fits the needs of the student alone. The passive student who seldom volunteers answers or asks questions may become an active learner when seated at the computer. The student who may not hear "well done" from the teacher may hear those words in many ways when working at the computer. The student whose learning style is different from the teacher's primary mode of delivery may understand the information more clearly when the computer uses a different style of instruction (Dunn and Dunn, 1987). In the individualized setting, the computer is the perfect tool for the introduction of a skill or its practice as a form of remediation or enrichment. Types of software that adapt well to individual use include drill-and-practice packages and tutorials such as those shown in Figure 3.10.

Using one computer for individual instruction does pose some problems in scheduling, especially in a classroom of twenty-five or more students. How can all twenty-five have the same amount of individual time

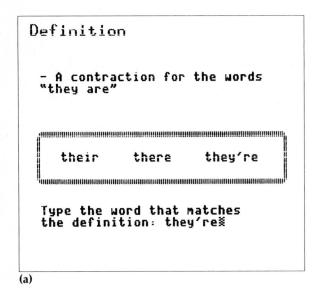

(a)

(b)

Figure 3.10 The software programs illustrated here—screen (a), WORD HERD: SOUND-ALIKES (MECC); screen (b), GRAMMAR GREMLINS (Davidson); and screen (c), SENTENCE COMBINING (Milliken)—provide the individual with guided practice.

> This program will help you learn how to put sentences together to make new sentences.
>
> Suppose you wrote these sentences:
>
> **Mary likes cats.**
> **Mary likes dogs.**
>
> You could put them together like this:
>
> **Mary likes cats and dogs.**
>
> PRESS [SPACE] FOR NEXT PAGE

(c)

at the computer? Perhaps they can't. And to be quite honest, perhaps they shouldn't. When the computer is used for individual instruction, the needs of one learner will not match those of another. Therefore, any formal schedule of computer use needs to be flexible enough to meet the needs of the individuals. We know of one teacher who uses a "people" schedule, with the names of those students who will be using the computer on a given day or week posted near the computer station. The schedule includes only the student's name and the lesson or software program assigned. During the students' work period, they take turns working at the computer. They are responsible for completing their assigned lesson and informing another student on the list that the computer is available. The schedule is student managed and does not create an additional burden in classroom mangement for the teacher.

This discussion assumes that a single computer is placed in a learning center in the classroom. When computers are arranged in other configurations, other possibilities arise. These additional arrangements are discussed in *The Computer in the Classroom* (Vockell and Schwartz, 1988).

The Computer in the Cooperative Learning Model

Since communication is a vital characteristic of a language-rich learning environment, using the computer strictly for an individualistic approach may promote learning of factual information or provide a means of motivated drill but may do little to encourage language skills. On the other hand, using the computer with small groups of students promotes frequent, open, and effective communication (Johnson and Johnson, 1986). Furthermore, since few classrooms have the number of computers necessary to set up a one-to-one ratio of computers to students, it is feasible for students to work in groups at the computer. As we've already pointed out, small-group interaction partnered with the cooperative learning model creates an advantageous classroom environment.

When used with small groups, the computer still offers most of the advantages described for individual learners, especially opportunities for frequent responses and individualized feedback. In addition, learners can attain the advantages of cooperative learning, which, when applied to computers (Johnson and Johnson, 1986) often consists of two to four students working interdependently to complete an assignment. Each student has a role (keyboarder, recorder, checker, encourager), and these roles are rotated among all members. Before entering information into the computer, all members of the group must be in agreement. This model is highly interactive, requiring group members to assist each other in working toward a common goal. Members have a vested interest in the performance of the group and in their own performance. Note that because the cooperative learning model, by its very nature, demands the use of language arts skills, the development of communication skills is one of its benefits. Therefore, students using this model can practice language arts skills even when they are studying entirely different subjects, like science or mathematics.

Many language arts activities lend themselves to a cooperative approach on the computer. The word processing of group stories allows peer editing in the creation of a document that will be published for the entire classroom. Word processing packages also allow teachers to create prompted lessons geared to the specific needs of their students. The proper use of programs that highlight higher-order thinking skills, such as THE FACTORY (Sunburst), promote peer interaction. Programs like this and lesson plans for using them are discussed in *The Computer and Higher-Order Thinking Skills* (Vockell and van Deusen, 1989). Additional computer activities that promote collaborative skills will be discussed in later chapters of this book.

The Computer in Large-Group Instruction

Large-group computer activities have often been overlooked in the language arts classroom. Perhaps many teachers are not aware of how simple it is to connect a computer to a large-screen monitor or a TV screen, which turns the computer and software into a presentation tool. As a lead-in or for demonstration, this method is highly motivational. An even larger display is provided by liquid crystal display (LCD) projection systems placed on overhead projectors (these devices are becoming more affordable for classroom use). However, most of the currently available LCD systems do not project color displays—and color is a useful component of much, but not all, software designed for elementary students. Both the large-screen monitor and the LCD projection system broaden the management possibilities for computer use in the language arts classroom. Both can also provide an opportunity for reviewing content in a large-group format. Programs like the GAME SHOW by Advanced Ideas are perfect for reviewing specialized vocabulary controlled by teacher input.

The initial presentation of almost any skill (and especially higher-order thinking skills) should be monitored by skillful teacher supervision. Often this introduction takes place without computerized assistance, but sometimes the computer can be an effective tool, even for an entire class. As we pointed out in Chapter 2, there is an important difference between the learning phase of instruction, when teacher supervision and feedback is critical, and the practice phase, when it is less so. Not all software is easily adaptable to large-group instruction; and teachers must often carefully plan their use of software on a large screen in front of an entire class or carefully select software that is effective for large-group instruction. Tom Snyder Productions is one software publisher that emphasizes software for the "one-computer classroom." For example, the DECISIONS, DECISIONS series is designed to foster interaction among all the members of an entire class.

The large-group use of computers does not necessarily contradict the principle of individualization. The key requirement of individualized instruction is that each student be working at his or her maximum level of performance on tasks related to his or her needs. Students involved in individualized instruction can also definitely benefit from interacting with peers; for example, they may profit from modeling, from motivating social interactions, or from feedback. They can also benefit from interacting with a knowledgeable teacher, who can keep them on task, model useful strategies, and provide feedback and insights as needed. For higher-order skills, a large-group, inquiry approach will often be effective initially, because it is likely to meet the needs of the students. Individualization comes from the interaction with a skillful teacher using the software with the students, not from the program itself.

Table 3.1 summarizes the three basic configurations in which computers can be employed and the conditions under which each is appropriate. As this table indicates, there are relatively few circumstances under which solitary use of the computer is the most desirable strategy. For programs that teach language arts skills, small groups are almost always preferable to individual students working at the computer. For initial presentations of higher-order thinking skills, however, large-group (whole-class) presentations are usually preferred. But once important skills have been thoroughly learned by some members of the class and at least partially mastered by everyone, small groups may provide a better use of academic learning time than a continued large-group session.

Table 3.1　Three basic configurations for classroom computer use and the situations appropriate for each.

Individual use

When the conditions for small-group use are present, but students are working on objectives that are of interest to them alone and not to other students in the same class at the same time.

When the very nature of a program demands solitary use (e.g., a game played by one person that would be boring for others to watch).

Small-group use

When students are learning factual information and specific skills that they can easily teach to other students.

When students are learning factual information and specific skills for which the computer provides enough structure to explain details and provide remedial feedback as necessary when learners express a lack of knowledge or a misconception.

After students possess a sound initial understanding of the thinking skills involved in the program, and they need additional practice to make the skills part of their automatic, individual repertoires.

After students have initially learned a thinking skill, there may be four or five good programs that provide additional practice; and it may be better to let students choose one or two of these programs that interest them rather than forcing the whole class to run a single program.

When cluster grouping is used for gifted students, there may be times when these students should work together on a project while the rest of the class pursues tasks that these students have already thoroughly mastered. (The term *cluster grouping* refers to the strategy of putting "clusters" of gifted students in heterogeneous classrooms with a trained teacher who will stimulate them intellectually and encourage them to interact with one another. This is a soundly based alternative to putting them in special classes for gifted students.)

When slower students need additional practice to master skills for which faster students need no more practice.

Large-group use

When students are still in the learning stage, especially when trying to master a higher-order skill, and they are likely to need the structured feedback and guidance that can best be provided by a teacher.

When the computer will serve as an effective "electronic chalkboard," as in the demonstration of geometric principles.

When some motivational factor makes it desirable for the whole group to work together, as when the program presents an interesting game that spectators might enjoy.

Off-Computer Activities

Once the grouping technique (individual, small-group, or large-group) has been determined (see the software implementation plan in Figure 3.6), the teacher's next step is to decide which precomputer and/or postcomputer activities are warranted. These activities are often referred to as "off-line." Both the pre and postcomputer activities illustrate the need for a complete plan. As Figure 3.7 showed, there are actually nine instructional events in any well-designed lesson. The computer can be employed to present all or part of any of these nine events. Although it is possible for a single program to encompass all nine, it is by no means necessary; and it is rare for a program to do so. The following is a list of the nine instructional events with examples of how the computer can assist with each:

- *Gaining student attention:* The computer may provide a game, an interesting screen presentation, or a puzzling problem that makes students want to proceed with the program or refer to some other source to learn more about a topic.
- *Sharing objectives:* The program may state a specific set of objectives to help students focus their attention as they run the program.
- *Recalling prerequisite knowledge:* The program may provide a pretest to see if students possess basic skills. These may be skills needed to run the main program itself or skills needed to perform an activity that will be conducted completely off the computer.
- *Presenting content:* The computer provides a tutorial on the information or skill to be studied.
- *Providing guidance:* The computer recommends study strategies or provides mnemonic devices or branches the student to information particularly suited to that student's needs.
- *Eliciting performance:* The computer presents questions for the student to answer. These can be questions embedded in a tutorial, to ascertain that the student is progressing properly through the tutorial, or the questions can be part of a drill on material taught completely off the computer.
- *Providing feedback:* The computer evaluates student performance, usually to questions asked on the computer during the previous phase. However, it is also possible for the computer to provide feedback for performance conducted completely off the computer, as in the case of personalized feedback letters generated on a word processor.
- *Evaluating performance:* The computer evaluates the performance either after individual tasks or after a whole series of tasks. Evaluation overlaps with feedback, and the teacher often merely has to make sure that the learner makes the necessary comparison or judgment of feedback that constitutes evaluation.

- *Enhancing retention and transfer:* The computer provides opportunities to respond in new situations with information or skills learned in an original instructional setting. Often the student learns something in one program and then applies it in another. Or the student learns something off the computer and later applies it while running a computer program.

An actual lesson of instruction is very complex, and these activities may be presented through many different media. The value of examining all nine instruction events is that a breakdown in learning may occur if any one of these events fails to take place. Therefore, the teacher's role is to make sure that all the events are incorporated into an effective lesson plan. The computer should play a role as needed. A common occurrence is that the teacher will ascertain that several events are presented effectively off the computer, but that the computer can make a distinct contribution by presenting one or two other events.

Figure 3.11 provides a detailed lesson plan in which the computer is integrated with print and audiovisual media into a complete instructional unit. As you can see, this outline covers all nine instructional events, some in which the computer plays no role and others in which it is dominant.

Depending on the software and how it is being used, pre and postcomputer activities may be involved in any one or a combination of these events of instruction. A brief discussion of objectives, or a description of how to use the software, may be all the student needs before going to the computer. Sometimes role playing is suitable and sometimes the use of manipulatives helps. There are times when a large screen can be used to walk through a particularly tricky portion of a program or to preview vocabulary. Few software packages are effective when used with absolutely no pre or postcomputer activities.

SUMMARY

As this chapter illustrates, using the computer effectively for language arts instruction is dependent on several factors. Establishing a language-rich learning environment sets the stage for well-designed lessons based on software wisely selected for the objective stated. Careful selection of software helps assure that the computer will provide effective instructional materials related to the objectives of the language arts curriculum. Well-organized lesson plans help integrate these materials into the language-rich learning environment.

Figure 3.11 A sample software implementation plan.

Objective: To differentiate among the uses of *their*, *there*, and *they're*.

Title: MAGIC SLATE (or other word processing program)

Publisher: Sunburst   Grade: Fourth

Type:
Drill	Tutorial	Utility	Management
Simulation	Game	X Application	

Software will be incorporated in the following lesson structure:
    Gaining student attention
    Sharing objectives
    Recalling prerequisite knowledge
X Presenting content
X Providing guidance
X Eliciting performance
X Providing feedback
X Evaluating performance
X Enhancing retention and transfer

Interaction: X Individual   X Small-Group   X Large-Group

Other peripherals required: An LCD (projection system) for large-group introduction.

Student involvement time: Approximately forty minutes

Precomputer activities: Distribute among small groups of three or four students sentence strips (large type fonts on construction paper) that contain the proper uses of the target words. Have students read the sentences within the groups and predict what the goal of the lesson is. Discuss the use and spelling of each of the homonymns (*there*, *their*, and *they're*).

Computer activity: On the LCD, display an exercise in which several sentences use the wrong homonymn. Have students in the large group point out the misuse of the words and discuss why each is wrong. Have students correct these errors on-screen. Assign each group to create a paragraph on MAGIC SLATE misusing the homonymns *there*, *their*, and *they're* and save the exercise on a disk. Groups will trade paragraphs and make corrections on the screen so that the final printout is a revised exercise with the corrections included.

Follow-up activities: This format can be used with any specific focus on word usage. Encourage students to create their own proofreading exercises to exchange with peers.

REFERENCES

Dudley-Marling, C., and D. Searle. "Enriching Language Learning Environments for Students with Learning Disabilities." *Journal of Learning Disabilities* 21 (1988): 140–143.

Dunn, K., and R. Dunn. "Dispelling Outmoded Beliefs About Student Learning." *Educational Leadership* 44 (1987): 55–62.

EPIE Institute. *TESS: The Educational Software Selector.* New York: Teachers College Press, 1986.

Gagne, R., and L. Briggs. *Principles of Instructional Design.* New York: Holt, Rinehart and Winston, 1979.

Johnson, R. T., and D. W. Johnson. "Comparison of Computer-Assisted Cooperative, Competitive, and Individualistic Learning." *American Educational Research Journal* 23 (1986): 382–392.

Mayer, J. S., and R. S. Brause. "Learning Through Teaching: Is Your Classroom Like Your Grandmother's?" *Language Arts* 63 (1986): 617–620.

Vockell, E. L., and E. Schwartz. *The Computer in the Classroom.* Watsonville, Calif.: Mitchell, 1988.

Vockell, E. L., and R. van Deusen. *The Computer and Higher-Order Thinking Skills.* Watsonville, Calif.: Mitchell, 1989.

CHAPTER 4

READING

BECAUSE OF THE RELATIVE newness of computers in reading instruction and because of the huge amount of software available, implementation of the computer in the reading curriculum is often difficult. It has been easier to generate vast quantities of software than to explain how the software is best used. To determine the computer's best use for reading instruction, teachers must first gain practical teaching experience, acquire knowledge of reading theory, and understand the potential of the microcomputer.

Five basic guidelines underlie the best current applications of the computer to reading instruction:

1. One of the greatest strengths of the microcomputer is as a word processor.
2. Reading should be taught in contexts that are meaningful to students—that is to say, not as isolated units with no relevance to each other. Units of instruction should be integrated. Background and interest should already exist or be developed as part of the unit.
3. Inexpensive synthesized speech can have a dramatic impact on beginning reading instruction, especially to very young readers.
4. The teacher and the student must remain the key figures in the instructional process. The computer is a tool, not a replacement for an effective teacher who coordinates instruction and facilitates learning.
5. Teachers and school administrators need to be sufficiently prepared to use the microcomputer successfully in the classroom. This requires more than token support.

By following these guidelines, schools can greatly enhance the effectiveness of their reading programs.

BASIC APPROACHES TO READING

There are eight major approaches to reading instruction:

- *Basal Reader Approach:* Designed for the average child, this approach is highly structured, skills oriented, and well organized. Its components are student texts (readers), teacher manuals, and a great variety of supplemental materials—workbooks, tests, management systems, duplicating materials, software, cassettes, games, charts, and so on. These materials are acquired as a package from a major publisher and often include computer software to supplement the program.

- *Language Experience Approach:* Students learn to read stories created either individually or in cooperation with classmates, usually with the guidance of the teacher. The underlying theory is that writing, not reading, is the natural step between speaking and reading; that is, if people can speak, they can write; and if they can write, they can read. This approach is highly recommended by experts, and both teachers and students usually like it. Its major disadvantage is that, because it is hard to "package," publishers are reluctant to endorse it—and many teachers find it annoying to work without a structured set of textbooks. However, the language-rich classroom includes many opportunities and materials that can support this approach.
- *Modified Alphabet Approach:* Additional or altered symbols have been added to the alphabet in order to provide a one-to-one sound-symbol correspondence. After the students are able to read simple stories, these special symbols are phased out and students learn to read words with traditional letters and spellings.
- *Phonics Intensive Approach:* Students learn techniques for "sounding out" or decoding unknown words. Phonics systems isolate the smallest meaningful sounds and teach rules or clues to identify these sounds in print.
- *Linguistics Approach:* Larger groups of letters (phonograms), rather than individual sounds (phonemes), are used as patterns for decoding. *The Cat in the Hat* by Dr. Seuss relies heavily on such linguistic patterns.
- *Programmed Instruction Approach:* Highly individualized, this approach permits students to control the pace and sometimes the order in which information is presented. It is usually designed to be self-directed and requires a great deal of built-in "branching" or alternatives for students to move ahead or go back as they interact with the text.
- *Individualized Instruction Approach:* Students read selections, usually of their own choice, then share them with teachers and classmates. Teachers prompt students to undertake reading activities, provide interaction and feedback, and offer instruction in areas in which students need help.
- *Multi-Media Approach:* Machines such as tape recorders, filmstrip projectors, language masters, and so on are used in an integrated attempt to teach reading skills.

These approaches overlap and are often employed simultaneously. For example, teachers using the Basal Reader or Language Experience approaches are likely to use phonics methods as part of their instruction. Although the Language Experience Approach is the most widely recommended by experts and is obviously compatible with the concept of a language-rich environment, practical considerations make the Basal Reader Approach the most prevalent in American schools. However, many teachers use the Language Experience Approach to supplement basal reading. In addition, there appears to be a tendency among publishers to incorporate some of the principles of the Language Experience Approach into their basal series.

Regardless of which approach teachers use, computers can play a vital role in delivering certain types of reading instruction, and this chapter will discuss these briefly. For greater detail on the major approaches and strategies for integrating reading instruction with computers, see *The Computer in the Reading Curriculum* (Whitaker, Schwartz, and Vockell, 1989).

The following pages describe specific reading skills. Teachers will generally employ one or more of the approaches described above when teaching these skills. And although good teachers have effectively taught reading without computers for many years, the computer can be introduced to enhance the quality of academic learning time and help students learn to read.

Comprehension—understanding, inferring, communicating, predicting, internalizing, applying, appreciating, and the like—is the purpose of reading. How to best achieve it has been debated for decades. Experts agree that no matter how children are introduced to words, starting very early in the program and continuing throughout its duration, they should have experience with reading the words in meaningful contexts. As this chapter will show, the computer can be a useful tool at any stage of this process; but it is only a tool. It must be integrated with other proven strategies, such as parents reading to their children, students interacting with their teachers, children reading to children, and students applying their reading skills in meaningful ways to their basal readers and other textbooks, to their own writing, and to literature.

LETTER RECOGNITION

The ability to visually discriminate one letter of the alphabet from another is often considered the first skill in the hierarchy of reading skills. Students who cannot correctly recognize and discriminate among letters simply cannot go on to the higher skills of giving meaning to written symbols. Nevertheless, the mastery of simple skills such as letter and word recognition does not guarantee that students will be able to read—these basic skills are a necessary but not a sufficient condition for correct reading performance.

Although essential to reading, basic skills such as letter discrimination do not necessarily have to be taught to all learners during the initial stages of reading instruction. After hundreds or thousands of hours of being read to while on their parents' laps, some students simply acquire these skills without formal instruction. Reading skills, even as elementary as letter recognition, need to be taught only to those students who require instruction in order to get meaning from what they are reading—in order to comprehend. However, the average student will no doubt require some instruction and practice in letter discrimination and most other basic reading skills. This usually takes place at the "readiness" stage of instruction, most often during kindergarten. Learning to identify the names of letters and their associated sounds and developing knowledge of the alphabet are the most popular reading readiness activities.

While there has been a great body of reading readiness material developed, the current opinion is that much of it has little to do with beginning to read. The learning of colors and color names, for example, may even have a negative effect on the large number of color-blind children who, in frustration, may actually come to believe that they will not learn how to read because they cannot discriminate colors! It is now believed that prereading activities such as language development are more beneficial for young children. In other words, it may be more useful to give children an opportunity to use words than it is to teach them to tell right from left or to recognize arbitrary words out of context. Geoffrion and Geoffrion (1983) suggest that instruction should focus on four aspects of reading readiness: developing an awareness of print, learning to identify the letters of the alphabet, developing an initial reading vocabulary, and increasing language comprehension skills.

There are many software programs that effectively teach and give practice in letter recognition. These programs combine color, animation, and sound to teach skills useful in reading. With the addition of peripherals, such as speech synthesizers, programs can engage children's senses even further. Moreover, good computer software lets children *control* their own learning by letting them set their own pace and actively participate in each operation.

STICKYBEAR ABC from Weekly Reader Family Software is a good example of a program that introduces young children to the letters of the alphabet. When a child presses a letter key on the keyboard, the computer provides an animated picture involving a word that begins with that letter (see Figure 4.1). The program is merely an electronic and interactive version of the old "A is for Apple" books and the "Sesame Street" television program. The major advantage of the computer is that children can feel that they themselves are generating the examples. The traditional approaches need not be discarded, but it seems reasonable to believe that the interaction and animation will hold children's interest and lead to increased learning.

MUPPET WORD BOOK and Muppet Learning Keys from Sunburst provide similar practice in letter recognition. Many of the Muppet programs from Sunburst use a colorful, lightweight, plastic input device called Muppet Learning Keys that serves as a simplified, alternative keyboard. It employs an alphabetical arrangement of letters and large keys, which children use to direct the computer instead of using the standard keyboard. The Muppet Learning Keys device is plugged into the joystick port at the back of the computer with a cord that is long enough to allow it to be passed around in a small group of children. Once in place, this device can be used for other software from Sunburst as well.

With the addition of a speech synthesizer, another sense—hearing—can be employed. The ability to listen to words and sounds is particularly important for young children. Furthermore, some programs rely entirely upon computer-spoken (synthesized) directions, so that even the youngest child can run the programs without individualized adult supervision.

Figure 4.1 STICKYBEAR ABC (Weekly Reader Family Software) responds to keystrokes by displaying a picture of something beginning with the same initial letter.

An example of teaching and practicing letter recognition with the aid of a speech synthesizer is Disk I ("ABC Discovery") of DR. PEET'S TALK/WRITER by Hartley. The first program on this disk, "ABC Song," presents the letters of the alphabet one at a time on the screen in both upper and lowercases and simultaneously says the name of the letter (see Figure 4.2). In "Big Letters," children merely type any letter they wish on the keyboard and it is shown and spoken. When they press the Return key, the letters are repeated in the order in which they were typed. "Find Letters" requires students to type a letter—for example *O* for *orange*. The computer rewards correct answers by displaying a clever graphic. An added bonus of this program is that children gain familiarity with the computer keyboard.

Older speech synthesizers, while useful in many respects, were also frustrating because they sometimes produced a robotlike or unclear sound. A child with auditory discrimination problems would not be helped very much by such faulty sound. Improved speech synthesis, such as that often found in programs for the Apple IIGS computer, goes a long way toward solving this problem.

Another useful peripheral, called a "touch window," allows children to use their sense of touch to better discriminate and internalize letters of the alphabet. Like the Muppet Learning Keys, this input device enables young children to interact with a microcomputer in a special way (see

Figure 4.2 In "ABC Discovery," one of the programs on DR. PEET'S TALK/WRITER (Hartley), children have many opportunities to practice letter recognition.

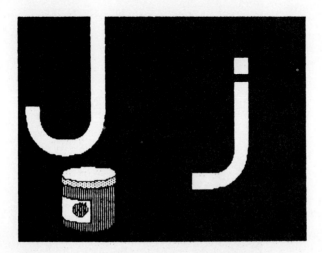

Figure 4.3). Students merely touch the transparent plastic sheet (the touch window) covering the screen to indicate their answer. Like the Muppet Learning Keys, the touch window simply plugs into the computer joystick port.

With a program entitled TOUCH 'N WRITE from Sunburst (Figure 4.4), students can use the touch window to actually learn letter formation. Students must correctly trace each letter in a well-organized presentation before going on. If they go outside the designated lines, they receive corrective feedback. As students complete lessons, they are rewarded with screen graphics and even a printed coloring and practice page. Student work can be monitored by means of a built-in management system.

With the addition of peripherals such as speech synthesizers, simplified keyboards, and touch windows, the computer can provide young children with opportunities to learn letter recognition and related skills in the learning modes they prefer—visual, auditory, or kinesthetic. This adaptation to individual learning styles can make an important contribution to early reading skills.

Figure 4.3 An example of a touch window. The student interacts with the program by touching areas on the special screen instead of (or in addition to) typing information at the keyboard.

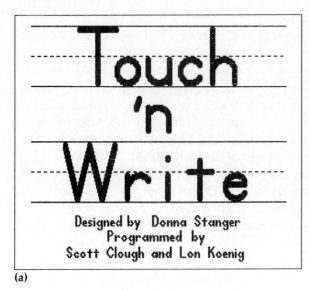

(a)

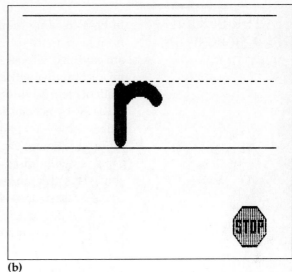

(b)

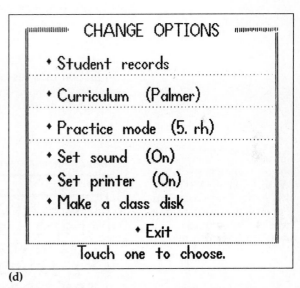

(c)

(d)

Figure 4.4 TOUCH 'N WRITE by Sunburst provides self-directed practice in manuscript writing.

LETTER-SOUND RELATIONSHIPS (PHONICS)

In basal reading sequences, phonics instruction usually spans the years from kindergarten through third grade. By the end of this time, students are expected to possess the basic skills to decode most English words. A microcomputer with a speech synthesizer is an excellent device for teaching students to read through phonics. With software such as TALKING TEXT WRITER by Scholastic, students can "make the computer talk" by typing letters and then replaying them. The synthesizer will use built-in phonetic "rules" to attempt to pronounce what has been entered. In this way children can eventually discover, even invent, principles of letter-sound relationships! This program is so easy to use that it can be employed at kindergarten or below (see Figure 4.5).

SOUND IDEAS by Houghton Mifflin is another software package that uses the voice synthesizer to provide phonics lessons to young children. Because most of the directions are spoken, little or no adult supervision is required. The system consists of a package of software diskettes, a guide, and a student activity workbook. The lessons are variations of the same format throughout the series; that is, the student is required to match a "target" picture, letter, or word to one of three pictures (see Figure 4.6). In addition, teachers can easily view each student's performance score upon completion of a lesson. At the end of each lesson, students are given a spoken reference to a specific page in their activity workbook.

Figure 4.5 Children enjoy the voice capabilities of TALKING TEXT WRITER (Scholastic). The words that appear on the screen are also "read" to the students through a speech synthesizer.

Figure 4.6 Students using SOUND IDEAS by Houghton Mifflin are continually aware of their progress. On-screen graphics post their scores.

A great many programs for phonics drill, such as MECC's PHONICS PRIME TIME series, do not require a speech synthesizer. Typically, such programs require the student to identify a picture and match it with a specific letter or letter combination, for instance, initial or final sounds.

FIRST LETTER FUN from MECC is unusual and interesting because it guides children through a colorful graphics "story" wherein they are periodically required to identify the first letter of the word for a particular object highlighted in the picture on the screen (see Figure 4.7). Programs

Figure 4.7 Children pick the letter that matches the picture shown in MECC's FIRST LETTER FUN.

from MUPPET WORD BOOK deal with beginning consonant and vowel sounds and have the additional advantage of permitting young students to enter words from an alternate keyboard with the letters arranged alphabetically instead of hunting for letters on a standard keyboard.

WORD MUNCHERS from MECC enables children to practice vowel sounds in a gamelike atmosphere. Figure 4.8 shows a screen from this program in which the learner is supposed to "gobble up" all the words that have the long *A* sound, as in *cake*.

READER RABBIT (Figure 4.9) is an extremely popular program for helping students develop letter-sound recognition. In the example, students choose a word containing the short *a* sound, as in *sat*, and that word is added to the train. For users with an Apple IIGS, READER RABBIT also comes in a "talking" version.

The Basal Reader Approach is built around phonics instruction; so teachers emphasizing that approach can use computerized phonics programs to supplement the basal readers as needed. However, since basal readers are generally thorough in their phonics instruction, most students may have little need for such supplementary programs. Unlike this approach, the Individualized Instruction and Language Experience approaches do not emphasize phonics instruction; teachers employing these approaches may want to use computerized phonics programs to help their students develop decoding skills.

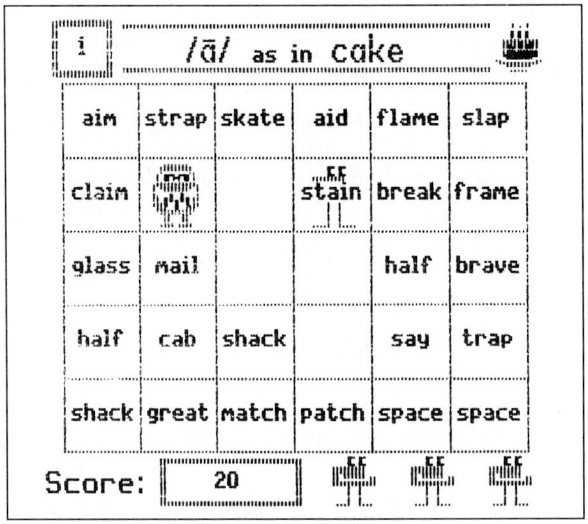

Figure 4.8 WORD MUNCHERS (MECC) is a popular way to review vowel sounds. Students find words with the key sound while trying to avoid being "eaten" by the Troggles.

Figure 4.9 Matching short vowel sounds is one of the activities that READER RABBIT (The Learning Company) uses to motivate students.

Although sounding out words is useful, many of the most common words are nonphonetic. One way to deal with these exceptions is to use an overall phonics approach in which the exceptions are taught as "sight words." Another approach is to use a modified alphabet or orthographic system. In such a beginning reading program, students are taught an extended alphabet, which represents the exact number of speech sounds in the English language. The theory is that students will have less difficulty with beginning reading if each sound has only one symbol. Later, students are eased into standard spellings.

IBM's WRITING TO READ is an entire computerized beginning reading program based on the modified alphabet for kindergarten and first grade. Students spend about thirty to forty minutes per day in a lab setting rotating through five "stations." At the "Computer Station" students are taught, through interactive software and synthesized speech, the forty-two speech phonemes developed for the program (Figure 4.10). At the other stations—"Work Journal," "Listening Library," "Writing/Typing," and "Make Words"—students engage in other reinforcement and reading-related activities.

The program's supporters claim that by the end of the first grade, WRITING TO READ graduates are ready to read second-grade materials written in the standard alphabet. In schools in which it has been implemented, the WRITING TO READ program has met with an apparently high degree of success. A major difficulty with the program, however, is that it

Figure 4.10 The "Computer Station" of the WRITING TO READ program introduces students to the forty-two phonemes used in our language.

requires the exclusive use of one brand of computer hardware and software. Most schools cannot afford to install more than one brand of computer—not many schools, for example, can install an IBM lab for reading *and* an Apple lab for mathematics. Obviously, hardware vendors would like to keep customers to themselves, but teachers may not want to be restricted to the software written for a particular machine (for example, a teacher restricted to IBM software could not pick and choose among more popular programs written for the Apple II computer).

Regardless of their approach to phonics, educators must take care to not burden or bore students with large amounts of unnecessary phonics instruction. Most students simply need a basic grasp of phonics as a reading tool. There is no reason to believe that advanced phonics skills make young children even better readers. In addition, the amount of phonics skills needed by individual students varies considerably. Furthermore, if children have extreme difficulty learning through a phonics approach, it often makes more sense to use a different technique with those pupils rather than to work harder on the phonics. For instance, children with auditory discrimination problems often find it extremely frustrating to discern many of the subtle sound discriminations required in some phonics programs—unaccented syllables, for example. Differences in regional dialects and pronunciations present another problem. All that phonics can be expected to do is help children get approximate pronunciations.

Phonics instruction from workbooks necessarily involves an inherent paradox: How are children supposed to know if they have sounded out a word correctly if they merely read it and write an answer in their workbooks? In fact, most workbook phonics activities lack important feedback. The most useful practice in phonics occurs when students are able to read aloud and receive feedback from a teacher or tutor, but this requires too much personal monitoring to be useful in the typical classroom. The computer has not done much to solve this problem. New courseware that takes advantage of larger computer memories (e.g., READER RABBIT for the Apple IIGS) helps by providing high-quality audio feedback to learners; but at the present time there are no effective programs that permit learners to say what they think they have read and then indicate to them whether they were correct. Although such programs would be useful and are conceptually possible, their actual development appears to be a long way off.

Keeping in mind the danger of overdoing phonics instruction, the teacher can then proceed to include it when necessary with very positive results. As this chapter has indicated, the computer can often help with this process.

WORD RECOGNITION

The ability to recognize and give meaning to words is essential to the development of reading skills. If students at any level are to read well, they must develop a large, flexible vocabulary of sight words. Reading instruction becomes a much more reasonable task when readers recognize the vast majority of words as "familiar friends" and have to deal only occasionally with unfamiliar words.

At any level of reading instruction, word recognition refers not only to the ability to quickly pronounce a given word but also to attach an accurate (contextual) meaning to it. If readers do not have this ability, comprehension suffers.

Probably the most effective teaching of word attack skills occurs when a teacher applies basal strategies *during* the reading lesson—at the time when students need to attack a new word. Because of its interactive capacity, the computer can supply word attack assistance similar to that of an expert tutor at the very time when readers are experiencing difficulties. However, at the moment such programs are not widely available. One technological development that will assist in this strategy is *hypertext*, which is discussed in Chapter 11. But until such programs are available, teachers can use a wide variety of programs largely designed for word recognition drill and practice. Whenever possible, programs should provide context clues.

The computer can play an important role in developing word recognition skills. Several programs are especially designed to help students develop a good sight vocabulary. For example, Random House's WORD BLASTER (Figure 4.11) presents a definition and several words on the screen; the learner must "shoot" the correct word before it reaches the bottom of the screen. WORD ATTACK PLUS by Davidson, WORD QUEST by Sunburst, and WIZARD OF WORDS by Advanced Ideas likewise help young readers develop their sight vocabulary. Such programs as the Sunburst's WORD-A-MATION and WORD DETECTIVE provide a similar service for older readers.

Figure 4.11 With an arcade format, WORD BLASTER (Random House) encourages students to develop a good sight vocabulary.

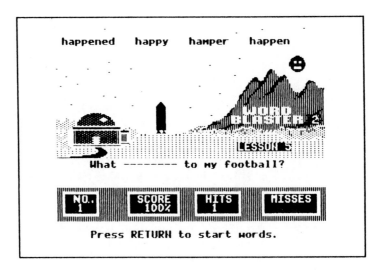

However, once they get beyond mere sight recognition, word recognition computer programs are not always so successful. A major problem is that

> word identification instruction has become the most popular domain for computer-based programs. Unfortunately, current commercial offerings are dominated by programs that overemphasize phonic and spelling cues without comparable concern for the role of meaning in word identification. These programs deprive students of important semantic and discourse cues. (Geoffrion and Geoffrion, 1983, p. 66)

Computerized cloze programs may come closest to addressing this problem. The cloze technique is a respected strategy for helping students develop word recognition and comprehension skills by inserting missing letters or words into passages. In order to perform this activity, students have to examine the context and think carefully to determine what ideas are being expressed by the passage. The precise nature of the learning task depends on the nature of the passage, the letters or words omitted, and the types of clues given. Two good examples of computer programs that employ the cloze technique are M-SS-NG L-NKS and CLOZE-PLUS. Sunburst's M-SS-NG L-NKS (shown in Figure 4.12) is the simpler of the two. It omits letters, and students fill them in to complete words and sentences. The number and pattern of letters omitted is determined by the

Figure 4.12 The cloze technique is incorporated in M-SS-NG L-NKS (Sunburst). Students supply the missing letters to complete the passage.

```
   I C E   C R E A M   < 1 >
Over one hundred y█-rs -g-, -m-r-c-ns,
-n th- -v-r-g-, -t- 1-ss th-n -
t--sp--n -f -c- cr--m p-r p-rs-n --ch
y--r. N-w th- -v-r-g- -m-r-c-n --ts
m-r- th-n f-ft--n q--rts -f -c- cr--m
- y--r. N- -th-r c--ntr- c-ns-m-s -s
m-ch -c- cr--m -s th- -n-t-d St-t-s.
```

user. The passages are interesting to the students—many of them are taken from reputable children's literature. In addition, an editing program permits teachers (or parents or children) to enter texts of their own.

Milliken's CLOZE-PLUS is a slightly more sophisticated program. It uses structured cloze and vocabulary-in-context activities to help students develop the ability to derive meaning from context clues. In addition to having students complete sentences, the program asks the student to give the meaning of words in context. Whereas M-SS-NG L-NKS simply gives the correct passage as a reward, CLOZE-PLUS also supplies pictures related to the story. CLOZE-PLUS does not have an editing system, but it does have a management system that keeps track of student performance.

In FAY'S WORD RALLY by Didatech Software, students try to select the proper word missing from a sentence at the bottom of the screen by moving as quickly as possible through a maze of words. The eighty sets of word lists are based on the Ginn 720 reading series levels 2–9, but sets for higher levels are available or teachers can create their own. In addition, there is a built-in management system for up to forty students.

You will notice that the cloze and context-clue programs overlap heavily with the comprehension programs described next in this chapter. As we stated earlier, word recognition and comprehension are not strictly independent or hierarchical. Readers often get the meaning of words from the context as well as from words themselves. Thus, programs like these teach comprehension skills as well as word recognition skills. They do not, however, provide a complete solution to the word recognition problem.

COMPREHENSION SKILLS

Comprehension, not only explaining but also interpreting and interacting with written material, should be the goal of reading instruction at all grade levels. When comprehension is not taking place, the teacher must identify the problem and provide instruction to overcome it. Reading comprehension skills are typically taught in a hierarchy based upon the intellectual or developmental level necessary for understanding. Specific, subordinate skills are important, but it is sometimes best to give this instruction only as the need arises. If the focus of reading instruction is not on comprehension, children often develop specific, segmented skills that serve no useful purpose.

Reading comprehension has two major components: (1) giving meaning to words and sentences, and (2) interpreting these in the context of previous knowledge. These two components overlap. Giving meaning to a sentence or passage is a highly individual activity.

Reading comprehension is correctly defined as a higher-order thinking skill. Goodman and Burke (1980) describe reading as a problem-solving process that actively involves the reader in predicting, confirming, and interpreting. A reader involved in active reading parallels the writer involved in creative writing. The reason many persons don't read well is because they don't think well, and vice versa. Improving thinking skills will improve reading abilities, and improving reading comprehension will improve thinking skills. A detailed discussion of using the computer to enhance thinking skills can be found in *The Computer and Higher-Order Thinking Skills* (Vockell and van Deusen, 1989).

In many current reading classrooms, while lip service is given to the importance of comprehension, not enough time is devoted to this higher-level skill because beginning readers are so busy mastering lower-level skills. At higher-grade levels much more attention is typically devoted to comprehension skills. A major impediment at all levels is that reading comprehension skills are often taught as discrete skills rather than as integrated processes that must be coordinated to facilitate understanding.

There is on the market an abundance of computer programs described as reading comprehension software. It is important to remember that most of this software is drill and practice and is probably best used *after* specific skill instruction. Programs that support reading comprehension will be effective to the extent that they enhance academic learning time related to comprehension. This means that the software should enable students to attend to and practice vocabulary, language skills, schemata development, critical thinking, and problem-solving activities with a high rate of success. If computer programs do not enhance academic learning time in this way, teachers should use other means to help students develop comprehension skills.

Reading comprehension is a *process* skill. That is, the goal of a reading comprehension lesson is not to enable students to understand and remember the content of a particular passage but rather to help them develop strategies for understanding what they read after leaving the instructional setting. When teaching factual information, teachers (and computer programs) must rely heavily on feedback and reinforcement of correct answers. However, when teaching the *process* of comprehension, reinforcing specific correct answers is not as important as helping students to focus on the processes that enable them to perform their tasks more correctly.

When teaching process skills, teachers (or computer programs) must focus on the skills to be acquired, help students develop a motivation to want to learn these skills, demonstrate them, and give students opportunities to practice them. The most important type of feedback in a reading comprehension lesson occurs when a student realizes that the use of a particular strategy has led to a satisfying and more complete comprehension of a passage that would otherwise have been less fully understood. This kind of feedback makes it more likely that the student will apply the same strategy when reading a similar passage in the future.

Also note that in Chapter 2 we made a distinction between the learning phase and the practice phase of instruction. While students often can work relatively independently during the latter, they usually require much more support during the former. It is important to keep this distinction in mind with regard to comprehension skills. Even the best programs described in this chapter are not likely to effectively *teach* comprehension skills. Although it is theoretically possible to develop materials that will teach comprehension by providing prompts, engaging students in active inquiry and discourse, providing feedback, and branching to remedial information and more prompts, we are unaware of any programs that teach it as effectively as a good teacher. However, many of these programs are very useful for permitting individual students to *practice* comprehension skills, once they have learned these skills in another context. It is also possible for a teacher to use these programs in an instructional context to *teach* the skills.

KITTENS, KIDS, AND A FROG by Hartley (Figure 4.13) provides practice for first and second graders in the following comprehension skills: main idea, detail vocabulary, sequence, cause/effect, inference, drawing conclusions, making judgments, predicting outcomes, and pronouns. A management system keeps track of student scores in each of these areas as the student reads a selection and then answers questions.

THOSE AMAZING READING MACHINES by MECC (Figure 4.14) offers a novel approach to practice of sequencing and testing strategies in a way available only through computer technology. The software is designed for grades 3 through 6. It consists of Rube Goldberg-type diagrams of "machines" that students analyze to get them to "work."

Scholastic's TALES OF DISCOVERY (Figure 4.15) takes advantage of the microcomputer's rapid branching ability by presenting stories in which readers become a character and work their way through the story by making choices. It is a "twist-a-plot" type of presentation that guides

(a)

```
Jan has a blue car.
Jim has a red car.
Jan's car can go fast.
Jim's car can not go
    fast.




Press <RETURN>.
```

(b)

```
What car will win?

    a. Jill's car
    b. Jim's car
    c. Jan's car


answer : _
```

(c)

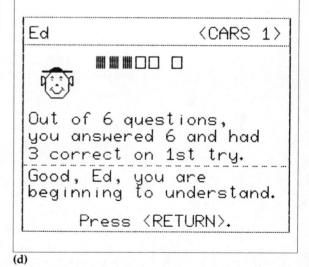

(d)

Figure 4.13 Children respond to questions in KITTENS, KIDS, AND A FROG (Hartley) after reading one of the eighteen stories available on the disk.

students through plot development. The disk contains one selection on each side. TALES OF ADVENTURE is similar.

With THE PUZZLER from Sunburst (Figure 4.16), the student chooses a story from a menu and proceeds to solve the puzzle by a series of

Figure 4.14 The whimsical machines used to check comprehension in THOSE AMAZING READING MACHINES (MECC) capture students' attention and encourage them to invent machines of their own when their session at the computer ends.

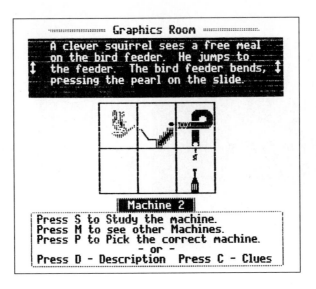

inferences. After learners make predictions about the solution, they receive another part of the story. As the story evolves, some earlier predictions are no longer consistent with the current text, and the students use syntactic, semantic, contextual, and pragmatic clues to revise their earlier predictions. After each inference or revised inference, they continue to receive additional segments of the story until they finally settle on a single solution; they then are shown the computer's answer. Each story can have more than one correct answer. This program provides a highly motivating format to promote generalization of thinking skills.

The relative absence of good comprehension software is not tragic. At the present time, this absence simply means that teachers must continue to teach comprehension skills by their own efforts. However, they *can* use the available reading comprehension computer programs as tools—suggested by the teaching models described in Chapter 1—to supplement their traditional teaching methods and to help students develop the lower-level (but still important) skills described in earlier sections of this chapter.

Logo (discussed in detail in Vockell and van Deusen's *The Computer and Higher-Order Thinking Skills*) is a programming language particularly suited to young children. A recent version of Logo, entitled LOGOWRITER (Figure 4.17), enables children to integrate the programming and artistic aspects of Logo with the writing capabilities of a simple word processor. LOGOWRITER can be especially effective in teaching integrated com-

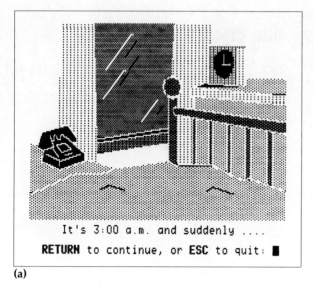

(a)

(b)

... you're dripping with sweat.

You dreamed you saw Brad trapped in the old, abandoned Belmore House. He was screaming to you for help.

But was it really a dream?

RETURN to continue, or **ESC** to quit: ■

It's 3:00 a.m. and suddenly ....
RETURN to continue, or **ESC** to quit: ■

Figure 4.15 Students become a part of the story in TALES OF DISCOVERY (Scholastic). As the story unfolds, students make decisions that influence the plot and learn that many endings are possible.

What do you want to do?
1. Go back to sleep.
2. Call Brad to check.
3. Go directly to the Belmore House.
   Type **1**, **2** or **3**, or **ESC** to quit: ■

(c)

prehension skills through the Language Experience Approach. However, as pointed out in *The Computer and Higher-Order Thinking Skills*, in order to use Logo, teachers have to spend considerable effort learning the language themselves. When teachers are able to devote time to this (typically at least thirty hours), they are often pleased with the outcome. On the other hand,

Yes, Fred had made an appearance in June! Early in the morning, when droplets of dew still clung to the green blades of grass, he was seen on the step outside the workshop. A little thinner perhaps, but then the hot summer days would provide a lot of tasty delights. Fred's behavior hadn't changed. He was as quiet and sly as ever, just waiting for someone to carry him about and leave him in interesting places – under a straw hat, on a picnic table or in a baseball mitt.

p. 2 of 5   ← Predict →

(a)

(b)

Figure 4.16 Higher-order thinking skills are tested in Sunburst's program called THE PUZZLER. As more information is disclosed, students find that they must update their predictions to fit the current situation. Multiple "right" answers are possible . . . just like in real life!

teachers who expect to be able to begin using Logo immediately after purchase are usually frustrated. It is probably accurate to say that, as far as *reading* objectives are concerned, other programs described in this chapter

Figure 4.17 LOGOWRITER combines the features of a word processing program with the capabilities of the Logo language. The result can be a delightful expression of student imagination.

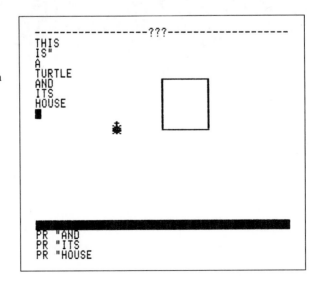

are at least as useful as Logo and are definitely easier for the teacher to employ.

Besides the programs described in this chapter, several other software packages promote comprehension by teaching study skills and higher-level reading skills. These programs are discussed in Vockell and van Deusen's *The Computer and Higher-Order Thinking Skills*. In addition, many of the programs described in subsequent chapters of this book as aids to speaking, writing, and communication skills are obviously relevant to reading instruction.

SUMMARY

A solid foundation in reading is vital to the language arts curriculum. This chapter has examined the major areas of the reading curriculum and has suggested ways in which the computer can help enhance academic learning time by providing opportunities to practice reading skills. The computer can become a part of a language-rich learning environment that permits even very young children to learn to read and understand ideas as effectively as possible. To be useful, the programs described need to be integrated with the overall instructional principles of effective teaching described in Chapter 1.

REFERENCES

Geoffrion, L. D., and O. P. Geoffrion. *Computers and Reading Instruction*. Reading, Mass.: Addison-Wesley, 1983.

Goodman, K., and C. Burke. *Reading Strategies: Focus on Comprehension*. New York: Holt, Rinehart & Winston, 1980.

Vockell, E. L., and R. van Deusen. *The Computer and Higher-Order Thinking Skills*. Watsonville, Calif.: Mitchell, 1989.

Whitaker, B., E. Schwartz, and E. L. Vockell. *The Computer in the Reading Curriculum*. Watsonville, Calif.: Mitchell, 1989.

CHAPTER 5

LISTENING AND SPEAKING SKILLS

HUMAN BEINGS SPEND A major portion of each day communicating. Think about it. We begin the morning with conversation at the breakfast table and continue to *speak* to peers, family, friends, and business associates all day. In turn, we *listen* to those same peers, family members, friends, and business associates. We *read* the newspaper, personal and business correspondence, and the latest best-seller. We *write* letters, memos, and notes when conversation is not practical.

These skills are intertwined rather than isolated from each other. We naturally connect speaking with listening, and reading with writing. But there are other pairings possible. "Listening is the foundation for reading skills at all levels of comprehension, just as talking skill is the foundation for writing skill at all levels of composition" (Moffett and Wagner, 1976, p. 72). It is also fairly obvious that children learn to *think* by listening, talking, and reflecting upon what they are doing during these activities. As foundation skills, listening and speaking deserve the same emphasis in the language arts curriculum that reading and writing receive. The fact that these skills intertwine encourages a variety of activities that motivate students to develop them.

The computer can connect students, peers, and teachers in the process of teaching and learning communication skills. It can be a tool, facilitator, motivator, or instrument of instruction in a language-rich classroom.

COMPUTERIZED SPEECH PRODUCTION

The computer can provide a synthesized "voice" for listening and speaking activities. Before exploring the basics of listening and speaking skills and the computer's role in instruction, let's briefly examine the speech production capabilities of the computer.

There are three methods of speech production with microcomputers: text-to-speech, digitized speech, and linear predictive coding (Salpeter, 1988). When the computer interfaces with random access technology, speech can also be delivered by direct recording and reproduction through such devices as CD-ROM and interactive video. Since these last two strategies will be described in Chapter 11, the present chapter will treat only those discussed by Salpeter. *Text-to-speech* uses algorithms to translate written words to sounds or phonemes. This method produces a very robotic sound but its minimal memory requirement permits the flexibility necessary in "talking" word processors. *Digitized speech* uses a method similar to digitized audio recording. However, the realistic sound devours memory, with one second of digitized speech equaling ten thousand bytes. Even when the process allows compressing, the memory requirement is prohibitive. *Linear predictive coding* (LPC), sometimes called custom-encoded speech, takes a recording of human speech and compresses the sound. It is then stored and reconstructed by way of a special speech synthesis chip. This method requires less memory space than the digitized production and sounds better than the text-to-speech output, but to use it the special chip must be added to the computer.

A surface understanding of the ways in which the "voice" is produced by the computer should prove helpful in reviewing the popular synthesizers on the market today.

Models include the following:

Echo IIb and Echo + for the Apple IIe and Apple IIGS
Cricket for the Apple IIc
PC+ for the IBM PC and the Tandy 1000 SX
Echo PC for the IBM PC, IBM PC JR, and most compatibles
Echo 1000 for the Tandy 1000 EX and Tandy 1000 HX
Mac Recorder for the Macintosh

IBM offers digitized and LPC speech through a board that attaches to the PS/2 series. The Ufonic Voice System by Educational Technology offers a high quality LPC voice for the Apple II series. Commodore, Amiga, and the Apple IIGS come with sound chips that can accommodate digitized speech. With all these possibilities, computerized voice production can be a realistic tool in the language arts classroom.

This discussion may appear somewhat technical. While it is in some respects useful to understand the distinctions covered in the preceding paragraphs, it is no more necessary to understand the subtleties of electronics when using a speech synthesizer than when using a microwave oven or automatic color control on a television set. What teachers and students really care about is the quality of the sound they hear, the ease with which it can be attained, and the cost of the materials. As a practical matter, it is important to know that some computer programs require specific components to generate synthesized sound; if you want to run these programs, you must be sure to have the proper hardware connected to your computer.

Appropriate use of speech synthesizers as well as other computer-related activities can support the development of listening and speaking skills in the language arts classroom. Separating listening and speaking activities into distinct categories is difficult at best but can be done if they are introduced from the perspective of the listener or speaker. Let's examine activities from each perspective to determine the computer connection in learning and teaching these skills.

LISTENING

Listening is central to all learning (Devine, 1982). Proportionately, it consumes more of our waking time than speaking, reading, or writing. In fact, elementary students listen on the average of 60 percent of their school day! Listening is the first communication skill that infants acquire. Babies react to the sound of a human voice, especially that of a parent or sibling, by turning their heads or smiling. By the time children first attend school, they have had several years to practice listening. Unfortunately, these years of practice do not guarantee that kindergarteners will come to school equipped with effective listening skills. In fact, the majority are not good listeners. A steady diet of TV, without the beneficial interaction of parent or peer conversation, produces passive listeners, since it demands no response to its message and therefore cannot assure assimilation of ideas. Another negative impact of mass media is that it tends to produce conformity of thought rather than individuality. In addition, the way in which people learn to listen has a powerful effect on their ability to solve problems (Lundsteen, 1979). Therefore, the language arts teacher cannot assume that students will acquire listening skills *spontaneously*. Instead, teachers should provide systematic opportunities for students to *learn* listening skills.

Hearing sounds is only a small part of the listening process. Listening involves understanding the meaning of words, phrases, or sentences; evaluating their meaning; integrating ideas with existing knowledge; and responding. The response may be spoken words, a facial reaction, an extended thought, or a body gesture (Petty and Jensen, 1980). Each of the five steps—hearing, understanding, evaluating, integrating, and responding—requires multiple levels of physical and intellectual functions that seem to occur simultaneously.

Effective listening is dependent on the attention given to the listening act (Petty and Jensen, 1980). Since the computer is an ultimate attention grabber in the classroom, it can help focus attention for activities that develop listening skills.

Maxwell (1981) divides listening skills into four categories: basic listening, expanded basic listening, critical listening, and listening for information. We'll use these categories as a basis for examining computer-related activities.

The proper way to develop listening skills is to devote high-quality academic learning time to this task by employing strategies such as those described in Chapter 2. The computer is simply one of several options to be considered as an instructional tool. If a cassette recording, the teacher's or a peer's voice, or some other method of delivery is more practical, it should be used. But when the computer has something to offer, it should be considered.

Listening Activities

Awareness of sounds, discrimination, and identification are not only basic listening skills but are prerequisites for reading readiness (see Whitaker, Schwartz, and Vockell, 1989). A word processing program that uses speech synthesis (e.g., TALKING TEXT WRITER by Scholastic, MY WORDS by Hartley, or LISTEN TO LEARN by IBM) offers unlimited practice in the basic listening skills. These programs allow the student or teacher to use appropriate keyboard strokes to input a letter, word, phrase, or entire story that can then be "read" aloud by the computer. The use of headphones can prevent the sound from disrupting the entire class while blocking out distracting noises so the student can concentrate on the lesson.

Lessons may be as simple as a list of word pairs in which the student listens and determines whether the words are alike or different (Figure 5.1). Or students might be asked to name the initial letter sound in the words. Still other lessons could revolve around the number of sounds heard in the word. The possibilities are endless, since the word processor will accept and repeat exactly what is entered from the keyboard on cue.

Computer-supported activities do not necessarily have to depend on speech synthesis. Students can use a word processor to respond to a listening exercise presented off the computer. The teacher can create printed materials that can be used in listening activities. Frequently at the primary level, students participate in listening games that require them to identify the letter that produces the initial sound of a word. The teacher says the word and asks the students to respond by choosing the correct letter. Creating individual sets of the alphabet for students to use in such activities is an easy task with the help of a graphics/text generator like SHOWOFF or PRINT SHOP by Broderbund. The latter also provides graphics that can be used in student-produced "letter books" (see Figure 5.2).

Figure 5.1 TALKING TEXT WRITER (Scholastic) can be used to create activities that provide practice in letter discrimination.

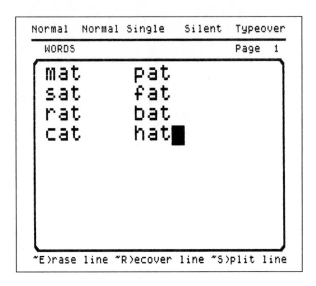

Maxwell (1981) lists the higher levels of listening skills (shown in Figure 5.3). Some of these are most effectively introduced and practiced using the teacher's voice or a recording. Others lend themselves to computer-related activities. In the examples provided in the following paragraphs, the computer often plays a relatively *indirect* but important role in the development of the designated skill. Instead of teaching a skill directly, the computer frequently provides a stimulating setting in which the teacher, by exercising normal pedagogical ingenuity, can help students seize opportunities to develop these skills.

As with more basic listening skills, the talking word processor can play a role in helping develop these higher-level skills. For example, students can listen for rhyming words in a list created by their teacher. Adding an asterisk or another symbol to each rhyming pair would indicate their understanding. After the lesson is completed, students can add their names to the end of the lesson and print out the final copy to turn in to the teacher. To add variety, the students themselves can dictate lists of words for the teacher or aide to type and save on the word processor. By trading lists, the students would be exposed to a wider variety of words.

Following Directions

Oral directions are integral to the normal classroom routine. Giving directions to describe a computer-related activity ties the computer to the broader listening activity of following directions. Directions may be as

Figure 5.2 Letter books created by the teacher or students offer a way to personalize materials. In this figure PRINT SHOP by Broderbund simplifies the process with choices in graphics and alphabet styles.

simple as listening for the choice of program assigned on a particular piece of software or the number of "problems" to complete in a program. Oral directions may include what to do after the student has completed the activity (check the schedule for the next user, record your activity, etc.). Not surprisingly, students tend to listen more attentively to oral directions when they know that they will be directly involved in the activity described and held accountable for following the directions.

Advertising Techniques

Outside the classroom, the students' listening skills are tested daily by advertisers, politicians, and other "persuaders." The language arts classroom is the perfect place to arm young consumers with strategies that put their listening skills to use in identifying the six categories of propaganda techniques described by Devine (1982):

Figure 5.3 Maxwell's higher-level listening skills.

Extended Basic Listening Skills
- Rhyming sounds
- Following directions
- Auditory memory
- Who, what, where, why
- Sequence
- Listening for specifics
- Listening and categories
- Reversibility of thought via listening (recalling and manipulating information)

Listening for Information
- Main idea
- Major details
- Sequence of events
- Differentiation of major and minor details
- Drawing conclusions
- Determining cause and effect
- Distinguishing fact from opinion
- Interpreting mood and tone

1. *Glittering generality:* connects the concept or product with simplistic, general truths
2. *Testimonial:* a celebrity endorses the product
3. *Name-calling:* associates the concept or product with a "bad" label
4. *Transfer:* attempts to transfer love, authority, or prestige from one person to another or one object to another
5. *Plain folks:* persuader appears as just an ordinary person
6. *Card stacking:* uses only positive facts, ignores any negatives to support product or point of view

The computer can assist in preparing lessons to help recognize these propaganda categories. Students can use PRINT SHOP by Broderbund to create posters or banners depicting imaginary products the students are "selling." A word processor can be the chief tool in creating the ad copy. Students complete the activity by orally sharing their ads and having the class identify the propaganda technique used. This is great practice for watching and evaluating the barrage of ads that students see every day on TV.

Collaborative Projects

Although development of listening skills may not be their major objective, projects involving partners or groups in a cooperative learning strategy force students to communicate with each other. Listening in order to understand another's viewpoint, question, or solution to the problem at hand provides valuable practice in critical listening skills. In collaborative projects, students depend on each other to contribute vital parts of the final solution to the problem. Communication is essential.

An example of a collaborative project related to the computer is provided by WHERE IN THE WORLD IS CARMEN SANDIEGO? by Broderbund (Figure 5.4). Students must track down a notorious international thief who has stolen a national treasure. In doing so, they must remember clues about the suspect, analyze geographic clues regarding the suspect's next destination, and have an understanding of the vocabulary used. This program lends itself well to cooperative learning, with each group member taking a specific task and being responsible for reporting to the group as the adventure unfolds on the computer screen. Each group member must listen to what others are sharing, so that they can contribute to joint decisions throughout the game.

With suitable software and a little imagination, the computer in the language arts classroom can encourage and support the development of

Figure 5.4 Students use a variety of clues to track down the thief in WHERE IN THE WORLD IS CARMEN SANDIEGO? by Broderbund.

effective listening skills, not in isolation but in relation to the general curriculum. Let's turn now to oral communication skills and explore the role of the computer in their development.

ORAL COMMUNICATION SKILLS

Oral communication requires interaction. There is little reason to speak if no one is listening! Children begin communicating as infants when a cry initiates a response to their needs. As the child matures, the garbled syllables of baby talk become real words and eventually phrases and sentences. Children usually enter school with years of experience in oral communication.

The manner in which parents interact orally with their children at home creates the foundation for children's oral skills. If the parents have included children in discussions, encouraged them to share questions and opinions, and have held them responsible for explaining their behavior verbally, those children find language a comfortable vehicle for expression. On the other hand, other children—whose parents did not encourage them to talk, or allowed siblings to speak for them, or generally excluded them from discussions—will find their language development impeded (Tough, 1979).

Even though teachers cannot change a child's prior language development, they can make a difference in the way a child perceives and uses oral communication. A warm, friendly classroom atmosphere, a variety of experiences, and respect for and acceptance of the individual foster the process. The language-rich environment described in Chapter 3 encourages children to express themselves in a number of ways, including verbally. Only with practice can children develop the self-confidence necessary to effective oral communication skills.

Competence in oral communication takes many forms in everyday life. Wood (1984) identifies five categories of oral communication (see Figure 5.5). As with listening skills, computer activities may not be the most appropriate choice for *directly* developing any of these oral skills. However, a wide variety of computer-related projects and activities can help students *practice* speaking skills. Often the oral communications activity is a flip of the listening activity. In order to develop listening or communication skills, there must be something to listen *to,* to listen *for,* and to share. In the classroom, that "something" is often found in a peer's oral presentation:

Figure 5.5 Categories of oral communication (Wood, 1984).

1. *Controlling:* communication that influences others, such as refusals, bargaining (advertising, conversation, discusssion)
2. *Sharing feelings:* communication that expresses our own feelings or responds to others (conversation)
3. *Informing/Responding:* communication that reports information or responds to it (reports, interviews)
4. *Ritualizing:* communication that perpetuates the social mores (small talk, introductions)
5. *Imagining:* communication that deals with reality through a creative mode (storytelling, drama)

the same activity that develops listening skills encourages the development of speaking skills.

Oral activities are not designed to promote development in specific areas of language arts. Rather they are created to provide a familiarity with the process of communication and nourish an ease in its use (Petty, Petty, and Beckeny, 1976). The computer again becomes a tool of support in creating visual aids to enhance the presentation.

Oral Communication Activities

Advertising Techniques

As with listening skills, propaganda techniques can help students practice their oral communications skills, particularly Wood's (1984) first skill category—controlling. Students can use the computer to create visuals that enhance the points they make verbally. Of course, the students to whom the presentation is made get to practice their listening skills while the presenters hone their oral skills.

Dear Abby

Sharing feelings orally in the classroom happens spontaneously when there is an atmosphere of trust and mutual respect. In the primary grades, children are more apt to share their personal experiences and feelings as well as respond to the feelings of others. In the intermediate and higher grades, students are more guarded and need nonthreatening assignments and activities to draw them out. One such activity is based on the popular "Dear Abby" advice column. Students use a word processing package, such as MAGIC SLATE by Sunburst or BANK STREET WRITER by Scholastic, to write and then print out letters stating real or imagined problems. The printed letters protect the author, since there is no handwriting to match to the writer. The teacher or students read the letters to the class and students respond orally, sharing their feelings about the problem and proposing possible solutions. Even the student who wrote the letter can offer advice to the "letter writer," since the computer conceals the writer's true identity.

Oral Reports

Reports are perhaps the activity used most often to practice Wood's third skill category—informing/responding. Petty, Petty, and Beckeny (1976) recommend that when preparing for an oral report, students should follow the five steps shown in Figure 5.6. Although students have made oral reports for decades without the use of the computer, it can support each step and simplify preparation. Oral reports appear in many areas of the school curriculum: book reviews, current events, explaining "how to," and sharing other information are all likely topics and can be useful in social studies and science as well as in language arts. With the help of a word processing program to outline and write the report and a graphics generator to create maps, pictures, or graphs, students can enhance their presentation and increase their confidence in, as well as the quality of, their oral reports.

Figure 5.6 Five steps to follow when preparing an oral report (Petty, Petty, and Beckeny, 1976) and software suggestions to accomplish them.

1. List questions that the report should answer (students can use a word processor such as MAGIC SLATE by Sunburst or BANK STREET WRITER by Scholastic)
2. Check references (students can perform an on-line search using Grolier's ELECTRONIC ENCYCLOPEDIA as discussed in Chapter 7)
3. Organize the report; outline (students can use a word processor or prewriting software such as FIRST DRAFT by Scholastic or THE WRITING WORKSHOP by Milliken)
4. Match to time frame; reorganize or delete when necessary (students can use a word processor)
5. Create visuals to enhance the report (students can use a graphics generator such as THE PRINT SHOP and its GRAPHICS LIBRARIES disks by Broderbund, BIG PRINT by Springboard, EASY GRAPH by Grolier, or THE SLIDE SHOP by Scholastic)

Brainstorming

Brainstorming is another activity used for development of oral communications skills. Moffett (1976) defines brainstorming as a method for collecting a large number of possible solutions to a problem. After stating the problem, all solutions are accepted without judgment. Then students take time to reflect on the suggestions, organize, evaluate, and refine them to create a practical solution to the problem. The computer can facilitate this process. With a word processing program and either a large-screen monitor or liquid crystal display (LCD) projection system, the suggestions given during the initial brainstorming session can be displayed for all to view. The advantage of this method over use of the chalkboard is the ease with which the computer saves, alters, and prints the information. Each student could then receive an individual copy of the suggested solutions and immediately begin the second stage of brainstorming: refining, evaluating, and finally choosing the logical solution to the problem.

Interviews

Knowing how to ask the right question to obtain needed information is one of the skills practiced in the oral communication activity of interviewing. Students can collect facts or opinions through verbal surveys of classmates, relatives, friends, and so forth. A specific program designed to help students collect data this way is SURVEY TAKER by Scholastic. To report the information they gather, students can use a word processor, a database (BANK STREET FILER by Scholastic), or a graphics program for creating graphs and tables (MECC GRAPH; see Figure 5.7).

Informal Talk

When students talk informally at the computer station, they are developing their communication skills. Simply explaining to a student partner how to use a particular piece of software provides practice in giving directions or in making explanations. The "domino" method relies on the ability of each student to explain the directions clearly. In this method the teacher explains software to one student, who in turn shares it with another student, who in turn shares it with yet another student, and so on. Students get immediate feedback when their partners are able to successfully use the software package. Note, however, that simply telling students to gather and talk will not necessarily result in productive conversations. Rules for group activities, such as those delineated in Johnson and Johnson (1987) and Slavin

Figure 5.7 Using a student survey as a data-gathering instrument, MECC GRAPH (MECC) offers a tool for presenting the information in graphic form.

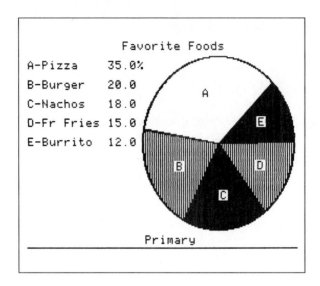

and his colleagues (1985) are helpful to ensure that informal talk actually leads to improved communication skills.

In situations where the students are talking informally, the teacher must act as a transparent guide whose main role is to keep the students on task without interfering. This is especially true in the case of cooperative learning projects in which the goal is collaborative. In addition, by providing immediate feedback and guiding activities, the computer can help keep students on task. The programs in the DECISIONS, DECISIONS series by Tom Snyder Productions lend themselves to cooperative ventures that encourage peer interaction and interdependence.

Choral Reading

An appropriate activity for all ages, choral reading is a more formal approach to the use of talking. It teaches students to interpret words and phrases, improves diction, and increases vocabulary and understanding (Petty and Jensen, 1980). Word processing simplifies the generation of materials for choral reading. Students or teachers write, save, and print the text the group will use. Easy editing is a major advantage of any good word processing program, allowing teachers or students to make quick changes in speaking assignments, phrasing, and vocabulary as the choral reading exercise develops. The word processor can also easily generate short segments of the text for individual readers and present large-letter, double-spaced copies that are easy to read.

Dramatics

Creative dramatics arise from a combination of imagination and oral communication skills. Add one more ingredient, the computer, and student productions take on a new dimension that uses the text and graphic capabilities of a variety of programs. Let's examine the connection between dramatics, oral communication skills, and the computer.

Puppetry ranks as one of the most effective activities in stimulating oral expression (Petty and Jensen, 1980). Students who may otherwise be quite shy find little trouble in letting a puppet do the talking for them. If the puppet is part of a play being produced by a group of students, there is even more opportunity to develop oral communication skills during the discussions necessary for preparation.

Stick puppets can be easily produced with the help of graphics programs. There are literally hundreds of choices available on the PRINT SHOP GRAPHICS LIBRARY disks from Broderbund. People, animals, and inanimate objects can be printed, cut out, and colored or painted, then mounted to a stick, ruler, or tongue depressor. In this way, students can create a classroom collection of puppets to use in planned or spontaneous puppet plays.

In addition, the graphics capabilities of programs designed for, say, creating a book can instead be used to create scenery for puppet plays. ONCE UPON A TIME by Compu-Teach (Figure 5.8) allows the student to create a farm, jungle, or street backdrop for a story that the student types

Figure 5.8 This farm scene and story were created by a first grader who felt very comfortable using ONCE UPON A TIME (Compu-Teach) as a creative tool.

```
I WENT TO SEE MY COUSIN. HE LIVES ON THE
FARM.  HE HAS A PIG AND A HORSE.`

    PRESS <ESC> WHEN DONE WRITING
```

on the screen. KIDWRITER by Gessler provides a hundred choices of graphics to include in a scene.

Word processing programs can assist with script generation as well. In addition to the usual word processing advantages, scripts can be printed out for easy reading. For primary students, the twenty-column version of MAGIC SLATE (Sunburst) is appropriate: the large letters are easier to read and the program is simple to use. However, teachers with more powerful word processors, like APPLEWORKS by Claris or MICROSOFT WORD by Microsoft, can select options to print information in larger print for easy reading by the members of the cast.

PLAYWRITER'S THEATER (Prescription Learning) presents a unique approach to both speaking and listening skills. In this program students may choose the scenery, characters, stage commands, and even dialogue from a predesigned list. The play is animated, and a voice synthesizer by Ufonic presents the dialogue. Students become writers and producers, using a combination of the speaking and listening skills discussed in this and the previous chapter.

Storytelling, an ancient art largely ignored by our society, combines many of the communication skills discussed in this chapter. The speaker practices verbal skills while the audience listens. In preparation for storytelling, students can write their stories first on a word processing program, using the printout to practice telling their story before they present it orally. In addition, they can create printed visuals on the computer to enhance their presentation. Or, with programs like GRAPHICS EXHIBITOR by Koala, SHOWOFF by Broderbund, or CARTOONER by Electronic Arts, students can create a slide show or animated cartoon to accompany their story. Likewise, teachers may use graphics generated by the computer as beginnings for round-robin stories in the classroom. The computer definitely serves as a support in storytelling.

SUMMARY

Listening and speaking skills allow us to communicate person-to-person. Even though children develop these very human skills before ever entering a classroom, we as teachers have a responsibility to offer activities that motivate, encourage, and nourish the further development of these skills in each of our students. The computer can play an indirect but important role in supporting these efforts. By providing a language-rich environment based on a variety of opportunities including those that use the computer,

The Play's the Thing!

Miss Babbitt's fifth-grade class was going to write their own play. On Monday, during a brainstorming session that Miss Babbitt tape recorded, the whole class discussed the play. That evening Miss Babbitt played the tape while sitting at her computer; she entered the twenty-seven ideas for the main plot into her APPLEWORKS word processor. The next day she distributed this list to her students. After all students voted for their top three choices, a plot was selected—a ghost story. At another brainstorming session, the students elected Mary Jane as writer-producer. While the children were at recess, Miss Babbitt typed the main ideas for the ghost story into her word processor. After lunch Mary Jane broke the plot into five basic parts. Miss Babbitt then divided the class into five groups, and on Wednesday each group of five or six students worked on one of the basic plot parts. The students wrote by hand, without using the computer at all. By Friday Mary Jane's folder contained a large number of ingenious ideas.

By the following Monday, Mary Jane had a handwritten play that she liked very much. While the other students did seatwork, Mary Jane and Miss Babbitt entered the play into the word processor. It came to five double-spaced pages. On Tuesday morning each student received a copy of this first draft, with instructions to make suggestions and revisions. When Mary Jane was flooded with new ideas, Miss Babbitt showed her how to enter changes into the computer. To follow up, Mary Jane interviewed individuals and small groups to get more ideas. She then held a casting session and assigned acting roles. When rehearsals began, Mary Jane generated large-print versions (by entering a few commands into the computer) for the players to read while practicing. During rehearsals, new ideas frequently came up, which Mary Jane simply added by hand to the script. However, every few days she generated a new, current copy of the play for herself and the players.

Meanwhile, Henry and Jake agreed to supervise ten other students as stage hands. Their work with scenery and stage props required that they have a current copy of the script, which Mary Jane gave them whenever changes occurred. This enabled them to effectively integrate the props with the play.

Marty and Maria agreed to handle the play's publicity. They did all the posters with PRINT SHOP. Bill and Hans used the word processor to take care of the program, tickets, and invitations. They used a mail merge program in conjunction with a database to invite teachers and parents to the play and to thank them afterward for their support.

The play was an immense success. An anonymous student even used CERTIFICATE MAKER to give Mary Jane an "Oscar" for her production. Miss Babbitt thought it was almost as much fun as the play she had starred in twenty years ago when she was in the fifth grade herself—but she wondered how she had managed in those distant days without a computer.

we can achieve our main objective: students who can communicate effectively in their world!

REFERENCES

Devine, T. G. *Listening Skills Schoolwide*. Urbana, Ill.: ERIC Clearinghouse on Reading and Communication Skills and the National Council of Teachers of English, 1982.

Johnson, D. W., and R. T. Johnson. *Learning Together and Alone: Cooperative, Competitive, and Individualistic Learning*. Englewood Cliffs, N.J.: Prentice-Hall, 1987.

Lundsteen, S. W. *Listening*. Urbana, Ill.: ERIC Clearinghouse on Reading and Communication Skills and the National Council of Teachers of English, 1979.

Maxwell, M. J. *Listening Games for Elementary Grades*. Washington, D.C.: Acropolis Books, 1981.

Moffett, J., and B. J. Wagner. *Student-Centered Language Arts and Reading, K–13*. Boston: Houghton Mifflin, 1976.

Petty, W., and J. M. Jensen. *Developing Children's Language*. Boston: Allyn & Bacon, 1980.

Petty, W., D. C. Petty, and M. F. Beckeny. *Experiences in Language*. Boston: Allyn & Bacon, 1976.

Salpeter, J. "Making the Computer Talk: Some Common Approaches." *Classroom Computer Learning* 8 (1988): 32.

Slavin, R. E., S. Sharan, S. Kagan, R. Hertz-Lazarowitz, C. Webb, and R. Schmuck (Eds.). *Learning to Cooperate, Cooperating to Learn*. New York: Plenum, 1985.

Tough, J. *Talk for Teaching and Learning*. Hong Kong: Ward, Lock, and Drake Educational Associates, 1979.

Whitaker, B., E. Schwartz, and E. L. Vockell. *The Computer in the Reading Curriculum*. Watsonville, Calif.: Mitchell, 1989.

Wood, B. "Oral Communication in the Elementary Classroom." In C. Thaiss (Ed.). *Speaking and Writing K–12*. Urbana, Ill.: National Council of Teachers of English, 1984.

LANGUAGE DEVELOPMENT: PLAYING WITH WORDS

AS A RESULT OF their elementary language arts programs, children are expected to develop competencies in reading, writing, and the five areas discussed in this chapter—vocabulary, spelling, word usage, punctuation, and capitalization. But in too many classrooms, teaching strategies are such that students have little interest in or commitment to learning these skills. As our chapter title suggests, this does not have to be the case—learning *can* be fun. We will attempt to show how the computer, in conjunction with a language-rich classroom environment and a whole language approach, can create student enthusiasm for learning the basic language arts skills.

Although children enter school with a vocabulary of between three thousand to seventeen thousand words, they acquire most of the vocabulary they will use as adults during their school years (Petty and Jensen, 1980). In the primary grades, teachers may begin word study with a predetermined list; their efforts may be nothing more than verifying that all their students do possess a common core vocabulary. Traditionally, in the intermediate grades teachers often use an isolated approach to vocabulary development. Taught as a separate subject, it usually consists of looking up a list of new words in the dictionary and using them in original sentences. Students engaged in this activity seldom see much connection with their active vocabulary. Likewise, spelling often focuses on a predetermined list of twenty to twenty-five words per week that students use in a variety of paper-and-pencil activities. Practice in word usage, punctuation, and capitalization usually consists of copying exercises from a text. Handled in this manner, these topics are isolated from the natural opportunities that are available daily in a language-rich elementary classroom.

Although the computer can certainly play a significant role in these traditional language development activities, it can do even better: it can help students and teachers integrate words more actively into their classroom environment. In the most effective setting, the teacher is the guide; and the computer, once again, is a tool for instruction. This chapter examines the role of the computer in the development of vocabulary, spelling, word usage, punctuation, and capitalization skills and identifies software packages that nurture this development and promote a positive attitude.

VOCABULARY DEVELOPMENT

While there is certainly some merit in "studying vocabulary words" or in having a "word for the day," teachers in a language-rich classroom will focus more on helping students to understand the words they hear, read, and write rather than on strictly imposing a "word list" approach. Furthermore, vocabulary development involves much more than simply encouraging students to use new words in the school setting. In a real sense vocabulary development is conceptual development. With an ever-increasing vocabulary, students grow in their understanding of the world around them. Teachers facilitate this growth by providing real opportunities as well as vicarious ones that encourage vocabulary development. Petty and Jensen (1980) identify seven areas that provide vocabulary enrichment (Figure 6.1). The final category—encouraging children's interest in and curiosity about words—is one that the computer supports effectively. To foster this, the teacher uses activities centering on the following topics:

1. Context clues
2. Synonyms, antonyms, and homonyms
3. Prefixes, suffixes, and root words
4. Dictionary skills (including pronunciation)

The computer can play an active role in each of these areas. It can offer guided or individualized practice as well as an opportunity to explore new ideas. Even though extended practice of an isolated skill may be valuable at times, the activities that we present are most effective when fully integrated into experiences of personal interest to the learner. In other words,

Figure 6.1 Seven areas that provide opportunities for vocabulary enrichment (based on Petty and Jensen, 1980, p. 286).

1. Manipulative activities that involve handling various materials, tools, and equipment; learning new names and understanding directions; discussing plans and results
2. Social experiences within the classroom: show-and-tell, a daily news period, free conversation periods, and general class discussion
3. Development of social responsibilities: receiving and greeting guests, extending courtesies, and helping one another
4. Development of interest in the natural environment and community activities by means of field trips, discussion of plans, training in observation, and a discussion that summarizes the total experience
5. Observation and handling of specimens and articles brought into the classroom in connection with science or social studies
6. Science or hobby displays that involve classification, organization, and labeling
7. Encouragement of children's interest in and increased curiosity about words

just as it is conceivably possible to develop vocabulary skills by reading a paperback vocabulary book in isolation, it is conceivably possible to use the computer programs discussed in this chapter as isolated units of instruction. However, it is far better to incorporate these programs within a language-rich classroom, to pique students' interest or as tools to help them master skills that they themselves determine to be valuable as their language experiences expand.

Context Clues

Examining unknown words in context rather than in isolated lists is the most productive way to expand vocabulary. Unless students connect the meaning to their personal experience or see a need to know, the word does not become an active part of their vocabulary. To find the meaning of unknown words in a written or oral passage, students collect clues from the surrounding words. The classroom provides many opportunities to expand vocabulary through this strategy. Besides the areas listed in Figure 6.1, reading for leisure or instruction offers an everyday way to increase vocabulary through context clues. However, teachers should not assume that students automatically understand new words simply because context clues are available. By pointing out the unfamiliar words and discussing them, teachers can encourage their students to approach vocabulary development in a systematic as well as an incidental manner.

The computer offers several formats for focusing on context clues. One includes a story with questions based on the student's understanding of the vocabulary, of which TIGER'S TALES (Sunburst) is an example. Each of the five stories, about a cat named Tiger, encourages students to use context clues to determine the story's outcome; and each story includes a vocabulary section. Sunburst's NEWBERY ADVENTURES: A WRINKLE IN TIME, CALL IT COURAGE, A CRICKET IN TIMES SQUARE, and ISLAND OF THE BLUE DOLPHINS (see Figure 6.2), provide context clue exercises after students have read assigned chapters in the designated book. MULTIPLE MEANINGS (Hartley) (see Figure 6.3) has a similar format, but it concentrates on descriptive sentences instead of a complete story for its springboard into context clue practice. Since vocabulary develops by adding new words and understanding that words have multiple meanings, this particular software package (and others such as the vocabulary component in BRICK BY BRICK by Hartley) is especially valuable.

M-SS-NG L-NKS (Sunburst) provides a hint of its format in the title. Three different versions challenge students to effectively use context clues to fill in the missing parts of words. M-SS-NG L-NKS: MICRO ENCYCLO-

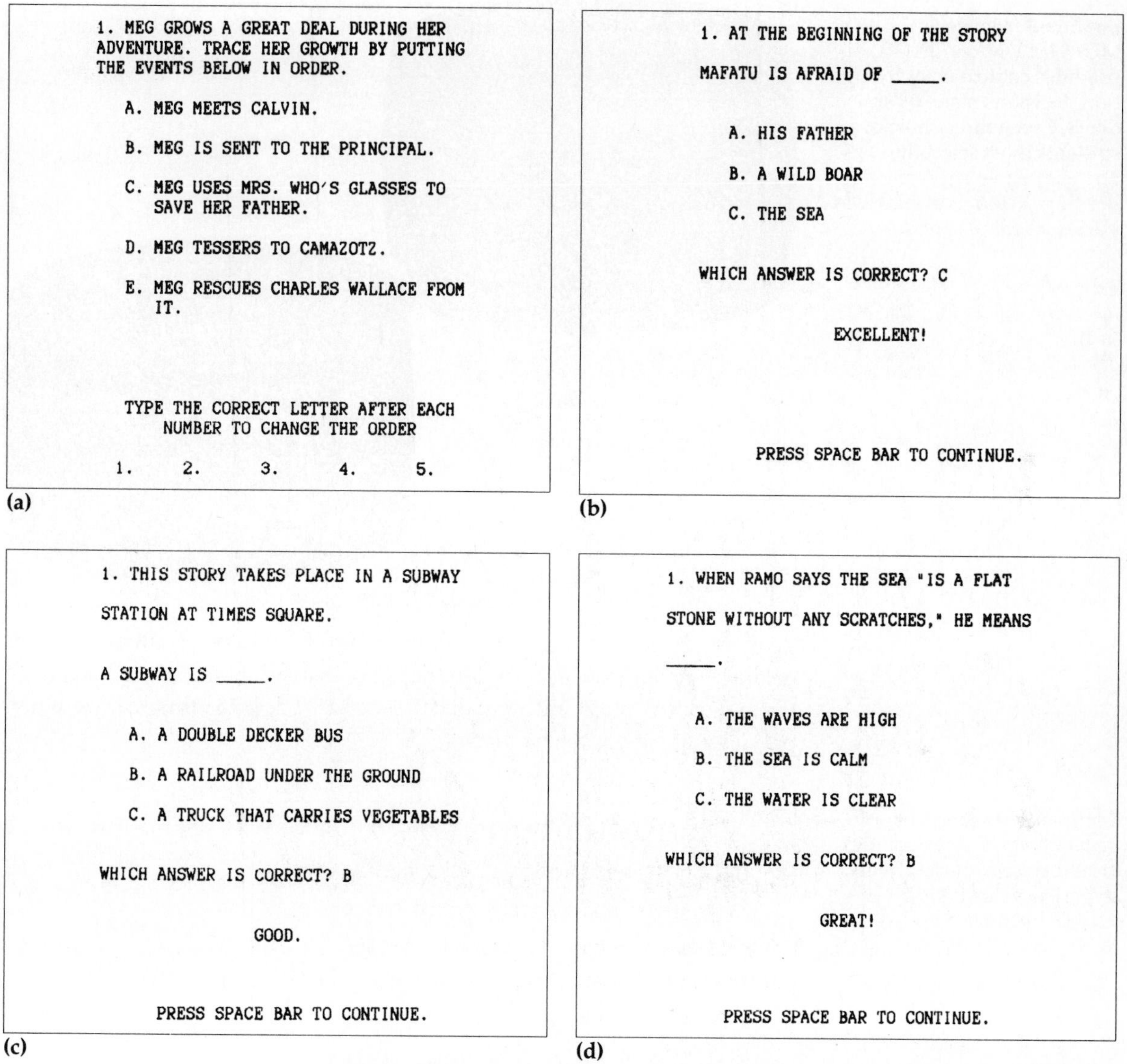

```
1. MEG GROWS A GREAT DEAL DURING HER
ADVENTURE. TRACE HER GROWTH BY PUTTING
THE EVENTS BELOW IN ORDER.

   A. MEG MEETS CALVIN.

   B. MEG IS SENT TO THE PRINCIPAL.

   C. MEG USES MRS. WHO'S GLASSES TO
      SAVE HER FATHER.

   D. MEG TESSERS TO CAMAZOTZ.

   E. MEG RESCUES CHARLES WALLACE FROM
      IT.


   TYPE THE CORRECT LETTER AFTER EACH
      NUMBER TO CHANGE THE ORDER

   1.     2.     3.     4.     5.
```
(a)

```
1. AT THE BEGINNING OF THE STORY

MAFATU IS AFRAID OF _____.


   A. HIS FATHER

   B. A WILD BOAR

   C. THE SEA

WHICH ANSWER IS CORRECT? C


       EXCELLENT!




   PRESS SPACE BAR TO CONTINUE.
```
(b)

```
1. THIS STORY TAKES PLACE IN A SUBWAY

STATION AT TIMES SQUARE.

A SUBWAY IS _____.


   A. A DOUBLE DECKER BUS

   B. A RAILROAD UNDER THE GROUND

   C. A TRUCK THAT CARRIES VEGETABLES

WHICH ANSWER IS CORRECT? B


       GOOD.



   PRESS SPACE BAR TO CONTINUE.
```
(c)

```
1. WHEN RAMO SAYS THE SEA "IS A FLAT

STONE WITHOUT ANY SCRATCHES," HE MEANS

_____.


   A. THE WAVES ARE HIGH

   B. THE SEA IS CALM

   C. THE WATER IS CLEAR

WHICH ANSWER IS CORRECT? B


       GREAT!



   PRESS SPACE BAR TO CONTINUE.
```
(d)

Figure 6.2 The intriguing stories told in Newbery winners are reviewed through computer activities from Sunburst. A WRINKLE IN TIME, CALL IT COURAGE, A CRICKET IN TIMES SQUARE, and ISLAND OF THE BLUE DOLPHINS are illustrated here.

PEDIA (Figure 6.4) uses "Ice Cream" and "Whales and Sharks" as themes. Familiar pieces of literature are used in M-SS-NG L-NKS: YOUNG PEOPLE'S LITERATURE. Teachers have authoring capabilities in the third

Figure 6.3 Hartley's MULTIPLE MEANINGS provides context clues to support decisions made by students. Given three choices, students must select the correct use of a word. A record-keeping system is available to track student progress.

Case · a lawsuit
Which sentence uses this meaning?
a. There was a court case against him.
b. The nurse brought in the next case.
c. The apples were packed in a case.

answer:

The correct answer is:
There was a court case against him.

By exchange:
There was a court lawsuit against him.
This makes the most sense.

Press < RETURN >

version, M-SS-NG L-NKS: ENGLISH EDITOR. Authoring capabilities are desirable on any vocabulary program, because teachers *and* students have the power to create individualized practice. Look for this feature when previewing software for purchase.

Figure 6.4 Teachers or students can create activities from personal or classroom experiences with M-SS-NG L-NKS by Sunburst.

```
    INVENTIONS <6>
Th█ f-rst m-ch-n-c-l cl-cks w-r- q--t-
-n-cc-r-t- -nd -s--ll- c--ld n-t b-
r-l--d -p-n t- k--p t-m- t- b-tt-r
th-n f-ft--n m-n-t-s p-r d--. -n f-ct,
m-n- --rl- cl-cks w-r- s- -nr-l--bl-
th-t th-- h-d -nl- -n- h-nd, -nd th-
d--l sh-w-d -nl- h--rs -nd q--rt-r
h--rs.
```

Games are another popular format for vocabulary practice, and they often use context clues. Arcade games, TV game shows, and traditional board games have inspired the computer formats for these software packages, whose graphics and feedback motivate students to continue to expand their vocabulary. One such package is MAGIC CASTLE (Learning Well), in which students must answer vocabulary questions to reach the enchanted castle. THE GAME SHOW (Advanced Ideas) bases its format on the old "Password" TV game show. Students try to guess the word that fits the clues given by the computer. Built-in lists of words may be used, but this program also has an authoring option so that teachers can create original word lists and clues based on the experiences of their students.

Synonyms, Antonyms, and Homonyms

Defining words through the use of synonyms, antonyms, and homonyms is a common approach to vocabulary development. Once again, the computer offers activities that reach beyond the traditional paper-and-pencil exercises to motivate students. Hartley's Language Arts Series II contains a program, ANTONYMS/SYNONYMS, that provides practice in identifying certain synonyms and antonyms and distinguishing among them. Another program by Hartley, OPPOSITES, presents twenty-five lessons in which students identify antonyms. Students compare and contrast homonym pairs in WORD HERD: SOUND ALIKES by MECC. It provides students with context clues and graphics to help them find the correct term. WORD-A-MATION by Sunburst (Figure 6.5) combines five "machines" that allow students to create word chains using synonyms, antonyms, and homonyms.

Prefixes, Suffixes, and Root Words

An effective technique for identifying unknown words is to break the word into its root word and affixes. By establishing the meaning of the root word, prefix, and/or suffix, students develop a strategy that can be transferred to other words with similar roots or affixes. Because mastering this strategy takes time and especially practice, the computer is a good tool. FOCUSING ON LANGUAGE ARTS: PREFIXES/SUFFIXES (Random House), WORDS AT WORK: PREFIX POWER (MECC), BOPPIE'S GREAT WORD CHASE (Developmental Learning Materials [DLM]), and ROOTS AND AFFIXES (Hartley) give students practice in dividing and defining words and allow teacher input, from inserting original lists of words to choosing which predesigned list will be presented to which student.

Figure 6.5 Students can explore word relationships using the "machines" in WORD-A-MATION (Sunburst).

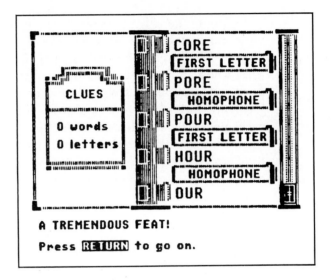

A word processing program can also be used to divide and define words. Given a list of words, students can use the program's editing features to divide the word into its root, prefix, and/or suffix. Then they can insert the meaning of each component and finally combine the meanings to define the original word. This basic format could be expanded or modified depending on the level of the student's understanding. Word families based on a common root word can be saved as separate files to be retrieved when needed. Word origins, a fascinating topic to many students, can also become part of the file. Students can keep individual files based on their own word awareness, or a collaborative class project could be initiated. In either case the use of the computer simplifies the process of editing so that all students can contribute easily.

Databases such as BANK STREET FILER from Broderbund, MASTERTYPE'S FILER by Scarborough, and FRIENDLY FILER from Grolier present yet another option for developing skills in identifying and defining word parts. With a database, students can create an electronic filing system for words with common roots, suffixes, or prefixes (Figure 6.6). Depending on the software's search capabilities, students can expand their vocabulary by comparing and contrasting words with common roots and affixes. New words that contain familiar components easily become a part of the students' active vocabulary. Reports can be generated to produce a class booklet containing words that the students have identified and defined. Such a booklet serves as a good resource for students as they continue to confront unknown words.

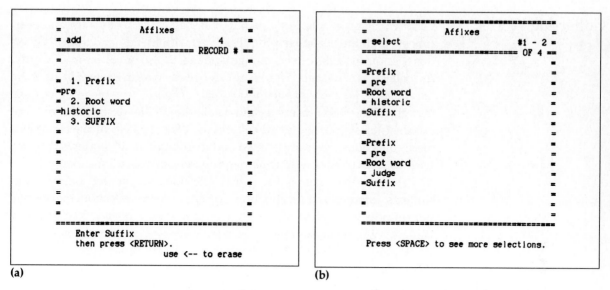

Figure 6.6 The database format of FRIENDLY FILER (Grolier) allows students to create their own collection of words that exemplify the affixes that they use in their writing.

Word Games

Graphics, animation, and sound supply the positive feedback that encourages students to stay on task while using the many word games that are on the software market. Although educators sometimes disparage educational games, they cannot deny the power of these games to motivate students. And many of these programs have built-in editing options so that the teacher or student can edit the existing word lists or create lists from scratch.

A variety of formats are available in vocabulary games. In WORD SPINNER by The Learning Company, students add words to a "wheel" that contains a word family. HINKY PINKY GAME by Learning Well presents hints (context clues) for arriving at an answer containing a funny, rhyming word pair. WIZARD OF WORDS from Advanced Ideas consists of five games based on a "Royal Registry" of thirty-eight thousand words. The games range from simple scrambles to a hangman format. WORD CRUNCH by Teacher Support Software uses a Scrabble format to entice students to practice using vocabulary words. Containing simple word processing features, MECC's PAINT WITH WORDS allows students to use words to create a picture on the screen. Each of these programs extends vocabulary while keeping the student interested.

Collecting Words

Children are great collectors: stickers, baseball cards, rocks, cars, and even rubber bands are treasured, proudly shared with friends, and traded. Given this passion, teachers can encourage students to also be collectors of words. As collectors, students "trade in" the tired, overused words in their vocabularies for more explicit terms that reflect the true meaning of their thoughts. The word processing and database activities described earlier are excellent for supporting word collections. With the help of the computer, these collections are easily printed and distributed to all students and can serve as resources for writing stories, reports, poems, and the like.

The possible themes for word collections are limited only by the students' interests and imagination. To begin a word collection, the teacher can introduce the class to *The Book of Lists* (Wallechinsky, Wallace, and Wallace, 1978) as an example of the wide variety of possible themes.

Or the teacher can initiate the project with sample list titles such as the following:

Rainbow Words

This collection of color words ignores the overused *red, blue,* and *green* by emphasizing words like *auburn, indigo,* and *teal.*

Words That Go Bump in the Night

Onomatopoeias (*bang! crash! splat!*) are fun to collect as students attempt to describe the sounds they hear in the classroom, cafeteria, playground, at home, and so on.

Lions and Tigers and Bears, Oh My!

Words that describe scary scenes, creatures, or events stretch the imagination.

Uhmmm Good

This list includes words that describe food—its taste, aroma, texture, and appearance.

Touchy Words

A hands-on activity, in which students touch objects and items such as sandpaper, silk, and cotton balls, initiates a list of "touchy" words.

Petty and Jensen (1980) also suggest some themes, including quiet words, sports words, alliterations, rhyming words, and figurative language (similes and metaphors). Students will have their own themes to pursue as well. The more fun students have while collecting words, the broader their vocabularies become.

With the help of PRINT SHOP COMPANION by Broderbund or CALENDAR MAKER by CE Software (Figure 6.7), students can use the word collection activity in a different framework. Teachers create a weekly or monthly calendar highlighting a "word of the day," either teacher- or student-generated, for students to define and use verbally or in a written assignment that day. Students often enjoy fitting these new and unusual words into their personal conversations, classroom discussions, and written work. Themes can be chosen from the list above or taken from subject areas being studied, or from holidays, field trips, or other topics of interest. It is important to choose words that are meaningful within the context of the students' lives. An arbitrary list of strange words does little to expand vocabulary.

Word collections may also take the form of word booklets created with programs that combine text and graphics, such as PRINT SHOP by Broderbund. With the hundreds of graphics choices available in its GRAPHICS LIBRARY programs, students are able to create pages for their booklets that include illustrations (Figure 6.8). Desktop publishing programs like PUBLISH IT! by Timeworks Platinum further facilitate the mixing of text with graphics.

Flash cards, a traditional format for vocabulary practice, offer another word collection activity that the computer can enhance. This activity is especially helpful to students with special needs, who require additional practice to learn and use words that other learners acquire almost automatically. Students benefit most from this activity when the words are individualized according to their needs and experiences; and commercially printed cards may simply not meet these needs the way teacher-designed cards would. Since vocabulary develops from the students' experiences, using predetermined sets of cards may not make sense, but the time-consuming task of manually printing individual cards for twenty-five students is prohibitive. Enter the computer! There are several programs on the market that facilitate the printing of flash cards and allow the user to choose the words and add definitions when appropriate. MAKE-A-FLASH from Teacher Support Software (Figure 6.9) gives teachers or students the opportunity to create flash cards using prescribed basal text words or words created with a word processing program.

The greeting card generator on PRINT SHOP also offers a format that lends itself to making flash cards. The user creates a "greeting card" that

Figure 6.7 A calendar program like CALENDAR MAKER (CE Software) allows students to expand their vocabulary with a "word of the day." This exercise is most meaningful when the words directly relate to student activities rather than being chosen arbitrarily.

October 1990						
Sunday	Monday	Tuesday	Wednesday	Thursday	Friday	Saturday
	Word of the day: ghost	Word of the day: haunt	Word of the day: vampire	Word of the day: sorcerer	Word of the day: magic spell	
	1	2	3	4	5	6
	Word of the day: apparition	Word of the day: eerie	Word of the day: ghoul	Word of the day: enchantress	Word of the day: haunted	
7	8	9	10	11	12	13
	Word of the day: phantom	Word of the day: ebony	Word of the day: monster	Word of the day: wizard	Word of the day: prank	
14	15	16	17	18	19	20
	Word of the day: spook	Word of the day: trick	Word of the day: witch	Word of the day: warlock	Word of the day: specter	
21	22	23	24	25	26	27
	Word of the day: spirit	Word of the day: hallowed	Word of the day: Halloween			
28	29	30	31			

has a word on the front and the definition or a related graphic inside. The teacher can either cut the card apart and mount the two on the front and back of an index card or keep the greeting card intact. The greeting card feature allows the user to choose the font (typeface), border, and graphics to further enhance the card. The program is so simple that students can generate their own cards for practice. This activity can support a vocabulary

Figure 6.8 Each PRINT SHOP GRAPHICS LIBRARY (Broderbund) program contains over a hundred graphics, which can be incorporated into assorted PRINT SHOP posters, banners, greeting cards, or letterheads.

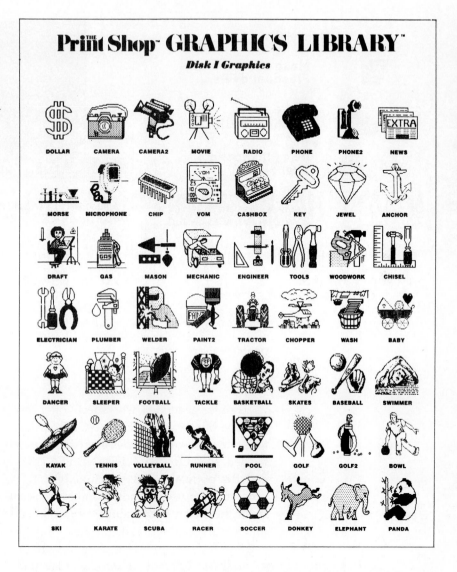

list in any subject area and encourages students to take responsibility for their own learning. Also note that the graphics can tie in with ideas from contemporary research emphasizing the value of graphic mnemonic strategies in vocabulary development (e.g., McDaniel and Pressley, 1989).

Students can practice vocabulary at the computer keyboard instead of using paper flash cards with QUICK FLASH from MECC (Figure 6.10). Screen "flash cards" may be added and deleted as the students progress.

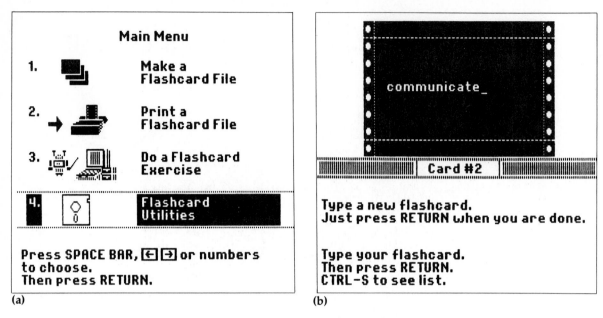

(a)   (b)

Figure 6.9 When students need to work with a highly individualized vocabulary, a program like MAKE-A-FLASH (Teacher Support Software) simplifies the process.

Printer-generated worksheets offer yet another form of vocabulary practice. Mindscape's CROSSWORD MAGIC (Figure 6.11) is a simple way to create crossword puzzles that contain exactly the words and definitions needed. MECC's PUZZLES AND POSTERS uses both crossword puzzles and the popular word search activity to generate puzzles. Both these programs are user-friendly. Moreover, assigning students themselves to create these forms of vocabulary exercises serves as an additional means of practicing vocabulary skills. Students enjoy creating puzzles for each other and benefit from the level of understanding necessary to create them, especially in the case of the crossword format. Another interesting program is Hartley's PRINT YOUR OWN BINGO, which permits students or teachers to generate "bingo" games based on vocabulary development or other language arts skills.

Dictionary Skills

"Look it up in the dictionary" is the response often given when a student asks a teacher what a word means, how it is spelled, or how it is

Figure 6.10 Students who wish to practice vocabulary words on-screen can use MECC's QUICK FLASH.

```
          Authors
  Name the author of this
  work of literature:
  Pilgrim's Progress

  ※

  Press Return to see answer.
  Press the Escape key to quit.
```

pronounced. Because students are often reluctant to write words they cannot spell or to say words they are unsure of pronouncing or defining, they need dictionary skills. However, if they are asked simply to look up lists of words in the dictionary, they often fail to connect the exercise with their own needs and soon lose interest.

The computer can provide the needed motivation and variety of activities that enable students to practice skills necessary to use the dictionary. For example, an automatic understanding of alphabetical order is necessary to promote efficient use of the dictionary. Programs that reinforce alphabetical order include FOCUSING ON LANGUAGE ARTS: DICTIONARY I–II by Random House and WORD ORDER by Teacher Support Software. Using computer-generated flash cards or word-processed worksheets to produce a hands-on activity to arrange words in alphabetical order is another way to involve students physically as well as mentally in the process (see Figure 6.12).

As dictionaries become computerized and are available on electronic databases, new opportunities for computer-assisted instruction are likely to arise. In addition, hypertext strategies (discussed in Chapter 11) will make it possible, and easy, for students to look up words at the very time they are most interested—when they run across a word they don't know while reading a difficult text, such as an electronic encyclopedia.

Figure 6.11 Creating clues for CROSSWORD MAGIC (Mindscape) forces students to have a good understanding of the terms used.

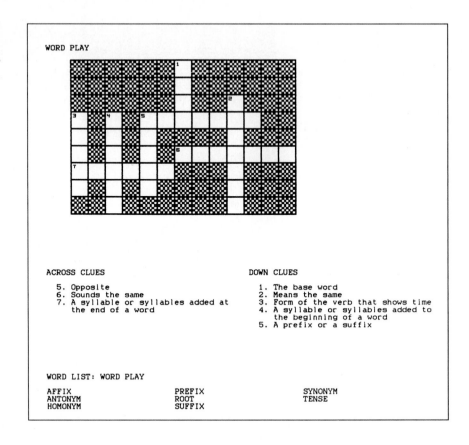

WORD PLAY

ACROSS CLUES

5. Opposite
6. Sounds the same
7. A syllable or syllables added at
   the end of a word

DOWN CLUES

1. The base word
2. Means the same
3. Form of the verb that shows time
4. A syllable or syllables added to
   the beginning of a word
5. A prefix or a suffix

WORD LIST: WORD PLAY

AFFIX   PREFIX   SYNONYM
ANTONYM   ROOT   TENSE
HOMONYM   SUFFIX

SPELLING

Students are often hesitant to write words they cannot spell. In addition, as students grow older they face the practical problem of being evaluated negatively if they spell poorly. Therefore, a goal of an elementary spelling program is to give students the confidence and necessary skills to spell the words they write. This can be done in a number of ways. In the whole language approach, teachers often recognize this hesitation and encourage their students to use "invented spelling." Students simply write the words as they think they are spelled, so they can focus instead on communicating their ideas. If lists of words are used at all for spelling and vocabulary development in this kind of program, they are taken from the students' own experiences. Under the guidance of their teacher and as their writing matures, students begin to compare their invented spelling with the correct

Big Words for Little Children

Mrs. Rawlings felt that her third graders needed to learn to use the pronunciation keys found in the glossaries of their textbooks and in dictionaries, but few of them felt motivated to do so. It really didn't make much sense to eight-year-olds to use a pronunciation key to pronounce a word they already knew. Nor did it make much sense to them to use a key to pronounce a word they didn't know, if they had no need to know that word.

Mrs. Rawlings noticed that her students were fascinated by constellations and by dinosaurs, so she brought into the classroom computer programs like MECC's URSA. It was easy to locate the brightest stars of some constellations (for example Rigel, Betelgeuse, and Bellatrix in Orion or Procyon of Canis Major), and the children were eager to go home and point these out to their friends and family. This motivated them to learn about and use these big words, which in turn motivated them to use a pronunciation key to decode the names of these stars. She found that DINOSAUR DISCOVERY provided similar stimulation.

A pair of computer programs almost completely unrelated to language arts had provided students with a stimulus to learn to use ordinary, noncomputerized pronunciation keys.

spelling of words in other contexts. For some students the transition to correct spelling is natural. Others need additional help to develop spelling strategies.

Another approach to spelling is primarily phonetic, associating letters and sounds while learning the rules that govern our language. Its advocates point out that since words very often follow rules of orthodox spelling, it would be extremely inefficient to ignore the existence of these rules. Often this approach is accompanied by spelling workbooks or predetermined lists of common words. In Figure 6.13 Petty and Jensen (1980) identify objectives that guide this approach. Although the whole language and the phonetic approaches seem poles apart, in reality teachers can benefit from both. For example, in a whole language approach students can certainly learn "spelling rules" when these fit needs identified within their original writing; and students using traditional spelling books will certainly learn their spelling words better if the words they study are closely related to their own experiences. No matter which approach or combination of ap-

(a)   **(b)**

Figure 6.12 A word processing program like MAGIC SLATE (Sunburst) can help create activities for students to complete at the computer or with paper and pencil.

proaches is used, computer activities can support spelling instruction in a number of ways.

A prerequisite skill for spelling—letter recognition—is addressed by the following programs: FIRST LETTER FUN (MECC), GETTING READY TO READ AND ADD (Sunburst), KIDS ON KEYS (Spinnaker), KINDERKONCEPTS (Midwest), LETTER RECOGNITION (Hartley), STICKYBEAR ABC (Weekly Reader Family Software), and READER RABBIT (The Learning Company).

One rather sophisticated program that teaches spelling rules and provides practice is THE SPELLING SYSTEM by Milliken, which focuses on consonants, short and long vowels, and irregular spellings in a well-structured set of lessons. Entertaining graphics provide positive feedback. The list of spelling words covered by the program is based on the most commonly used words for the elementary grades.

Another program that teaches rules and provides practice is S-P-E-L-L, THE READING WRITING CONNECTION by Sunburst. This program is a year-long fourth-grade curriculum that contains a management system to track student scores. Worksheets, tests, and suggestions for off-line activities are included.

Figure 6.13 Objectives of a good spelling program (based on Petty and Jensen, 1980, pp. 442–443).

Attitudes: Each child should
- recognize the necessity for correct spelling in effective communication;
- show a desire to spell all words correctly;
- believe that spelling correctly is something he or she can accomplish.

Skills and abilities: Each child should be able to
- recognize all the letters of the alphabet in upper and lowercase in both printed and handwritten materials;
- write legibly all the letters of the alphabet in both upper and lowercase;
- alphabetize words;
- hear words accurately;
- pronounce words clearly;
- see printed words accurately;
- group and connect the letters of a word properly;
- use punctuation elements that are necessary for spelling;
- use a dictionary, including diacritical markings and guide words;
- pronounce unfamiliar words properly;
- use knowledge of sound and symbol relationships;
- use knowledge of orthographic patterns that recur in language;
- use the most effective spelling rules;
- use effective procedures in learning to spell new words.

Habits: Each child should habitually
- proofread all writing carefully;
- use reliable sources to find the spellings of unknown words;
- follow a specific study procedure in learning to spell new words.

A language-based approach is highlighted in another Sunburst product. THE SCHOOL SPELLER (Figure 6.14) provides a structure for using the student's writing to create spelling lists. The program contains a spelling dictionary that can check a student's composition created with the word processing program MAGIC SLATE; a printout of spelling mistakes; and a management system. This program is the first to offer spelling in a language-based format.

Control of the on-screen word list is important to the successful connection of software to the spelling program. MASTER SPELL (MECC), CREATE SPELL IT (Hartley), SPELLAKAZAM (DesignWare), SPIDER HUNT SPELLING (Gamco), and WIZARD OF WORDS (Advanced Ideas) all allow teachers or students to add lists to the existing game format. In this way, whether spelling words are based on a text, a workbook, or experience-based lists, students have a variety of motivational games and puzzles to assist them in learning to spell.

Figure 6.14 SCHOOL SPELLER (Sunburst) connects correct spelling with the student's original writing. The program compiles misspelled words so that students can concentrate on words that are actually in their active vocabulary.

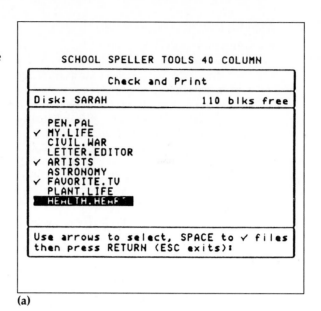

(a)

(b)

Many spelling games are based on prescribed lists. Even though the teacher may have no choice in the words used, the lists are often well planned and do include the most commonly used words. Educational spelling games include SPELL IT (Davidson), WORD LAUNCH (Teacher Support Software), ALPHABET ZOO (Spinnaker), POP R SPELL (Milliken), and SPELLOGRAPH (DesignWare). In addition, most spelling programs include an editing system that permits teachers and students to enter their own word lists.

In real life, people identify a word and then figure out how to spell it. Having a word flashed briefly on the screen, identifying the *in*correctly spelled word from a list, playing hangman—all these are imperfect approximations of real-life spelling. It is far more realistic for the teacher to say, "How do you spell . . . ?" However, since the computer may be available when the teacher is busy with something else, the programs cited above enable students to increase the time they spend practicing their spelling skills. Computers with speech synthesizers can actually "say" the words aloud, just as a teacher would. Speech synthesis may be especially valuable when a student has a learning disability or when English is the student's second language. SPELLING ATTACK by Educational Technology and SPELLER BEE by First Byte Software use voice output and should be seriously considered for special students. With improved speech synthesis, we expect to see better "talking" spelling programs.

Word processing programs are an excellent resource for creating spelling activities for students. As a teacher utility, such programs can be used to design worksheets, tests, or puzzles. Teachers can create and save on-screen exercises that use the editing features of the word processor (Figure 6.15). Students can also use word processing programs to develop their own practice exercises to share with classmates.

Spelling Checkers

Spelling checkers identify and help correct possible spelling errors in documents composed on a word processor. A spelling checker does not automatically spell words correctly as some educators believe. It simply attempts to match words in the word processing document to an extensive word list contained in its database. If there is no match, the program isolates the word and may inform the user of words that closely resemble the misspelled word, allowing the user to make the final decision (Figure 6.16). Many spelling checkers also have an add-a-word option that allows the user to add words that are not included in the existing list. The writer is the active decision maker in this procedure—the program simply offers alternatives. The spelling checker assures the writer that misspelled words will probably be identified for correction at a later time, allowing the writer to

Figure 6.15 A word processing program (MAGIC SLATE II by Sunburst). Note that the student uses editing features to complete the exercise.

```
Pg:001 Ln:010 Col:012 File:B
Replace the * with the correct
punctuation mark.↙
↙
1. The zoo is open every day from 9:00
to 5:00*↙
2. Will you go with me on Friday*↙
3. Wait until you see the polar bears*↙
4. They put on quite a show*↙
5. Please call me tonight so we can
make plans*

TYPEOVER - Use CTRL-E for insert,
Q-? for help, CTRL-Q for Main Menu.
```

focus on the expression of ideas without breaking the flow of thought to look up difficult words in the dictionary.

Two types of spelling checkers are available for classroom use. One is the individual package, like SENSIBLE SPELLER by Sensible Software, that works with several popular word processing packages. The other is built into the word processing package itself. The newest versions of

Figure 6.16 There is no magic involved in using spell checkers. As you can see, with Sunburst's SCHOOL SPELLER the student has ultimate control over the spelling of the word flagged by the checker.

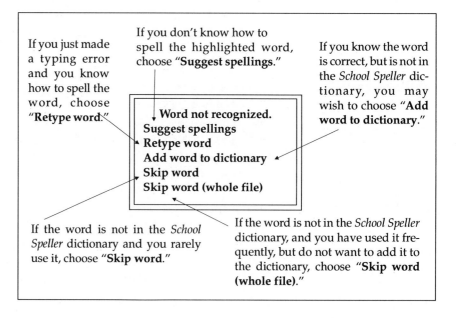

If you just made a typing error and you know how to spell the word, choose "**Retype word**."

If you don't know how to spell the highlighted word, choose "**Suggest spellings**."

If you know the word is correct, but is not in the *School Speller* dictionary, you may wish to choose "**Add word to dictionary**."

> Word not recognized.
> **Suggest spellings**
> **Retype word**
> **Add word to dictionary**
> **Skip word**
> **Skip word (whole file)**

If the word is not in the *School Speller* dictionary and you rarely use it, choose "**Skip word**."

If the word is not in the *School Speller* dictionary, and you have used it frequently, but do not want to add it to the dictionary, choose "**Skip word (whole file)**."

MAGIC SLATE, BANK STREET WRITER, APPLEWORKS, and many other word processing programs have built-in spelling checkers.

There's a slight danger that spelling checkers could become crutches for students, making them believe that spelling skills are not really necessary, since "the computer can find our mistakes for us." This is not likely to present a problem, provided the teacher helps students understand how spelling checkers really work. All a spelling checker can do is tell whether a word matches one of the words stored in the computer's memory. If a student accidentally spells a different word while misspelling the intended word, the computer will *not* catch the error. In addition, it is still much easier and enjoyable to spell words correctly the first time. A student who spells well will be faced by a small, manageable list of possible errors rather than one that is overwhelming.

The Computer's Role in Spelling Instruction

The lack of connection between pronunciation and actual spelling in our language is a source of frustration to students. Add to that frustration the multiple exceptions to any so-called spelling rule and you can see that the main role of the teacher is to build student confidence in the ability to spell correctly. Petty and Jensen (1980, p. 448) list five ways that teachers can accomplish this objective.

1. Make sure each child has a definite and efficient method of learning to spell.
2. Teach words that are necessary for the children's writing.
3. Make certain each child recognizes progress in learning new words.
4. Make spelling instruction meaningful and interesting.
5. Develop in each child an interest in language and a desire to spell and use words correctly.

Each of the computer-based spelling activities described in this chapter can support the teacher in developing student confidence.

WORD USAGE

To write and speak effectively, students must be able to choose appropriate words and structure them in a recognizable form. These skills often come under the heading "word usage," a catch-all phrase that includes subject-verb agreement, verb tense, pronoun-antecedent agreement, irregular verbs, and plurals.

As with other language-related skills, word usage certainly is a part of students' lives long before they enter school. The home environment largely determines the students' habits of word usage—and the school is sometimes unsuccessful in effecting changes toward more appropriate habits. Some differences in word usage actually arise from variations in dialect, and these are even more impervious to change. Effective teachers stress language that is appropriate for a given situation, provide opportunities to identify usage problems, and provide motivational practice that addresses the usage problems in as natural a language setting as possible (Petty and Jensen, 1980). They can do the latter by relating practice to the students' world, perhaps using a current subject of interest to create exercises. If students actually consider this linguistic conformity to be important and internalize the proper norms, they will begin to use "correct" English in their speech and writing.

For students who benefit from written practice, any word processing program can help create worksheets for individual practice. (A word processing program with speech synthesis would also give instructions and prompts out loud.) Teachers could have students with similar usage problems work in pairs at the computer, taking turns reading the exercises quietly to each other and mutually deciding on the correct response. Software for this type of activity includes VERBS and VERB USAGE (Hartley) (see Figure 6.17), FOCUSING ON LANGUAGE ARTS: USAGE I–II (Random House), and PRO-GRAMMAR and PRO-SENTENCE (South-Western Publishing).

PUNCTUATION AND CAPITALIZATION

Choosing the appropriate words and spelling them correctly require many skills and repeated practice. Observing punctuation and capitalization rules is also necessary to fully communicate thoughts in writing. Both capitalization and punctuation are most efficiently learned when the need for the skill arises, and both lend themselves easily to computer-related activities.

Figure 6.18 summarizes Petty and Jensen's (1980) suggestions of ways in which teachers can assist students in developing punctuation and capitalization skills. Good teachers have applied these strategies for many years; their implementation does not necessarily require the computer. However, the computer can help the instructional process by providing increased efficiency in the application of these strategies.

Figure 6.17 Although VERB USAGE (Hartley) could be an individual activity, many students would receive more benefit by discussing the choices on this screen with another student. Defending a response verifies students' thinking and allows them to verbalize their reasoning.

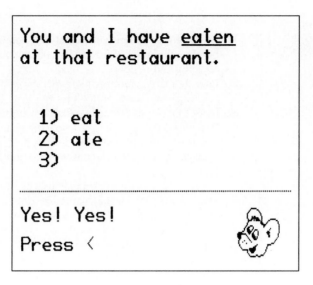

For example, Petty and Jensen recommend that teachers observe all written work carefully, not just errors made, and perhaps tabulate the types of errors. The teacher uses these observations as the basis for further teaching and review. With the help of a database or spreadsheet program (Figure 6.19), teachers can easily note and tabulate student errors. Letting the computer keep track of the details allows teachers more time to actually deal with the students' problems.

PROOFREADING AND RELATED ACTIVITIES

The most valuable editing skill for most students is to be able to find errors in spelling, usage, punctuation, and capitalization in their own personal writing—to be able to proofread and correct their own work. The editing features of a good word processing package and the legibility of the printed documents make this easier to do. For example, rather than rewriting an entire page by hand in order to correct errors, students can quickly add or delete capital letters or punctuation marks as necessary.

Similar to spelling checkers, grammar and style checkers identify possible errors in style, usage, punctuation, and capitalization in documents written on word processors. These programs are usually not integrated into a word processing program but must be run separately. They do not actually correct errors; they merely "flag" words and phrases and enable the writer to decide what action (if any) to take. In some cases they

Figure 6.18 Strategies for developing punctuation and capitalization skills (based on Petty and Jensen, 1980, pp. 425–426).

1. Observe all written work carefully, note errors made, and perhaps tabulate the types of errors. Use observations as the basis for further teaching and review.
2. Provide many proofreading experiences that emphasize the types of situations that seem difficult for pupils to handle.
3. Insist that pupils critically edit and proofread whatever they write.
4. Dictate exercises calling for specific skills (but avoid material that requires a lot of punctuation and capitalization).
5. Give children written exercises that require using capitals or punctuation.
6. Help children compile personal lists of words that they frequently fail to capitalize or that they capitalize erroneously. Introduce or review rules covering these situations and provide appropriate practice exercises.
7. Have students edit their own or other pupils' papers with special attention to capitalization. Sometimes students can do this individually; at other times they should work with a group.
8. Emphasize careful use of capitals and punctuation in all written work. Continually stress good form in writing.
9. Have pupils check their own writing after a dictation exercise. Emphasize self-diagnosis of difficulties.
10. Stress the relationship of sentence structure to punctuation and of both to clarity and smoothness of expression.
11. Give special attention to handwriting, if that is the cause of some capitalization faults.
12. Give frequent, short diagnostic tests on the major capitalization and punctuation items. Have pupils check their own work.
13. Make all practice periods short and relate them to specific needs. For example, use a five-minute individualized drill near the close of the day to work on errors observed during that day.

offer advice regarding the corrections the writer should make. At the present time these grammar and style checkers are nowhere near as useful as spelling checkers. Our experience is that only about one out of five or ten "errors" flagged by the computer is a genuine error. However, used constructively, these programs can help students zero in on and correct writing errors. These programs tend to be more helpful for high school and college students; they are discussed in greater detail in *The Computer in the English Curriculum* (Schwartz and Vockell, 1989).

As the next chapter will show, self-editing is a valuable part of the writing experience. However, most teachers feel that it is also a valuable

Figure 6.19 An example of error tracking using the APPLEWORKS database.

```
File:   ERROR TRACKING                                    Page 1
Report: ERR2

NAME: BILL JAMES
WRITING STRENGTHS: VOCABULARY, IMAGRY
ERR PERIOD END SENT:
ERR PERIOD ABBREV:
ERR PERIOD INITIAL:
ERR COMMA DATE:
ERR COMMA APPOSITIVE: X
ERR COMMA QUOTATION: X
ERR COMMA CITY,STATE:
ERR CAP FIRST WORD:
ERR CAP PERSON NAME:
ERR CAP PROPER NOUN:
ERR CAP TITLES: X


NAME: LAURA THOMAS
WRITING STRENGTHS: CLEAR THOUGHTS
ERR PERIOD END SENT: X
ERR PERIOD ABBREV:
ERR PERIOD INITIAL:
ERR COMMA DATE: X
ERR COMMA APPOSITIVE: XX
ERR COMMA QUOTATION: X
ERR COMMA CITY,STATE:
ERR CAP FIRST WORD:
ERR CAP PERSON NAME:
ERR CAP PROPER NOUN:
ERR CAP TITLES: X
```

experience for students to edit writings other than their own—that is, to look for and correct errors in sentences or paragraphs composed by someone else. In addition, finding and correcting errors is a valuable activity to prepare students for standardized tests. Finding appropriate material for student proofreading often takes time, time that teachers could better spend designing their own materials with the help of a word processing program. By creating numerous files or modifying commercially made ones such as WRITING ACTIVITY FILES FOR THE BANK STREET WRITER from Scholastic, teachers can suit the exercise to precisely the type of practice a particular student needs. The easily readable printed copy produced by word processing programs encourages students to edit their own as well as their peers' papers. Errors sometimes missed when reading cursive writing because of poor letter formation often seem to jump off the page when the document is generated by a printer. (In the next chapter we shall discuss in greater detail the advantages of using the computer for individual and group editing.)

Just as the computer can be used to create proofreading exercises, it also can be used to design specific exercises on particular capitalization and punctuation rules. This is especially valuable because many commercially created black-line master worksheets focus on multiple rules within one exercise—and much of this practice is merely wasted time for students who have already learned all but perhaps one of the rules emphasized. The computer and word processor allow teachers to focus an entire practice page on the specific rule or skill that a particular student needs to develop.

It is also useful to encourage children to compile personal lists of words that they frequently use incorrectly or misspell. The teacher can introduce or review rules covering these and provide appropriate practice exercises. Using words from this list, students can then create personalized stories or books on the word processor. For young students, CHILDREN'S WRITING AND PUBLISHING CENTER—with its word processing and graphics capabilities—may be the best resource. However, older students may want the more sophisticated features of a full-fledged word processing program. Both programs allow students to write and store their own lists, to which they can add words as the need arises, and both can print out a paper copy for students to review.

Teachers often like to give frequent, short diagnostic tests on usage, spelling, capitalization, and punctuation. (This process can include having pupils check their own work to reinforce self-editing.) Tests like these can be created and administered on the computer to give students more responsibility for their own learning. Petty and Jensen (1980) suggest making all practice periods short and related to specific needs. For example, teachers can use a five-minute individualized drill near the close of the day to work on errors observed during that day. Practice periods based on commercially produced programs fit this activity, although they may take more than five minutes. There are many programs that focus on usage, style, capitalization, and punctuation. With proper preview and selection, teachers can provide computer activities that meet their students' specific needs. The following programs are useful:

PUNCTUATION PUT-ON (Sunburst)
GRAMMAR GREMLINS (Davidson)
THE GRAMMAR EXAMINER (DesignWare)
FOCUSING ON LANGUAGE ARTS: CAPITALIZATION/PUNCTUA-
    TION I–II (Random House)
WRITING ACTIVITY FILES FOR BANK STREET WRITER VOL. 2
    (Scholastic)
CAPITALIZATION (Hartley Courseware)
BLACKOUT! A CAPITALIZATION GAME (Gamco)
CAPITALIZATION PLUS (Mindscape)

Note that it is not necessary by any means for students to run these programs in solitary isolation at individual computers. As we stated in Chapter 2, cooperative learning and peer tutoring can be tremendously effective in language arts—and many of the above programs can be used by students working in groups. The only time it is ideal to have students work alone is when the logic of the program requires a single person (as in some games) or when only a single student needs to meet the objectives covered by a program. In most other cases the judicious assignment of groups of two or three students to a computer can provide not only the more efficient use of computers but also the enrichment of the learning environment at the computer.

In addition, remember that during the *learning* phase of instruction, teacher guidance may be extremely important. And for "higher order" and "process" skills, such guidance is often essential. While students may be able to learn the meaning of new words by playing games at a computer, they are not likely to make subtle distinctions in word usage, to master the underlying principles behind punctuation, or to correct faulty habits in proofreading without a specialist helping them focus on and correct these problems. By connecting a computer to a large screen, a skillful teacher can often provide effective guidance to a large or small group of students. One strategy that is often successful starts with an active discussion of a program on the large screen and then lets students work at it independently, after they demonstrate that they are ready for the practice phase of instruction. Students should work alone or in small groups at the computer only if there is good reason to expect that they will benefit from this experience.

SUMMARY

To effectively communicate verbally and in writing—to be understood by listeners and readers—students must develop their vocabulary, learn to spell the words they write, follow standard usage rules, and adhere to capitalization and punctuation standards. Students can be motivated to learn these skills and even to take individual responsibility for their own instruction, if teachers can make the learning tasks interesting and vital. The computer can help teachers do this. By using commercial programs or by creating original activities with word processors and graphics packages, teachers can lead their students to "play with words" and develop important language arts skills while they play.

REFERENCES

McDaniel, M. A., and M. Pressley. "Keyword and Context Instruction of New Vocabulary Meanings: Effects on Text Comprehension and Memory." *Journal of Educational Psychology* 81 (1989): 204–213.

Petty, W., and J. M. Jensen. *Developing Children's Language*. Boston: Allyn & Bacon, 1980.

Schwartz, E., and E. L. Vockell. *The Computer in the English Curriculum*. Watsonville, Calif.: Mitchell, 1989.

Wallechinsky, D., I. Wallace, and A. Wallace. *The Book of Lists*. New York: Bantam, 1978.

CHAPTER 7

THE COMPUTER IN THE WRITING PROCESS

"THE WRITING ASSIGNMENT FOR today is . . . " You probably heard these words many times when you were a student. They were usually spoken by the teacher while you looked forlornly at an intimidating "blank page" that you had to fill with your thoughts within a designated time. The teacher, the sole audience, would then take this first draft and evaluate it as a final product, focusing on the surface features of spelling, punctuation, and grammar. If time permitted, you would rewrite the paper, correcting those surface errors, and then move on to the next assignment. Writing was just that, an *assignment*, which was given, read, and evaluated by the teacher alone.

In today's language-rich classroom environment, writing is not limited to the "writing assignment." It is an integral part of the daily classroom schedule and is a natural way for students to communicate with the teacher, with peers, and frequently with a broader audience. Writing is used to communicate learning in all subject areas, from mathematics to science. Students can document an interview with a grandparent for a social studies activity or include in a narrative the ways in which they observed mathematics being used at a baseball game. They may note their observations in a science experiment or create an advertisement for the book they have read. In language arts, writing projects can take many forms (Figure 7.1). Students may be committed to writing a personal journal in which they share their thoughts and feelings. The class as a whole may keep a classroom journal to be shared with parents and visitors. The opportunities for writing in the classroom are endless. We will explore these opportunities in language arts and across the curriculum.

Figure 7.1 Writing projects.

Story	Play	Phone Conversation
Essay	Limerick	Joke
Journal	News article	Myth
Fable	Interview	Invitation
Report	Booklet	Brochure
Recipe	Directions	Obituary
List	Memo	Description
Cartoon strip	Summary	Advertisement
Greeting card	Announcement	Haiku
Character sketch	TV commercial	Lyrics
Weather report	Ceremony	Slogan

The time frame and stages involved in writing depend on the project. A personal journal is constantly in progress and usually includes no rewriting or evaluation. But other projects normally involve many stages and the time frame is adjusted accordingly. Obviously, writing does not require a computer—but this tool can facilitate writing in numerous ways. It allows for better legibility, for multiple copies, and for streamlined editing. Publishing capabilities are within the reach of anyone with printer access. Computer graphics add interest to the final product. In the formal writing process, the computer can enhance each stage: prewriting, writing, rewriting, and publishing. We'll begin this chapter by examining the writing process and the computer's application at each stage.

THE WRITING PROCESS

As teachers view it today the writing process is a true *process*. It involves many stages that may not be entirely sequential. The writer moves back and forth between them: prewriting, writing, rewriting, and publishing. Interspersed among these stages are conferences with peers and teachers that facilitate each stage. The process centers on content, ideas, and style as well as the mechanics of spelling, punctuation, and grammar (Lewin, 1987). Writing requires an extended effort to communicate a clear message that includes reading, thinking, feeling, and talking (Turbill, 1983). The emphasis here is on "extended." A writing project may take minutes, hours, days, or weeks to complete. Because of this, Turbill suggests that writing should be a daily activity, so that students have the freedom to continue a long piece, to abandon a project that is not going well, or to begin a new piece. She also promotes student ownership, in which students control the topic, form, style, purpose, and audience. In today's classroom, the final product may reach a much broader audience. No longer is a student writing for the teacher's eyes only.

Prewriting

Rather than assigning a writing topic, many teachers have found that time spent in prewriting lays the foundation for successful writing ventures. Prewriting activities may be individual or group oriented and may involve discussion, listening, reading, or drawing. It is possible that, led by the teacher, a discussion about, say, a field trip, TV show, current event, or other topic might evolve into a session of brainstorming and clustering, both effective methods for eliciting ideas.

Brainstorming, a nonjudgmental approach to generating ideas, is an excellent prewriting activity. All ideas, thoughts, and phrases are written down and accepted by the group. Since no idea is judged right or wrong, students tend to share ideas generously and build on each others' thoughts. When the brainstorming session is over, individuals or the whole group "cluster" the ideas into categories that may eventually be used as a source for writing. Several software packages guide this type of prewriting activity. THE WRITING WORKSHOP: PREWRITING and THE WRITING WORKSHOP: ACTIVITY FILES by Milliken offer brainstorming, clustering, and branching activities (Figure 7.2). BANK STREET WRITER III ACTIVITY FILES (Scholastic), SEMANTIC MAPPER (Teacher Support Software), and THE WRITER'S HELPER (Conduit) also include prewriting activities. Any word processing program on the computer screen can be connected to a liquid crystal display (LCD) projection system to facilitate brainstorming. Because the ideas can be printed out by the computer, students won't be distracted from the discussion by having to write things down; and they can use the printout—or the electronic file on-screen—to help them branch out from the original ideas.

Free writing, in which students are asked to write whatever they are thinking, is another prewriting activity that can easily be adapted to the computer. A time limit is designated and students write until time is called. The purpose is simply to get them in the habit of writing without the pressure of evaluating their product. The more they write . . . the more they

Figure 7.2 Prewriting activities can be supported by software such as Milliken's THE WRITING WORK-SHOP: PREWRITING and THE WRITING WORK-SHOP: ACTIVITY FILES. Clustering and branching applications give writers a clear, graphic image of how their thoughts relate.

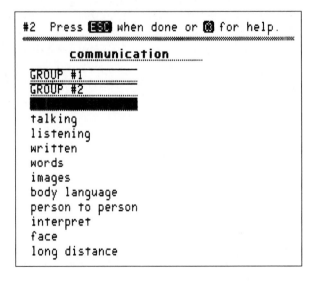

write! At the computer free writing requires only a word processing package and a timer. This activity takes on a new dimension when students turn off the monitor and continue to type, creating "invisible writing." This method helps prevent students from being so preoccupied with mechanics that creative thought is stifled. The hardcopy created from free and invisible writing can be used as a springboard for future writing topics and should not be graded in the traditional sense.

Prompted writing is another prewriting activity that is enhanced by the computer. Programs such as FREDWRITER by CUE and MAGIC SLATE II by Sunburst allow the teacher to create prompts to guide students at the prewriting stage (Figure 7.3). These prompts may be a series of questions or directions that require students to respond on the screen. After the activity, the prompts are removed and students have their responses in the form of a shell or outline, which they can use as a foundation for future writing. Dauite (1985) created sample questions and a checklist that can be adapted to prompted writing activities (see Figure 7.4). Sunburst has created a series of prompted writing activities that culminate in the printing of student-authored booklets. I CAN WRITE!, BE A WRITER!, WRITE WITH ME!, and WRITE A STORY! are included in this series.

Prewriting activities allow students to take time to think about their writing. It is a time for incubating, rehearsing, discussing, and researching before committing to the writing task (Turbill, 1983). By devoting time to prewriting, the following stage—the actual writing—flows more easily.

Figure 7.3 MAGIC SLATE II (Sunburst) can prompt writing. It allows the teacher to write directions and comments that initiate the students' written response.

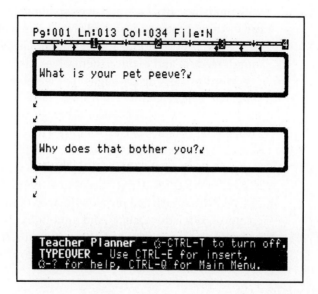

Figure 7.4 Topic-oriented prewriting prompts and checklist (Dauite, 1985, p. 82).

Prompts

1. What am I most interested in today?
2. Why is that interesting to me?
3. Why would someone else find that interesting?
4. What would be a good starting sentence for a story about this topic?

Checklist

1. Decide on a topic.
2. Write as many words as come to mind on that topic.
3. Group the words into categories of similarity.
4. Write a sentence that relates all the categories.
5. If the sentence expresses or suggests an idea you'd like to write about, use it to begin writing.

Instead of an intimidating blank page, students have a file and usually a printout filled with words, phrases, and thoughts that guide the writing of the first draft.

Writing

When we see writing as a process instead of an assignment, we can then view the first draft as an experiment for placing thoughts on paper—or in the case of the computer, on the screen. Just knowing how simple it is to make changes on the computer gives students permission to experiment with phrasing, structure, and even spelling. In the first-draft stage, students can focus on content, ideas, and style. Later they can address the mechanics of spelling, punctuation, and grammar. Usually students enjoy this new-found freedom and express themselves freely.

Word processing packages that facilitate this stage in the process are available to meet a variety of needs. These are discussed in greater detail in *The Computer in the Classroom* (Vockell and Schwartz, 1988) and in *The Computer in the English Curriculum* (Schwartz and Vockell, 1989). MAGIC SLATE II (Sunburst), LANGUAGE EXPERIENCE RECORDER (Teacher Support Software), THE WRITING WORKSHOP (Milliken), BANK STREET WRITER III (Scholastic), FREDWRITER (CUE), and AP-PLEWORKS (Claris) all provide the word processing features necessary to create a written document. And although it is important to choose a word processor suited to the level of the students, it is also useful to choose one that permits users to move up to more sophisticated procedures as their writing matures. In addition, it is sometimes helpful to select a program that will interface conveniently with the teacher's word processor or desktop publishing program. This compatibility makes it easier for the teacher to coordinate and share newsletters or booklets composed by students.

In addition, primary students often benefit from the use of voice synthesizers, large type, and graphics. Several packages offer one or a combination of these features. With such programs as DR. PEET'S TALK/WRITER (Figure 7.5) and MY WORDS (both from Hartley)—which combine speech synthesis with word processing—children type their thoughts and then the computer reads back their words or sentences. Programs like this not only help teach writing skills but are also ideal tools for the Language Experience Approach, which is highly recommended for reading instruction (see Chapter 4). In addition to reading the students' stories for them, TALKING TEXT WRITER by Scholastic contains such functions as a built-in dictionary that allows students to create, store, and recall a definition for any word used in the text. However, because these extra features make it a more complex program to operate, its word processor may be too difficult for students who are at the sound-symbol stage of reading. Once children have progressed beyond the DR. PEET and MY WORDS stage, they could simply learn the word processor they will be using in upper elementary grades and beyond—for example, MAGIC SLATE, MECC WRITER, LOGOWRITER, BANK STREET WRITER, FRED-WRITER, or APPLEWORKS. Word processors with speech synthesizers are useful for beginning readers who can benefit from the Language Ex-

Figure 7.5 This may look like a screen from any word processor, but the voice capabilities of DR. PEET'S TALK/WRITER make it especially helpful to young writers.

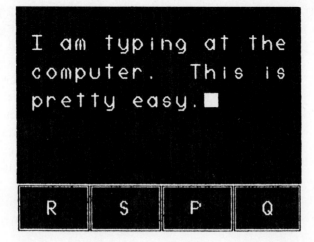

perience Approach, but it is not at all obvious that most typical readers beyond the beginning stage need this feature.

Children use a controlled vocabulary to create animated stories on THE STORY MACHINE by Spinnaker. KIDWRITER by Gessler and ONCE UPON A TIME by Compu-Teach allow students to choose the illustrations that will accompany their stories when they are printed out. The EXPLORE-A-STORY series from D. C. Heath permits students to write, modify, and share vividly animated stories. MUPPET SLATE by Sunburst includes large type, graphics, and borders to motivate young authors to write. PUBLISH IT! by Timeworks Platinum (Figure 7.6) combines word processing, layout design, and graphics into a desktop publishing program suitable for children.

Writing is, after all, the purpose of this stage. Any tool that allows students to easily record their thoughts in writing should be considered. The computer, compared with the traditional paper and pencil, offers the following advantages:

- Students are not distracted by handwriting concerns.
- Mechanics are less likely to interfere with the flow of thoughts.
- Students tend to experiment more with phrasing and structure.
- Students create longer documents.
- Hardcopy is easy to read and encourages thorough proofreading.
- In the rewriting stage, students are more willing to edit content as well as surface errors.

Peer and Teacher Conferencing

Once students have written a first draft and printed it, they need feedback to tell them whether they have communicated their thoughts clearly. Although the computer can provide multiple, easy-to-read hardcopies, it cannot evaluate the *content* of the writing—only people can do that, and conferencing is a good way to get the necessary feedback. Peers are readily available for this task. An excellent guide to peer conferencing is found in Madian (1987) (see Figure 7.7). Peer conferencing has two important results. As writers, students learn how others interpret what they have written and how they may change their writing to better communicate the message. As readers, students learn to evaluate content, which in turn is reflected in their approach to their own writing.

Students learn other valuable lessons while participating in peer conferencing. Offering suggestions and criticism in a positive manner is neces-

Figure 7.6 PUBLISH IT! (Timeworks Platinum) connects word processing, graphics, and layout design in an easy-to-use approach to desktop publishing for children.

George Rogers Clark School   April 1987
Clarksville, Indiana 47130

Computers ******
A Classroom Bonus

Mr. Dan Bullington, Principal

Fifth Grade Class of Dorothy A. Stemle

The fifth grade class of Mrs. Dorothy Stemle of George Rogers Clark in Clarksville Indiana recieved a grant from Indiana Consortium for Computer and High Technology Education. It is called, " COMPUTERS-A CLASSROOM BONUS."

It was to show how easy access to computers affects student performance. She was one of the nine teachers in Indiana to recieve the computer grant. Software and hardware were part of the grant. Some of the hardware received was three Image Writer II printers with Apple Talk boxes and 12 Apple IIe Computers . Apple Talk boxes are boxes that control the printers. Some of the software we received will be reviewed in this news letter.
By:Kyle Girten

Ghost Writers For Teddy Bears

Mrs. Stemle's 5th grade class interviewed Ms. Shultz's 1st grade class. We interviewed them on thier favorite teddy bears. We asked them what is the teddy

bears name, what is the 1st graders name, what the bear eats and more. After that we went back to our classroom and wrote a letter to the 1st grader that we interviewed and signed the teddy bear's name. Then we went back to the computers to type and print them out. After that we went the library and put the letters on the library tables. The first graders thought that it was there teddy bears who had wrote the letters but we really wrote them.
by Holly Harrison

LABEL LAB

Mrs. Stemle's 5th grade class helped on a project for our school office. We typed the names and addresses of all the students in the "BANK STREET FILER". Then we were able to use the "BANK STREET MAILER" to print out labels. When our secretary needs to mail letters to parents for conferences,she can just take them off the page and stick them on the envelope. She can find which students ride the bus,etc.   by Shelly Cawthorn

Our G.R.C.C news show goes on every Friday and is very popular around the school. The way we do our show is alot of fun. The best thing about doing the show is while were filming and writing our stories our English grade skyrockets.

We start our show with the anchormen and anchorwomen.then other reporters do their stories. For the last few weeks, we have had a little first grader come in and do his story or usually an interview on our show. We also have some commercials on our show. Bryce and I are the commercial directors, we don't always have funny commercials but our next going to be funny, but I'm not going to tell the press because our school is going to get a copy and I want it to be a surprise.

Everyone one in our class is on the GRCC-TV Staff. At the beginning of the year, we fill out an application for the TV staff jobs. We check jobs we are most interested in and the experience we have for it. There are four anchor people, sports reporters, meteorologists, commercial writers , actors, and artists. Everyone in the class is a reporter and everyone is a camera person at some time.

Our show reports each week on current events in the world and at GRC. We try to find stories that are happy and are interesting to our students.

We have specials with plays and music, etc. by our students from other classes on special holidays and Patriotism Week. The library is a great help when are doing research on many stories each week especially about historical events.

GRC CHANNEL 4 NEWS BROADCASTS FROM MRS.

STEMLE'S CLASS EVERY FRIDAY.

It's a Super Show!

See our new 1987 Show!

Figure 7.7 Peer-conferencing and peer-editing guide (Madian, 1987, p. 67).

In a word or phrase describe your impressions after the first reading:
- What did you like best about this piece?
- Was the intention of the writing clear?
- What details were useful?
- Was the progression of events or thoughts clear?
- Were there problems with punctuation, spelling, or penmanship?
- What was the writing about?
- How did you feel about the writing?
- Were any words overused?
- Were you confused by any aspect of the writing?
- Do you have any additional comments?

sary in our society, which is leaning more and more toward a cooperative, collaborative approach in the work world. Conferencing with peers, either one-to-one or in small groups, is excellent practice for many group-related skills.

Teachers may choose to conference with students individually or in groups. They may conduct these conferences—which should encourage student thinking—formally and informally throughout the writing process. Individual conferences most often deal with a student's specific problem, whereas group conferences permit teachers to introduce a concept, teach a skill, or encourage students to share their writing (Turbill, 1983). Because feedback is helpful at all stages in the writing process, conferences should not be limited to the first draft.

In addition, depending on the hardware and software configuration, teachers may be able to conference with students through computerized monitoring. While students work at separate terminals, the teacher can monitor all the screens from the file server or terminal and can send messages to individual workstations. However, this "electronic conference" should support rather than supplant the person-to-person conference.

Rewriting

After conferencing, students should immediately have the opportunity to rewrite their documents so that they can respond to issues brought to their attention by peers or their teacher. Word processing packages make this a much simpler process than paper-and-pencil revising. Students are encouraged to make the necessary transitions, restructuring, or other revisions because on-screen editing is easy. They are required to deal only with the improvement they wish to make rather than with rewriting the entire document or portions of it by hand.

Once students are satisfied that their writing clearly conveys their message, they can deal with the so-called surface errors. Peers or teachers can point out these errors in a second conference, which leads back to rewriting the document a second time with the help of the editing features mentioned earlier. For most writers, of course, the eventual goal of conferencing is to be able to proofread and correct their own documents.

The computer offers assistance to the individual proofreader in the areas of spelling, punctuation, capitalization, and usage. Depending on the program chosen, these areas may be addressed in a separate package such as MECC SPELLER by MECC (Figure 7.8), which includes a built-in ten-thousand-word dictionary to complement MECC WRITER. Other proofreading aids are included as part of more sophisticated word processing programs. HOMEWORD PLUS by Sierra On-Line includes a thirty-thousand-word dictionary with its word processing program. BANK STREET WRITER III by Scholastic has an on-line sixty-thousand-word glossary for its spelling checker plus a fifty-thousand-word thesaurus to aid in word choice. THE WRITING WORKSHOP: POSTWRITING from Milliken includes a spelling checker of forty-one thousand words; a mechanics checker that flags possible errors involving overused words, homonyms, sentence fragments, pronoun case, and punctuation; and a

Figure 7.8 With the help of MECC SPELLER, students become more confident in proofreading their work and less dependent on the teacher or peers. Perhaps teachers will hear the question "How do you spell . . . ?" less often with the assistance of a good spell checker!

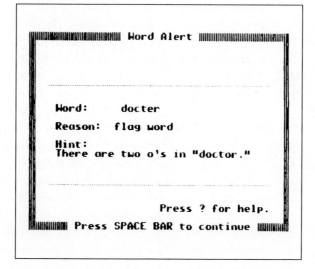

proofreader that guides students to examine each sentence in their documents by considering a list of leading questions. The LANGUAGE EXPERIENCE RECORDER by Teacher Support Software also indicates readability level, the frequency and number of unique words, number of sentences, and average length of sentences. Software is available to assist in almost any imaginable proofreading component from spelling to word choice. Note, however, that these computerized editing tools can only supplement—not replace—careful thought by the writer. Teachers should use them as aids to flag possible errors and to stimulate student thought.

Publishing

Because of the computer, publishing can be added to the writing process. Rather than have the document read by a limited audience of one (i.e., the teacher), the writer can think in terms of an audience that may include the classroom, the school, the community, and beyond! Multiple copies of a document can be printed right on the printer—however, using the hardcopy as a black-line master for the copy machine is a more cost-effective approach. Desktop publishing programs like PUBLISH IT! from Timeworks Platinum permit the production of documents with an even more professional appearance. Extending the audience gives a new purpose for writing and often a new sense of pride for the writer. The computer easily facilitates this step in the writing process.

In addition, through the use of a modem, it is possible to expand the audience farther—beyond school, state, and even national boundaries! Children in Iowa can send essays to pen pals in Australia and can reasonably expect a reply in a day or two. The Daedalus Project, operated out of the University of Connecticut, has used telecommunications to stimulate the writing abilities of learning disabled and physically handicapped students. This creative strategy is amazingly simple. Students were told that "Mysterious Mel" or someone else at the other end of the modem would answer any letters they would write. With this assurance, students who had previously never shown any interest in writing began doing so via modem. Not only did they improve their writing skills, they also showed dramatic improvements in self-esteem and social interaction.

In an educational setting, publishing a document for a broad audience is as attainable to a first grader as it formerly was to those who had special connections to a high school printing department. All that is necessary is a word processing program, a printer, and paper. The results of computer-generated publishing can be highly professional depending on the quality of the printer and the features available in the word processing package.

Fonts and special type effects, graphics libraries, and format choices can provide students with unlimited selections in the appearance of their final document. Students are pleased to see their words in boldface, underline, outline, and shadowed print (Figure 7.9). These common features are offered by many word processing programs, such as MAGIC SLATE by Sunburst and MULTISCRIBE by Styleware. Programs like PRINT SHOP by Broderbund also offer several font choices to add visual variety. The professional look of such features encourages students to think about the print that would be most pleasing visually as well as most supportive to the content.

The visual impact of a document often depends on illustrations as well as the text used. The computer has expanded this area for the nonartistic student as well as the gifted artist. Graphics libraries and clip art packages (PRINT SHOP GRAPHICS LIBRARY I, II, and III by Broderbund, and HOLIDAYS AND FESTIVALS by Right On) place hundreds of professional-looking illustrations at the students' fingertips. Many word processing programs such as KIDWRITER (Gessler) and ONCE UPON A TIME (Compu-Teach) include graphics in the package. These programs allow students to choose predesigned illustrations before writing their stories. For students who wish to create their own illustrations, programs like DAZZLE DRAW (Broderbund), KOALA PAINTER (Koala Technologies), and MACDRAW and MACPAINT (Claris) transform the computer into a drawing tool. Graphics created by these programs can be exported to the

Figure 7.9 The type style options available from MAGIC SLATE II (Sunburst) give a professional look to student work.

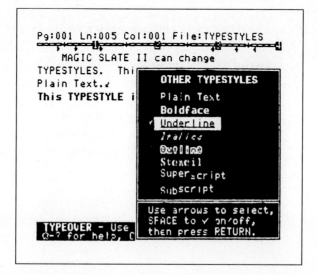

document to serve as illustrations. True artists and less-talented students alike benefit from the support the computer gives to creating graphics.

Choosing between pen and pencil and between single and double spacing were about the only "publishing" concerns before the computer became part of the writing process. Now the choices are more numerous. With the help of the computer, students can produce documents in formats other than that of the standard manuscript. Columns are now easily used by elementary students and "page design" is a phrase that has entered the writing process. Desktop publishing programs provide students with sophisticated tools to combine text and artwork. Student-designed newsletters, newspapers, illustrated reports, certificates, and flyers showcase writing in a professional manner. THE CHILDREN'S WRITING AND PUBLISHING CENTER by The Learning Company and PUBLISH IT! (Figure 7.10) by Timeworks Platinum include word processing, graphics selection, and page formatting. Because they are easy to use, both are popular desktop publishing programs for elementary students. The essentials for a desktop publishing program (based on Thomas, 1988; see Figure 7.11) define a good program and provide a way to evaluate programs for purchase. Although desktop publishing software is not necessary to the writing process, it can further motivate students to write and adds a level of professionalism to the finished product that simple word processors cannot.

WRITING ACROSS THE CURRICULUM

As stated earlier in this chapter, writing is not limited to the language arts curriculum. It should be used in every subject area and then not merely to write reports. It can play a much broader role in engaging the student in the learning process, no matter what the topic. A writing project in science, social studies, or mathematics gives students a different means of expressing their understanding of the subject. From the teacher's perspective, a writing project brings new insight into what students have actually learned. The computer is an efficient tool to facilitate the process.

Science

The study of science provides many opportunities for students to write (see Figure 7.12 for some suggestions). Students can explain how to set up an experiment or share the steps in the scientific method. To demonstrate their

Figure 7.10 With very little guidance, students can create their own class newsletters with PUBLISH IT! (Timeworks Platinum).

THE COMPUTER LINE

Greater Clark computer news

Vol.2 No.7, May 8, 1987

ELEMS HAVE 80 COLUMNS

Each elementary school in Greater Clark now has an average of four additional 80-column cards for its computers. This will allow teachers and staff to use more advanced word processing programs for letters home, forms, tests, etc. Older elem. students can also use 80-column programs.

HAS A MONSTER BEEN EATING YOUR COMPUTER?

If your computer has been in need of repair, you might want to send it in NOW, rather than waiting for summer maintenance. The Wilson Center Repair Shop has been working hard to improve the delay time we have been experiencing in getting our computers fixed. They assure me that they will try hard to get your computer back within one week.

I was at the shop last week and had a chance to watch them test a computer which had a particularly difficult problem to locate. The repair technician ran a great many tests over the course of two hours and eventually solved the problem.

I noticed that the backlog of yet-to-be-repaired equipment was no longer there. If you can spare your defective computer for a few days, this might be the best time to send it in.

Note: If your problem seems to be a disk drive, PLEASE send in the computer, disk drive, dd/card and cable. The problem could be any of these or a combination. And don't forget your work-order and repair tag.

Thanks,
Rhoda Meier

BUYING A COMPUTER SOON?

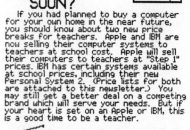

If you had planned to buy a computer for your own home in the near future, you should know about two new price breaks for teachers. Apple and IBM are now selling their computer systems to teachers at school cost. Apple will sell their computers to teachers at "Step 1" prices. IBM has certain systems available at school prices, including their new Personal System 2. (Price lists for both are attached to this newsletter.) You may still get a better deal on a competing brand which will serve your needs. But if your heart is set on an Apple or IBM, this is a good time to be a teacher.

THE "GAME SHOW" – revised version

The popular program THE GAME SHOW is now available in a new revised format. The graphics are much better than the older version and the program has a few more features than the original. The best part is that Advanced Ideas will allow you to trade in your old Game Show diskette for a new one for $15. Just send your old diskette and check to Advanced Ideas.

The program can also be purchased directly, at a list price of $35 (though such discounters as Fas-Track and Eastcoast Software have it for under $30.)

LAW OF THE HACKER:

Nothing is ever so bad that it can't be made worse by trying to fix it.

LAW OF BINARY OPERATION:

A computer operates on binary principles: it either works or it does not work.

LAW OF PRINTER PERFORMANCE:

A watched printer never jams.

Figure 7.11 Essentials for a desktop publishing program (Thomas, 1988, p. 34).

1. A word processor incorporating the following features: edit, insert, delete, copy, move, cut-and-paste, search-and-replace, center, and right/left justification
2. A variety of typefaces (e.g., Times, Helvetica), sizes, and styles (e.g., plain, bold, italic, underline)
3. The ability to import text created with a different word processor
4. An expandable spell checker with a minimun of sixty thousand base words
5. An art program with a wide variety of tools, colors, and shapes that, like the text, can be moved, deleted, copied, cut and pasted, and easily edited
6. An art file with several hundred basic pictures (e.g., people, animals, vehicles, everyday objects, and so on)
7. The ability to import art created with a different art program; or else a "scanning" program, which "digitizes" print materials such as photographs
8. The ability to "wrap" text—either horizontally or vertically—around art and to insert art anywhere into existing text
9. The option to choose whether to create text first, art first, or both as you go along
10. The ability to use the full power of your printer, particularly if you're lucky enough to own a laser printer

Figure 7.12 Suggested writing topics for science.

Students share their knowledge of particular topics by writing from an unusual perspective. They may choose a special event in science, an inanimate object, or a nonhuman living thing. Try these:

Ben Franklin's kite
Sir Isaac Newton's apple
A blood cell traveling through the body
A tree in summer, fall, winter, or spring
A cave during prehistoric times
A drop of water from an ocean, lake, or river
The first wheel, electric light, telephone, or other invention
An amoeba
A comet
A butterfly
A satellite

understanding of a concept, they can take the role of an inanimate object or nonhuman living thing and write from that perspective. Students can compose fictional interviews with renowned scientists and inventors, or pretend to be the researcher who finds the cure for cancer. Writing about a scientific breakthrough as if it were a current news release presents several possibilities. For instance, if the U.S. rather than the U.S.S.R. sent up Sputnik, how would our approach to the space program be different?

Some science programs are designed to deliberately stimulate writing. For example, THE DESERT by D. C. Heath (Figure 7.13) employs exactly the same strategies as the EXPLORE-A-STORY series, enabling children to write animated stories about desert life. Programs of this kind provide an ideal opportunity to integrate science with the reading and writing curriculum.

In science, as in other subject areas, asking the right question is frequently as important as knowing how to find the correct solution. By writing concise questions, students can share what puzzles them. They can also write sample test questions to be used in a review activity. Each of these writing projects personalizes the learning experience because the student has ownership in the process.

Social Studies

Social studies topics also lend themselves to written projects that go beyond the writing of reports. For instance, by putting themselves in the place of a historical person, students get a sense of history that cannot be matched in textbooks. To do this, students can write a dialogue for persons involved

Figure 7.13 THE DESERT (D. C. Heath) provides the backdrop for creative writing in the science curriculum.

in historic events—and to speak as those involved, students must have an understanding of the events and of the attitudes of the participants. Letters and journals are another way to get "inside" history. What would you have written to your family if you were on a slave ship bound for the U.S. or if you were stationed at a fort on the western frontier during the late 1800s?

Another approach is for students to "interview" a famous person from history. One student (or student group) looks up information about a historical figure, and another determines and then asks the appropriate questions during the interview. Writing short stories and plays about the era being studied forces the writer to understand more than just the dates on which important events occurred. Students might use the "what if" format (described in the science section) to explore, say, what could have happened if the British had won the Revolutionary War, or any other topic that catches their imagination. This approach gives life to projects by involving the student on a personal level. In addition, by using a word processor or desktop publishing program, the output from such projects can be incorporated into newsletters or newspapers.

Mathematics

Writing story problems and solutions that relate to the students' lives is one way to tie writing to the mathematics curriculum. When students explain in written form how to solve a problem and why the solution is practical, they prove they truly understand the concept. Or they might address how mathematics is used in any number of professions. Or, after taking notes on mathematics in their own lives for several days, they could write a summary of which mathematics area relates most to their everyday lives or which mathematics topic they would most like to explore. Responding to the data displayed on charts or graphs could be handled in written as well as numerical form. Students can also express their feelings about their mathematical abilities, an unusual assignment for a subject normally connected with the cognitive rather than the feeling domain.

THINKING SKILLS

Improved writing skills are not the only result of writing practice. By writing a first draft, reading it, thinking it over, and revising it to communicate their ideas more accurately, writers learn to *think* more clearly. If writers improve their writing by reflecting upon and revising their own writing, it seems fairly obvious that thinkers improve their thinking by reflecting upon and revising their own thoughts. Most teachers have certainly noticed that they come to understand an idea more thoroughly when they have written it down, found something wrong with the expression, and tried again. (For example, this paragraph itself has been revised several times, and the ideas expressed in it have become much clearer.) Written ideas are by their very nature more susceptible to reflection, revision, and improvement than are ideas that are spoken aloud or merely thought internally. One of the problems with modern technology is that children are encouraged to watch TV and to talk to others; rarely do they read and write. As a word processor, the computer can help reverse this process. Even very young students can discover that it can be an advantage rather than a nuisance to write their ideas down. Because their ideas are still on the disk, review and revision are easy. They simply read what they've written and make changes where necessary, without having to write the whole thing over. This process of self-reflection and revision can be an extremely important tool in the development of students' thinking skills.

SUMMARY

Writing in a language-rich classroom is process rather than assignment oriented. With the help of the computer and appropriate software, prewriting, writing, rewriting, and publishing are stages that flow easily from one step to the next. Students who use the computer for writing are encouraged by the ease of editing and the professional appearance of their final product. They tend to write longer texts, make more revisions to content as well as to surface mechanics, and show pride in their work. Their audience expands from their teacher to include their peers, parents, and even readers beyond their community. Although the product is important, the real learning takes place as students work through the process as writers and readers. Not only do students become better writers, they also become better thinkers; and the computer makes valuable contributions to this process.

REFERENCES

Dauite, C. *Writing and Computers*. Reading, Mass.: Addison-Wesley, 1985.

Lewin, L. "Rewriting—Using the Best of Both Worlds." In J. Madian (Ed.). *Making the Literature, Writing, Word Processing Connection: The Best of the Writing Notebook 1983–1987*. Mendocino, Calif.: Creative Word Processing in the Classroom, 1987.

Madian, J. "Responding, Correcting, and Evaluating." In J. Madian (Ed.). *Making the Literature, Writing, Word Processing Connection: The Best of the Writing Notebook 1983–1987*. Mendocino, Calif.: Creative Word Processing in the Classroom, 1987.

Schwartz, E., and E. L. Vockell. *The Computer in the English Curriculum*. Watsonville, Calif.: Mitchell, 1989.

Thomas, O. "Desktop Publishing: What? Why? Where? Which One?" *The Writing Notebook*. (November/December 1988): 34–36.

Turbill, J. *Now, We Want to Write!* Australia: Bridge Printery, 1983.

Vockell, E. L., and E. Schwartz. *The Computer in the Classroom*. Watsonville, Calif.: Mitchell, 1988.

CHAPTER 8

THE COMPUTER IN THE MEDIA CENTER

IN THE DISTANT AND mythical past, the elementary school library was a place where "treasures" were stored and guarded. The library might have been located in a refurbished storage room or unused classroom. Its shelves were filled with valuable resources, such as the school's one and only encyclopedia set—and children had to get special permission to take one of the volumes from the shelf. Needless to say, these precious volumes were never allowed to leave the library. But other treasures were! A student's signature was the only collateral required for *Little Women*, *The Hardy Boys*, or *Nancy Drew*. The library also housed a globe, an atlas, an almanac, and periodicals that couldn't be found anywhere else in the building.

The school library seemed a contradiction—it fostered skills of logic on the one hand and the appreciation of language and literature on the other. In an organized, no-nonsense manner, the librarian taught the skills of alphabetizing, locating a book in the card catalog, and finding it according to the Dewey decimal system. Yet it was the same librarian who led children to appreciate a particular author's storytelling ability by reading aloud to them. Although the library was a place to find concrete facts, it was also a place to dream: a place to practice the skills of reading, writing, listening, and speaking; a place where the language arts were seen, heard, and felt. A contradiction, yes, but a wonderful place for children to find treasures!

If you have stepped into an elementary school library recently, you are aware that treasures are still kept there. But rather than guarding them, the librarian shares them freely with students. Some libraries have become true media centers—with media specialists—offering teachers and students a wealth of *modern* treasures to assist them with various tasks, from choosing a book for leisure reading to gathering information for an assigned project. While the library continues to be a place where language arts skills are learned and practiced, it also reflects the technology of our era. Students looking for a book that matches their interests may first stop at the computer to respond to questions on an interest survey; then, using the electronic card catalog, the computer suggests titles for the student to pursue. Books are checked out literally with the wave of a wand, an electronic scanner that reads barcodes. Teachers and students can also use the library to preview a video tape, search a database via modem, or gather information from an encyclopedia stored on a compact disk rather than on a reserve shelf. Articles from such materials can simply be printed out to take home and review.

All the applications of technology described above are currently available. From automated circulation systems to on-line searches of databases located hundreds of miles away, the computer and related devices provide the keys by which students and teachers open these twenty-first century treasures found in the school library. To understand how all this works, we'll first look at library automation, including instruction in library skills and information literacy; then we'll examine how the automated library helps students discover the library's literature and provides teachers with an instructional resource in language arts.

LIBRARY AUTOMATION

Automated card catalogs and circulation systems—once limited to large public libraries—are now available to secondary, middle, and elementary schools, which find that an automated system can save time and money while teaching students the finer points of electronic search strategies and related communications skills. Let's take a brief look at library automation.

Computerizing or automating the school library means that functions normally completed by hand—such as book check out, overdue lists, and searches of the card catalog—are coordinated by a program or combination of programs on the computer. The decision to automate requires an objective look at the advantages and disadvantages, because not every school library should be automated. Small schools of 100 to 125 students, libraries with limited collections (less than two thousand books), and those staffed by part-time volunteers may not be time- or cost-effective when automated (Meddaugh and Way, 1987). For larger schools with adequate staff, automation is worthwhile and requires four steps in order to be implemented successfully: goals and objectives must be planned, software must be selected, hardware must be selected, and staff must be trained.

Media specialists Meddaugh and Way (1987) and Whaley (1988) agree that thorough planning is the first step in successful automation. Planning includes a realistic look at the process and the pitfalls (see Figure 8.1). By determining which aspects of the library system would benefit from automation and then proceeding carefully with a sequential plan, many of the pitfalls can be avoided. If possible, software selection precedes hardware selection. There is some advantage in having the media center use the same kind of computers that are used throughout the school, but this is by no means necessary. For example, if the media specialist determines that the

Figure 8.1 What to do and what to expect when you automate the library (Whaley, 1988, p. 3).

1. A salesman is a good initial contact, but your final decision should come after talking with other users of various software packages.
2. The cost of courseware is almost always more expensive than your estimates.
3. No matter how well you plan, something will not go as you expect!
4. You have plenty of answers. You just don't know the questions yet, and you will not find out until after you have purchased the software.
5. The quality of the data you put into the system will have a direct bearing on your final success with automation.
6. To be fully dependent on a machine will save time and energy—until it breaks!
7. Some vendors will go out of business.
8. Never look back. Someone will introduce a new system tomorrow that is better, faster, and less expensive than the one you just purchased.

circulation system can operate best with an IBM or Macintosh system, it makes sense to use this hardware, even though the school's other computers are all Apples. Since the media center computer will be devoted exclusively to library management tasks, the incompatibility will not be a problem.

Begin the decision process with a visit to an automated library to ask questions of the media specialists who use the system daily (see Figure 8.2). Once the software has been chosen, ask the software vendor to provide a list of the needed hardware. This list should include computers, monitors, cards, cables, adapters, hard drives, barcode readers, and printers. Delegating the hardware list to the software vendor circumvents any surprises concerning "missing pieces" when the system is set up. Software vendors may also handle the training of the media specialist and support staff, as well as provide assistance (for a fee) in entering the shelf list. Initial data entry seems to be the point of crisis in automation. Consistency is essential, since check out as well as searches pivot on the accuracy of the data entered. Depending on the size of the collection, some media specialists decide to rely on typing services provided by the software vendor.

Media specialists who work in an automated library find that the circulation tasks that once consumed their time no longer do so. Instead, they can spend more time providing students with opportunities to practice communications and thinking skills in a center that houses not only books but other information resources as well. Beyond the scope of "library" or

Figure 8.2 Questions to ask vendors and media specialists about library automation (Whaley, 1989, p. 4).

1. How long can your list of titles be?
2. How many different media types can be listed?
3. Can you vary the check-out time according to the media type?
4. Can you perform a "sort" on each media type?
5. How many different subject headings can be assigned to each entry?
6. How many characters can each subject field accomodate?
7. Can the system be networked without additional cost? Does any additional cost include the needed cards and connectors?
8. Do you buy your barcode labels from the vendor or can you print them on your own printer? What is the cost?
9. What reports can be generated from the system?
10. Does the overdue report also accumulate unpaid overdue fines?
11. Is a student with unpaid fines "locked out" from checking out more materials unless cleared by you?
12. Can the system generate catalog cards?
13. What security measures are in place to keep unauthorized users from accessing the system?
14. What is physically needed to do an inventory of the collection?
15. How are backups of the transaction file made? How are backups of the total system made? How much computer time and how much of your time will it take to perform either function?
16. Are there limits on the size of the collection?
17. When doing sorts and other operations on the data, which functions will require the student to access the catalog or the circulation module to be shut down?
18. Does the network require a dedicated server or can the computer double as a workstation?
19. How is the system restored in the event of equipment failure?

"media center," a new term for these technology-based collections of sound, print, and video is emerging: *information center.* The term is appropriate. We live in an information society, an era in which the wealth of data available to us increases exponentially every few years. The students we teach must deal effectively and efficiently with this information overload in order to solve personal and societal problems. The need to become "computer literate" has expanded to the need to become "information literate." Students must be able to locate, analyze, and use information that is resource rather than textbook based. In her review of research on the topic of information skills, Kuhlthau (1987) described information literacy in this way:

Helping students gain information literacy also means helping students learn to think. Learning to question, to weigh alternatives, to interpret inferences, and to seek further data can also help individuals cope with a continuously increasing wealth of information, and to survive in a world growing ever more complex.

The information skills listed by Kuhlthau in Figure 8.3 are practiced while using the computer as a tool to identify, access, and obtain data. An automated library speeds up the process of locating information housed on the shelf in printed form, but many such libraries have access to additional information resources. Putting encyclopedias on CD-ROM disks facilitates the search for pertinent information and simplifies cross referencing. On-line databases extend the students' reach for information not only beyond the library walls but across state and national boundaries as well. Both technologies require students to learn search strategies to obtain the information they seek. Let's take a closer look at these two forms of technology, the information that students can access through their use, and the skills required.

CD-ROM Technology

CD-ROM (compact disk-read only memory) is a direct descendent of the compact (music) disk (CD) and has two major advantages over the standard 5¼-inch floppy disk. The first advantage is its durability. The life expectancy of the 5¼-inch floppy is approximately eighty hours of interactive use. The estimates for the CD-ROM are between ten and fifty years (this technology has not been around long enough for a more precise prediction). The durability of the CD-ROM is based on the way the disk is read by the CD player. Rather than physically contacting the disk, the

Figure 8.3 Information skills necessary to use the computer to identify, access, and obtain data (based on Kuhlthau, 1987).

Information skills extend beyond that of simply locating information. For students to be able to solve problems and make decisions based on information, they must have the following:
- Knowledge of tools and resources with the additional skills necessary to plan a research strategy and evaluate information
- Acquisition of attitudes such as persistence, attention to detail, degree of skepticism
- Need-driven skills related to general and computer literacy

player reads the data with a laser beam. Although the user loses the ability to add, edit, or delete data on a CD-ROM, this lack of contact lengthens the life of the disk. (Tandy Corporation has announced a CD that does have editing capabilities. It is called a "write once—read many" or WORM.)

Storage is the second major advantage of the CD-ROM. A 5¼-inch floppy has about 360 kilobytes available for storage, whereas the CD-ROM has 540 megabytes or room for approximately 270,000 pages of text. The printed text for an entire encyclopedia takes up only 20 percent of the available disk space. And storage is not limited to text. A CD-ROM can also store video, graphics, numerical databases, sound, and computer programs.

Publishers have developed several categories of materials that take advantage of the CD-ROM's vast storage (Orwig and Baumbach, 1989):

- Reference materials such as encyclopedias, dictionaries, thesauri, and directories. Examples include BOOKSHELF (JMH Software), ELEC-TRONIC ENCYCLOPEDIA (Grolier), and MULTIMEDIA ENCYCLO-PEDIA (Compton)
- Indexing services such as abstracts, ERIC, and *Books in Print*. Examples include SILVERPLATTER (Silverplatter) and DIALOG ONDISC (Dialog Information Services)
- Visual databases that contain clip art for desktop publishing
- Software collections of public domain titles, such as PUBLIC DOMAIN FREEWARE/SHAREWARE (Alde Publishing)

A computer (preferably with a hard drive), software, printer, and a CD-ROM player are necessary components of a CD-ROM workstation. Add to this the cost of the CD-ROM disk itself and the total easily exceeds five thousand dollars. This is a sizable chunk if not the entire library budget for a school year (or two!). Therefore, the return in student learning must also be sizable. To guarantee this, the disks chosen by the media specialist must meet student needs.

One CD-ROM package that fits the needs of elementary students is Grolier's ELECTRONIC ENCYCLOPEDIA, an electronic version of Grolier's *Academic American Encyclopedia*. Sitting at the computer, students have an entire encyclopedia at their fingertips. They can use one of two search strategies: browse or word search. Each provides valuable practice in on-line searching skills. With *browse*, students search for information by using the first word of the entry they seek. This strategy forces them to think of a variety of titles for target information and to focus on key phrases. *Word search*, the second strategy, is more complex. Students search for a term or combination of terms in a form they determine. They may search for terms anywhere in the title, text, tables, bibliographies, or fact boxes found in this version of Grolier's. They can limit the search to a one-word match, narrowed by using the *and* function, or expand it by using the *or* function. While deciding on the most efficient search strategy, students are practicing the "information" skills described earlier in this chapter.

The Grolier encyclopedia has been criticized as "mere text on the screen" and inefficient in helping students zero in on desired topics. The Compton subsidiary of Encyclopedia Britannica now offers an entirely new software product, which may revolutionize our methods of gathering information. Compton's MULTIMEDIA ENCYCLOPEDIA is a complete encyclopedia on a 585-megabyte CD-ROM disk. It goes beyond the simple approach employed by Grolier. Besides nine million words of text, the disk includes fifteen thousand photographs, sixty minutes of audio, a United States history time line, a world atlas, science articles, an on-line dictionary, and even a built-in note pad so that students can take notes from articles and print them out for later use. In addition, the program permits the user to access information in several different ways. For example, students can use the key-word strategy (also available in the Grolier encyclopedia) to find all articles in the entire encyclopedia that mention a designated topic or combination of topics. But they can also follow more traditional approaches, such as moving from one topic to another (without having to pull another volume off the shelf), or moving from a general topic to a more specific topic as need and interest naturally dictate. The program provides seven different methods to access the information on the CD-ROM disk and permits the user to move easily from one method to another.

CD-ROM technology is not limited to encyclopedia-based resources. BOOKSHELF by JMH Software stores ten commonly used reference works. It also stores a word processing program that can be accessed while using the reference materials, so that students can create an original document or cut and paste information they access. The reference works stored on BOOKSHELF are:

The American Heritage Dictionary
Bartlett's Familiar Quotations
Roget's II: Electronic Thesaurus
The World Almanac and Book of Facts

U.S. Zip Code Directory
The Chicago Manual of Style
Business Information Source
Houghton Mifflin Spelling Verifier and Corrector
Houghton Mifflin Usage Alert
Forms and Letters

Teachers and media specialists who do their own research will find CD-ROM technology of special interest. Several components of ERIC can be found on CD-ROM. Although elementary students would not find this application beneficial, a school corporation might want to invest to meet the needs of its professional staff. The versions currently available are SILVERPLATTER from Silverplatter, OCLC (Online Computer Library Center) from OCLC, and DIALOG ONDISC from Dialog Information Services. Prices range from $350 to $950 for annual license fees and updates. The price of CD-ROM technology will no doubt decrease, and it will soon be a common reference tool in the school library.

On-line Databases

Accessing information beyond the walls of the library captures the imagination of students who are searching for data. On-line databases connect students via computer and modem to information in distant locales. Telecommunications—communicating long distances—literally access a world of information and deliver it to the computer screen. From there it can be stored on disk and printed for future reference. To enter this area of our information society, the school library must have a computer, modem, phone line, telecommunications software, and a subscription to an information service or phone number to access an on-line database. Students must know the log-on and password to correctly connect with the service. They must also learn the various search strategies unique to the service used. The school library, where students can practice their search skills with the support and supervision of the media specialist, is the perfect environment for on-line database applications.

Topics offered by information services vary, but most include environment, science, news, and industry. In Figure 8.4 we have compiled a list of information services that relate directly to the special needs of an elementary school. The cost for services varies according to subscription rates and long-distance charges.

Figure 8.4 Information services accessible via modem that relate directly to the special needs of an elementary school.

COMPUSERVE:	The largest information service with over five hundred thousand subscribers. It offers a students' special-interest group so that students can communicate on-line.
DIALOG:	Offers bibliographic information.
EINSTEIN:	An information service of eighty-five databases of interest to students and teachers.
PRODIGY:	Marketed by IBM and Sears, includes electronic mail and information on news, weather, sports, shopping, and education.
QUANTUMLINK:	Official on-line service for Commodore computers; offers access to public domain materials and homework tutoring by teachers.
NASA:	Offers daily updates on activities at NASA; science lesson plans can be downloaded.
AMERICA ON-LINE and APPLELINK:	Apple's information services offer technical support, news, special-interest groups, and electronic mail.

CAI in the Library or Media Center

Addressing information skills through the use of CD-ROM and on-line databases in the library is a practical use of technology, but because of a lack of funding it may not be affordable to all. Computer-aided instruction (CAI) is a less expensive application of the computer in this setting. Several programs focus on information skills and are compatible with hardware that may already exist in the library. To give students an opportunity to learn on-line searching skills with or without modem access, Grolier created the INFORMATION CONNECTION (Figure 8.5). This program lets students practice on-line, using passwords and employing search strategies. The program also includes telecommunications software so that students can use their new skills immediately if the proper equipment is available.

Choosing the most appropriate reference or resource book is an old research problem that can be approached in a modern way using CAI. Several software publishers offer programs that give students the opportunity to practice finding the correct reference:

HOW CAN I FIND IT IF I DON'T KNOW WHAT I'M LOOKING FOR? (Sunburst)
STUDY SKILLS (Houghton Mifflin)

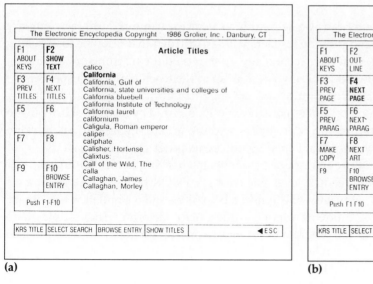

(a)

(b)

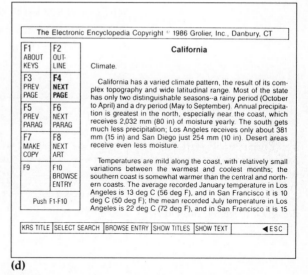

(c)

(d)

Figure 8.5 Gaining on-line skills can be done inexpensively with the use of Grolier's INFORMATION CONNECTION. Students practice skills that will be necessary for successfully using a telecommunications system.

LET'S LEARN ABOUT THE LIBRARY (Troll Associates)

SKILLS MAKER (Follett)

RIPLEY'S BELIEVE IT OR NOT! LIBRARY RESEARCH SKILLS (SVE)

THE COMPUTER AND LITERATURE

The computer can also help students learn the value of the library's literary treasures and provide teachers with an instructional resource for teaching children's literature. Technology meshes with the teaching of literature in predictably mechanical ways. It is up to the teacher or media specialist to share the affective portions of such instruction with the students. Although the computer cannot replace the emotions stirred by reading or listening to good literature, it can provide a medium for surveying interest, tracking accomplishments, and creating unique responses to books read.

Several programs assist students in choosing books that match their interests and reading level. For example, BOOK BRAIN by Oryx contains a database of twenty-one hundred book titles and a simulation of a library card catalog. Students respond to questions to determine interest and grade level so that the program can suggest appropriate titles. Students can also use standard searches for title, author, subject, or key word. There is even an option that allows students to comment on books; the comments are stored so that others can access them when trying to decide what to read. MECC's BOOKWORM (Figure 8.6) provides a similar database for books entered by students themselves. BOOKMATE by Sunburst matches students to books through one of four activities. Students can begin with a

Figure 8.6 The computer can be used in the media center to assist students in choosing an appropriate book geared to their individual tastes and interests. MECC's BOOK-WORM guides students through a list of questions designed to match students to appropriate books.

```
Call number    398 2A
Subject        FAIRY TALES
Author last    AARDEMA
Author first   VERNA
Title          WHY MOSQUITOES BUZZ IN
               OUR EARS
Reviewed by    WORMY BOOKWORM
Grade          3
Rating G-F-P   P
Description    TELLS WHY MOSQUITOES
  -> BUZZ IN OUR EARS

Do you want to search in all fields?
         (Yes or No) [N  ]
```

special day, movies made from books, headlines, or symbols to reflect their mood. The program then matches books to student responses.

Recording information relevant to the books read by students is another task that can be delegated to the computer. MECC's BOOKWORM can record information from classroom or library collections. Again, students' comments can be recorded for use by others. Actually, any database management program could be used for this purpose. APPLE-WORKS (Claris), BANK STREET FILER (Broderbund), or PFS: FILE (Software Publishing Corporation) are good choices. Each is easy to use and does not require unusual hardware configurations. In creating a personal database of books read, students are not bound by a publisher's choice of data categories. This freedom gives students the opportunity to choose the information that they deem important in the book. Much can be learned by simply reading their choice of categories.

However, teaching children's literature is much more than book selection. Vocabulary development, comprehension, character development, setting, and simple appreciation of a story well told are legitimate topics of instruction. We have found several programs that cover some of these skills.

Vocabulary development and comprehension skills are natural areas of instruction when working with children's literature. Sunburst Communications offers a series of programs based on Newbery winners that focus on these areas. After completing a book, students move to the computer to review vocabulary, be tested on their understanding of the plot and main idea, or engage in activities based on the action of the story. The NEWBERY ADVENTURE series includes CHARLOTTE'S WEB, MR. POPPER'S PENGUINS, ISLAND OF THE BLUE DOLPHINS, MRS. FRISBY AND THE RATS OF NIMH, and A WRINKLE IN TIME.

As children read, they often imagine themselves to be a character in the story. This is exactly what Tom Snyder Productions had in mind when it developed two new programs: JACK AND THE BEANSTALK and FLODD, THE BAD GUY (Figure 8.7). The reader's name is worked into the story. Activities are open-ended so that students can choose what will happen next. This branching feature offers an unusual twist to teaching plot development, allowing the teacher and student to explore "what would happen if . . . ?"

A more structured approach to linking literature and computer applications, Beaty's *A Link to Literature* (1988) is an excellent resource book, providing lesson plans that connect the reading of twelve popular children's books with computer-based activities. The lesson plans use

Figure 8.7 FLODD, THE BAD GUY (Tom Snyder Productions) is part of the series called the Reading Magic Library. In these interactive stories, students take the part of one of the characters and choose what will happen next.

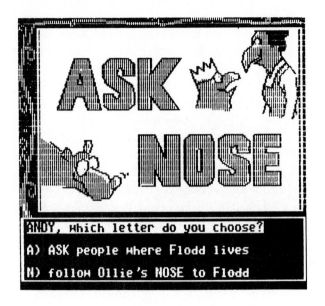

Teacher Support Software's Language Experience Series (SENTENCE STARTERS, GREAT BEGINNINGS, LANGUAGE EXPERIENCE RECORDER, READ-A-LOGO and MAKE-A-FLASH, THE SEMANTIC MAPPER, THE SEQUENCER, and WORD WORKS VOCABULARY series). With these, media specialists and classroom teachers can engage students in a variety of activities that encourage them to write, read, and listen to each other. The lesson plans provide solid models for anyone planning to use the Language Experience Approach in reading or literature instruction. Additional programs for helping students develop reading and literature skills are described in *The Computer in the English Curriculum* (Schwartz and Vockell, 1989) and in *The Computer in the Reading Curriculum* (Whitaker, Schwartz, and Vockell, 1989).

Book Reports

Responding to books with traditional book reports has often spoiled rather than enhanced the sense of accomplishment students feel when they have completed a book. However, there are many alternatives to writing an uninspired report, filling in blanks on a book report form, or—understandably—choosing to ignore the entire process. By responding innovatively to the story, characters, and setting, students enjoy literature more. And, as with many other learning activities, students don't need the computer in order to respond creatively—but it can certainly help, whether they respond orally, in writing, or with a project.

In *Developing Children's Language*, Petty and Jensen (1980) provide extensive lists of ways in which students can respond to books. Instead of recounting the story in detail, students can orally describe their favorite scene or character, give a speech that would be appropriate for a character in the book, or tape an "interview." As shown in Figure 8.8 a variety of written responses can be much more interesting than simply recounting the plot or describing the main characters. Petty and Jensen also point out that projects based on setting, characters, or any facet of the book can also take many forms, as summarized on the next page.

Figure 8.8 Alternatives to book reports (Petty and Jensen, 1980, p. 148).

1. Write a sketch of the most admirable character in the book (or the most unusual or the least admirable).
2. What did you learn from this book that you did not already know?
3. Describe the setting of the book. What did it look like and what kind of place was it? Was it happy, gloomy, lonely, or . . . ? Was the setting suitable for the story?
4. Did the characters in the book behave like real people? Give examples to support your answer.
5. Write a different ending that would fit the events of the story and the way the people in it behaved.
6. Write a dialogue for one of the incidents in the story as though it were a scene from a play.
7. Write a poem that shows how the book made you feel or that describes the setting or one of the characters.
8. Write a letter to one of the characters in which you discuss an event or situation that occurred in the story.
9. Write a portion of a diary that one of the characters might have kept. (This could be an entry from a single day or it could cover the period of time during which a particular incident occurred.)
10. Write a letter to the book's author; or illustrate and explain why you like the book.
11. Make an individual or class book of favorite words, phrases, or passages from books.
12. Produce a classroom newsletter containing book news (e.g., books read, new aquisitions, reports of experiences with authors or illustrators, announcements of book-related community events, book reviews, photos showing how books have been shared in the classroom, ads for books).
13. Conduct a survey to find out which books students think should win school book awards. Report the results.

Illustrate a Scene or Draw a Caricature:

This could be accomplished with a drawing program such as DAZZLE DRAW by Broderbund or KOALA PAINTER by Koala Technologies Corporation.

Create an Advertising Campaign for the Book:

PRINT SHOP by Broderbund provides the means for creating a letterhead, posters, and banners to make the "campaign" a visual experience.

Develop a Slide Show or Filmstrip:

Scholastic's SLIDE SHOP and Broderbund's SHOWOFF and VCR COMPANION help students create professional slide presentations on the computer screen or overlays for the VCR.

Draw a Comic Strip:

CREATE WITH GARFIELD from Developmental Learning Materials lets students manipulate their favorite Garfield characters and insert dialogue.

Design Models, Dioramas, and Other Visuals:

Graphics from THE PRINT SHOP or any of the PRINT SHOP GRAPHICS LIBRARY disks from Broderbund can assist the student in creating characters and settings.

Although each of the above ideas can be accomplished without the use of the computer, it is easy to see how valuable it could be to help students respond to literature by creating and sharing special projects. In addition, many of the written activities suggested by Petty and Jensen in Figure 8.8 would be easier to create with a good word processing program suitable to the grade level of the student.

SUMMARY

Whether it is called the school library, media center, or information center, the area designated to hold books and reference materials is being transformed by technology. Automated circulation and card catalog systems, on-line resources, and individual computer workstations share a compatible space with the treasured books on the shelf. This combination of modern and traditional treasures assures students that they will learn the information skills necessary to solve the problems facing them in the future. At the same time teachers are assured that the language arts skills supported by literature instruction will be nurtured.

REFERENCES

Beaty, J. *A Link to Literature*. Gainesville, Fla.: Teacher Support Software, 1988.

Kuhlthau, C. "Information Skills for an Information Society: A Review of Research." In *ERIC Digest* (digest by Susan Hubbard). Syracuse, N.Y.: ERIC Clearinghouse on Information Resources, December 1987.

Meddaugh, N., and D. Way. "Computerizing the Elementary Library." *The Computing Teacher* 14 (March 1987): 47–49.

Orwig, G., and D. Baumbach. "What Every Educator Needs to Know About the New Technologies: CD-ROM." Orlando, Fla.: UCF/DOE Instructional Computing Resource Center, 1989.

Petty, W., and J. M. Jensen. *Developing Children's Language*. Boston: Allyn & Bacon, 1980.

Schwartz, E., and E. L. Vockell. *The Computer in the English Curriculum*. Watsonville, Calif.: Mitchell, 1989.

Whaley, R. "The Media Center Automation Survival Manual, Part I: Preparing for Automation." *The Printout* (November/December 1988): 3–5.

Whaley, R. "The Media Center Automation Survival Manual, Part II: Selection and Implementation." *The Printout* (January/February, 1989): 3–5.

Whitaker, B., E. Schwartz, and E. L. Vockell. *The Computer in the Reading Curriculum*. Watsonville, Calif.: Mitchell, 1989.

CHAPTER 9

TOOLS FOR TEACHERS

ALL PROFESSIONALS RELY ON tools to assist them in completing a task. People in the fields of medicine, architecture, and manufacturing depend on the quality and accessibility of their tools to perform simple as well as complex activities. Everything from diagnosing a broken bone to building a skyscraper or producing a car requires a partnership of the human mind and the necessary tools. The field of education is no exception. Teachers rely on various tools to guide students to achieve their learning goals and to ease the burden of mundane teaching tasks.

Until the 1980s, tools for teachers were limited to visual aids such as maps, charts, and the ever-present chalkboard—tools typical of the industrial age—and films and overhead projectors—tools typical of the twentieth century. The advent of computers has created two new categories of teaching tools: peripherals and computer software.

The first category—peripherals—are devices that are added to the main computer system. The second category—software—includes packages that can assist teachers in instructional management, presentation techniques, and materials generation in all subject areas. In this chapter we will target these two categories of tools used by teachers in the language arts curriculum.

PERIPHERALS

The term *peripheral* refers to devices added to the basic computer system that expand its capabilities. This chapter focuses on three devices that currently enhance presentations in the language arts classroom: the liquid crystal display (LCD) projection system, the large-screen monitor, and the laser videodisc (laserdisc) player. Each has unique characteristics suitable for sharing information with small and large groups. Let's look at their advantages and limitations.

When people think of computer-assisted instruction, they usually envision a roomful of students seated at individual computers, actively and industriously pursuing the objectives of the curriculum. However, language arts teachers find that sharing a single program with a whole class is often a better way to use the computer. To do this requires a display mechanism—either a large-screen monitor or LCD projection system—that allows everyone to see the computer screen.

A large-screen monitor can be a 25-inch cathode ray tube or a television set with a large screen and an appropriate adapter. A major advantage of the large-screen monitor is that almost all schools already have one (or more) that can easily be wheeled into classrooms as needed. Another advantage is that a large-screen color monitor preserves a program's color graphics, especially important to programs for younger learners. A disadvantage of this screen is that students seated far from it cannot see it very well—especially if the on-screen information is printed in small letters, typical of some database management programs. In addition, the resolution of some of the older large-screen monitors—especially those designed primarily to show movies—cannot show text and diagrams as clearly as the computer's monitor. Finally, it is usually more trouble to set up and use those monitors than the simpler LCD projection systems.

To use a large-screen monitor, the output from the computer must be sent to the large screen rather than to the computer's monitor. In some cases, this may be as simple as unplugging a cable from one monitor and plugging it into the other (if the cable is too short, it should be replaced with a longer one). However—ideally—the output should appear on *both* monitors. This is usually accomplished by using a "Y splitter," which takes output from a single source (the computer) and sends it to two display devices (the computer monitor and the large screen). This enables the teacher to watch the computer monitor while the students watch the large screen.

Liquid crystal display projection systems are used in conjunction with conventional overhead projectors (see Figure 9.1). The major advantage of the LCD system is that it can project a very large display on an ordinary projection screen. The projection works just like an ordinary overhead projector—for instance, the teacher can make the display larger by simply moving the projector farther from the screen and focusing appropriately. In addition, the teacher can easily point to output by using a pencil or other pointer on the display device; or, using a transparency, the teacher can draw on the output without damaging the display device. LCD devices are usually easy to set up and provide very clear output. A major disadvantage is that, at the present time, the only LCD devices that project color displays are fairly expensive. Although the more affordable black-and-white display is no problem with some applications, it can be with others. Currently, less expensive color LCD devices are under development and should be available shortly.

The computer combined with a display device (either a large-screen monitor or LCD system) expands the way teachers share information with the whole class. For instance, by using a word processor in conjunction with a display device, teachers can not only demonstrate concepts or record brainstorming ideas or write down students' questions—as they did previously with transparencies and overhead projectors or the chalkboard—they can also save, edit, and copy the information. In these

Figure 9.1 An LCD projection system expands the use of the computer. With the addition of an overhead projector, the LCD can project a screen large enough for a classroom of students to view comfortably.

ways, teachers can combine "traditional" and technological strategies. For example, a teacher can project a student essay on the screen. To modify it the teacher can simply write corrections on a transparency placed on top of the LCD device, and these corrections can be projected directly onto the screen. Or the teacher can make corrections on the word processor, project them onto the screen, and save them to disk for future reference.

Using such display devices, the entire class could participate in writing a story or proofreading a draft. This is a definite advantage over the use of an overhead projector and transparencies, which are usually more presentation oriented and less interactive. In addition, with the computer configuration, each student can receive an individual product that extends the activity in a way that the overhead could not. Although teachers need not use the overhead display devices constantly, these peripherals are easily compatible with the strategies for prewriting and proofreading described in Chapter 7.

Activities centering on simulation software also benefit from the use of an LCD or a large-screen monitor. Involving the whole class or a small group in a program such as WHERE IN THE WORLD IS CARMEN SANDIEGO? by Broderbund or OREGON TRAIL by MECC can successfully be related to the language arts curriculum. Such programs offer a comfortable forum for practicing oral communication skills and can provide a common springboard for future writing projects.

In our discussion of group size in Chapter 2, we indicated that small-group and large-group work at the computer is often preferable to individual use. Especially during the learning phase of instruction, it may be desirable to use the computer with a large group (such as an entire class) under teacher supervision. The overhead projection devices and large-screen monitors are often valuable aids for this purpose.

In an indirect way the experiences that the LCD and large-screen monitor facilitate for the class as a whole also assist students when they use the computer individually. By using these devices for large display, teachers are better able to introduce a program that will eventually be used by a small group or by individuals. The entire class can preview the program and work through any difficulties before their allotted time on the computer. Introducing new software in this manner circumvents problems that might develop when students begin a new program without such preview.

Disadvantages in using these devices are minor and obvious, but teachers do need to be aware of them. Some LCD systems are notorious for overheating, which distorts the projected image. In the absence of a built-in fan, elevating the LCD an inch above the overhead's surface can solve this problem. Another disadvantage of the LCD is the lack of true color. Current devices use color contrast to represent rather than reproduce the computer monitor's output. Genuine color matching is still in the developmental stage.

A disadvantage of the large-screen monitor—which is able to reproduce color truly—is the size of the image it projects. Although the screen is certainly larger than the computer monitor's, it cannot compare with the size projected by the LCD. One solution is to use more than one large-screen monitor, so that students can see a screen easily from anywhere in the room. Another disadvantage is that teachers find it difficult and impractical to point to and write on large-screen monitors, whereas they can do so easily with an LCD system.

Perhaps the newest peripheral for classroom presentations is the CD-ROM player. As we mentioned in Chapter 8, a CD-ROM disk is a laser-optical disk, which closely resembles its ancestor, the compact music disk. The CD-ROM disk is virtually indestructible and can store a tremendous amount of material. The contents of the disk can then be read by a CD-ROM player, which uses a laser to read the data. At the present time the CD-ROM player cannot write to the disk, which means that information can be read from the disk but cannot be changed on it. The applications of CD-ROM to the library and media center were discussed in Chapter 8. At this point we should merely add that CD-ROM can bring major aspects of the library or media center into the individual classroom. Students and teachers can easily search encyclopedias and indexes at the time when their interest is piqued—without taking time to visit the library.

Laser videodiscs (laserdiscs) are larger than CD-ROM disks but not as widely used. Rather than a CD-ROM player, they employ the larger laserdisc player. Although both sides of a laser videodisc can store only one hour of video, the same disk can store up to fifty thousand still pictures or a vast number of words. Because these disks play and provide instant access to moving pictures, they are particularly useful for interactive video, which will be discussed in Chapter 11. In addition, it would be possible to expand CD-ROM applications tenfold by combining them with interactive videodisc applications either in the classroom or in the media center. For example, Compton's MULTIMEDIA ENCYCLOPEDIA (discussed in Chapter 8) could provide access to ten times as much of its already-impressive store of information if it were also interfaced with appropriate information on laserdisc.

To operate a CD-ROM or laserdisc workstation, the user needs a computer, a printer, some type of storage device such as a disk drive or, preferably, a hard disk, and a CD-ROM or laserdisc player. With the appropriate software these devices allow teachers to run interactive programs, to arrange slides, or to show motion pictures to support presentations. The teacher is able to select the exact portion of a video presentation suitable to the concept being taught. This feature alone can eliminate time wasted viewing an entire film or filmstrip when only a short segment applies.

Although teachers are experimenting with authoring programs that access laserdiscs for use as presentation tools, the time involved in preparing interactive programs for students often makes that application impractical. Laserdisc producers are beginning to see the commercial advantages of developing disks for use in education. Interactive hypertext-driven programs (see Chapter 11) have already been developed for the study of science. It is only a matter of time before language arts topics are addressed in the development of commercial laserdisc products. In the meantime, exploring laserdisc applications offers adventuresome teachers another technology frontier!

WORD PROCESSING

One of the most valuable tools for the teacher is a good word processing program, which can assist in materials generation, record keeping, and instructional management. APPLEWORKS (Claris), BANK STREET WRITER (Scholastic), MAGIC SLATE (Sunburst), FREDWRITER (CUE), MECC WRITER (MECC), and LANGUAGE EXPERIENCE RECORDER (Teacher Support Software) contain the features necessary to easily create, edit, and store a variety of documents. In addition to the instructional applications of the word processor (introduced earlier in this book), teachers can use a word processor to help them with some of their other tasks (see Figure 9.2). By storing documents that can be reused (for example,

Figure 9.2 Some tasks for which teachers can use a word processor.

- **Home-school communication**
  Letters announcing field trips, special programs, conference details, and extracurricular events are just some of the possibilities.

- **Worksheets**
  Unlike commercially prepared black-line masters, those designed by the teacher apply *directly* to the lesson.

- **Study guides**
  Guides can be personalized by the teacher to suit the needs of individual students.

- **Lesson plans**
  Even the most experienced teacher benefits from the recording of objectives, materials needed, and a lesson outline.

- **Project descriptions**
  Teachers easily modify projects for individual students by simply editing the original to suit the special needs of those students.

- **Class/student notes**
  A journal of class activities or individual behavior is often a good foundation for evaluation and conferencing.

a letter describing a field trip that is taken every year as shown in Figure 9.3), teachers save time—instead of rewriting the entire letter, they edit only the portions that change. Although this small task by itself involves relatively little time, add it to the numerous other written tasks that teachers perform daily and you can see how a word processing program would be a valuable time saver.

Some schools have created a collection of "templates" (predesigned documents that are altered to perform specific tasks) for letters, announcements, and the like (see Figure 9.4). Teachers must be sure that home-school communication is handled professionally and sensitively. At the end of a long day, choosing the most tactful wording for, say, requesting a parent conference may be difficult. If a template for such a letter is readily available in the school office, the teacher can easily edit the form, add personal details, and send it home confident of its content. Having each faculty member in a school contribute to such a collection of templates guarantees that it will reflect the needs of those who need it most. The suggestions in Figure 9.4 would be a good starting point for a template collection.

Figure 9.3 There are many annual events, trips, and celebrations that require communication with parents. By storing letters like the one shown, teachers can save time. They need only make minor changes and reprint the documents.

```
September 11, 1990

Dear Parents,

On Friday, September 14th, our class
will visit Spring Mill Park for an all
day field trip. We will meet at school
at 8:00 AM and return at 3:30. Please
be sure that your child brings a sack
lunch and a canned drink. This trip is
part of our study of Indiana and the
cost will be covered by our PTA. If
your child would like to buy corn meal
that is milled at the park, please send
$3.00. No other money is necessary.
We are looking forward to touring the
pioneer village. If you are interested
in joining us or if you have any
questions, please call me at school
after 3:00 on Wednesday or Thursday.


Sincerely,

Mr. Dewey
```

Figure 9.4 A partial list of templates that a language arts teacher may wish to have on file.

Grade reports to parents
Grade reports to students
Grade reports to or from resource teachers
Grade reports to central office
Individual educational plans
Inventories of supplies, texts, and the like
Class lists
Seating charts
Book reports
Lesson plans
Instructions to substitute teachers
Bibliographies
Tardy and absence reports
Requisitions for books and materials
Invitations to class functions
Instructions for science projects
Test formats (with instructions)

GRADE MANAGEMENT

Of all the tasks teachers perform, one of the most time-consuming is recording and calculating grades. The popular pocket calculator has certainly eased this burden but does little to assist teachers in reporting grades to students or parents. Software publishers have developed gradebook programs that incorporate the best qualities of the pocket calculator with the options of creating reports. The most effective programs include the following record-keeping tasks, summarized from *The Computer in the Classroom* (Vockell and Schwartz, 1988):

1. Allow the teacher to enter and edit class rosters, activities, and grades.
2. Duplicate rosters for classes with the same students. (In elementary classrooms this eliminates retyping the same names for teachers who have the same students for multiple subjects.)
3. Permit the teacher to weight grades according to their relative importance. (Homework assignments would have less weight than a quiz; the quiz in turn would have less weight than a chapter test, and so forth.)
4. Keep a cumulative average so that the current grade can be reported at any time during the grading period.

5. Provide the option of entering no grade or zero for students who fail to turn in assignments. (This option allows the teacher to decide if the assignment will be counted in the cumulative average.)
6. Convert averages to letter grades according to the teacher's grading scale.
7. Average categories of grades such as homework, tests, and projects so that they can be reviewed separately.
8. Print various reports such as an individual grade report, class grade reports, and class roster with options to include or exclude standard comments.

There are three basic issues that concern elementary teachers when they consider using a grade management program. Let's take a look at them in the form of questions and answers.

Does using a computerized grade management program mean that I can toss out my gradebook?

That depends on local regulations. Many schools require that teachers record grades in a standard gradebook. However, more and more school districts have discovered the advantages of a computerized grading system. In these districts teachers keep a hardcopy of their students' grades, which they update periodically. Depending on the program used and the report format, the hardcopies often look very similar to the standard gradebook but offer the teacher many more options.

How much time will I spend entering grades on the computer?

The average time spent by elementary teachers we surveyed was two sessions of twenty to thirty minutes each week—which is approximately the same amount of time a teacher would spend using a calculator to average student grades for a grading period.

What are the advantages to using a grade management program if the time involved is the same and the hardcopy looks like my gradebook?

The first advantage is eliminating that long session with the calculator at the end of a grading period. A good grade management program will display or print cumulative averages for individual students or the entire class with just a keystroke or two. Once the grades are entered, the teacher can avoid the irritating expenditure of time and the possible introduction of errors that would occur in calculating all these averages by hand. Therefore, teachers can easily report student progress to parents and students as often as needed.

That brings us to another advantage of grade management programs: reporting. An individual student report, complete with personal notes of encouragement and comments by the teacher, can be printed in a matter of seconds. Report formats are as varied as the programs available. Figure 9.5 illustrates sample reports from GRADE MANAGER (MECC) and REPORT CARD (Sensible Software). Since grade reports are personal communication with students and parents, teachers should pay close attention to a program's options and its variety of reports. Note the information that can

```
Progress Report for FLY, FREDDY
Class: SOCIAL STUDIES
Quarter: 1

Current Scores (*** means missing score)

Score/Possible (Percent Score)

Score Category: HOMEWORK

   1.  34/ 43 ( 79)

Score Category: TESTS

   1.  20/ 27 ( 74)

Score Category: REPORTS

   1.  40/ 50 ( 80)


Estimated Grade to Date: C

Comments:

        -------------------------------S---U--
        Attendance                  !   !   !
        Assignments                 !   !   !
        Daily Work                  !   !   !
        Class Participation         !   !   !
        Tests                       !   !   !
        Brings Needed Materials     !   !   !
        Attitude                    !   !   !
        Behavior                    !   !   !
        Alert and Attentive         !   !   !
```

(a)

```
                    CLASS: ENGLISH
                   DATE: OCT 1 1990

              STUDENT 1: MATT THOMAS

          NAME        WEIGHT    MARK    TOTAL     PERCENT
      ---------------  ------    ----    -----     -------
   1: HW 8/28/90         1        13     / 15       86.7%
   2: HW 9/4/90          1        14     / 20       70.0%
   3: HW 9/6/90          1        12     / 15       80.0%
   4: QUIZ 9/7/90        4        24     / 30       80.0%
   5: HW 9/11/90         1        15     / 15      100.0%
   6: EXB P46 9/13/90    1        16     / 20       80.0%
   7: PROJECT 1 9/18     4        20     / 20      100.0%
   8: TEST 1            10        35     / 40       87.5%
   9: CR WR 9/17/90      4        40     / 50       80.0%
  10: EXA P59 9/22/90    1        14     / 14      100.0%
  11: EXA P80 9/25/90                            --NO GRADE
  12: QUIZ 9/26/90       4        17     / 25       68.0%
  13: CR WR 9/28         4        20     / 25       80.0%

                 PERCENTAGE: 84 %
```

(b)

Figure 9.5 Up-to-date reports are readily available from GRADE MANAGER (MECC) and REPORT CARD (Sensible Software).

be shared by the report as well as the style in which it is reported. Remember that student evaluation is a task that requires human input and sensitivity!

Some grade management programs assist teachers in tasks other than grade reporting (Figure 9.6). REPORT CARD by Sensible Software offers the option of printing a class roster. This can save teachers time when a class list is needed to record lunch money or fund-raising efforts or any of the other record-keeping jobs that elementary teachers find themselves doing.

Figure 9.6 Some of the record-keeping tasks that an effective teacher might want a gradebook program to perform (based on Vockell and Kopenec, 1989).

1. Allow the teacher to enter grades for students as easily as would be possible with a normal gradebook.
2. Permit the teacher to make easy alterations of previously recorded scores to correct clerical errors or to accommodate retests or rescoring of previous work.
3. Computer averages for the students' work during an entire grading period.
4. Apply weighting formulas to grade computation (e.g., count the exam for 50 percent of the grade, homework for 10 percent, weekly quizzes for 25 percent, and class participation for the remainder).
5. Convert numerical grades to letter grades according to prescribed standards.
6. Provide records of performance (complete with current averages) for students at any time during a grading period.
7. When students are absent for tests or fail to turn in assignments, provide the option of counting this as either a zero, an *F*, or "no grade"—and compute averages accordingly.
8. Compute averages for the entire class for any recorded assignment.
9. Compute separate averages when requested by the teacher (e.g., quiz average, exam average, homework average) as well as record the overall performance of the students.
10. Provide hardcopy lists of student performance.
11. Provide anonymous printouts of student performance, so that the teacher can post scores with confidentiality.
12. With large classes (or multiple sections of the same class), provide both combined printouts for the entire class and separate printouts for subgroups.
13. Flag students with designated levels of performance on specific tests (e.g., students who were absent for a quiz, who scored above 90 percent, or who failed a test).
14. Flag students with designated levels of cumulative performance (e.g., students who have been absent for more than two quizzes or whose average is below 70 percent).

Figure 9.6 *(continued)*

15. Generate reports for individual students.
16. Generate reports that include standardized comments (such as how to interpret the grades, how to make an appointment to see the teacher, or whether the subsequent grades will be cumulative).
17. Generate personal letters to individual students, incorporating information about their grades and inserting specific comments based on these grades.
18. Allow the reuse of one set of names during another grading period without retyping all the initial information.
19. Include other information (such as phone numbers, names of parents, and student nicknames) in the same database with the grades.
20. Support different grading methods (e.g., percent, letters, points, pass/fail).
21. Create grids from the class list to keep attendance or record scores.
22. Allow for the recording and averaging of extra-credit work.

If the program has a "no grade" option, the teacher can use the individual student report to relay information beyond the typical grading format. Teachers often spend valuable time writing down the assignments missed by students who are absent. With the "no grade"option and well-planned labeling of assignments, teachers can simply print out the absent student's individual report for a particular subject to obtain a list of missed assignments.

Using the computer for grade management eliminates many burdens. At the same time grade management programs provide report formats that communicate a professional approach to a complex task. However, as *The Computer in the Classroom* (Vockell and Schwartz, 1988) points out, teachers who know how to use database management programs do not really benefit from using grade management programs. A simple database (perhaps supplemented with a gradebook template) will do everything that a grade management program will do. In addition, an integrated system such as APPLEWORKS can easily feed information from the database into the word processor and use a "mail merge" option to facilitate feedback and communication. Whereas grade management programs serve the single purpose of recording, calculating, and reporting grades, database management programs can serve a wide variety of purposes. The sole advantage of grade management programs is that they are initially easier to learn than database management programs. However, teachers who take the trouble to learn the latter invariably find that they have acquired a valuable tool for all sorts of record keeping and information organization.

CMI AND INTEGRATED LEARNING SYSTEMS

Teachers not only teach, they also "manage instruction." Simply stated, this means that teachers must assign students to appropriate tasks, observe performance on those tasks, and make new assignments. Because of its storage capabilities the computer is an excellent device for helping teachers manage instruction in the language arts curriculum.

Computer-managed instruction (CMI) comes in several forms. A very simple form keeps track of a student's performance on a particular skill or while working through a timed session, leaving teachers free to work with other students. At a more convenient time, the teacher can access the disk to review student progress, to alter assignments, and to provide more personalized follow-up. Programs that record and report student performance in this manner include these from Hartley: AFFIXES AND ROOTS, ADJECTIVES, FACT OR OPINION, ADVERBS, CAPITALIZATION, COMPOUND WORDS AND CONTRACTIONS, and ANTONYMS/SYNONYMS. JUNGLE RESCUE (Learning Well), SENTENCE COMBINING (Milliken), and WORDS AT WORK: PREFIX POWER and WORDS AT WORK: CONTRACTION ACTION (both by MECC) also include similar student record features. See Figure 9.7 for some examples of the student record feature.

Computer-managed instruction has acquired a more complex and in some cases controversial definition with the introduction of integrated learning systems. An integrated learning system (ILS) is a comprehensive package of computer-based instruction in basic skills that diagnoses student needs, prescribes lessons, tracks progress, and provides a wealth of statistical information for the teacher. Integrated learning systems rely on a networked configuration consisting of a host computer (loaded with the software and management system), student stations, and printers. Employed in the best way, these systems can provide a sophisticated form of support to the teacher and a structured, controlled, and highly motivational presentation of skills for the student. Teachers have access to information about student performance that can assist them in providing the individual, person-to-person attention necessary to integrate new skills into the general curriculum. On the negative side, an ILS can be a huge

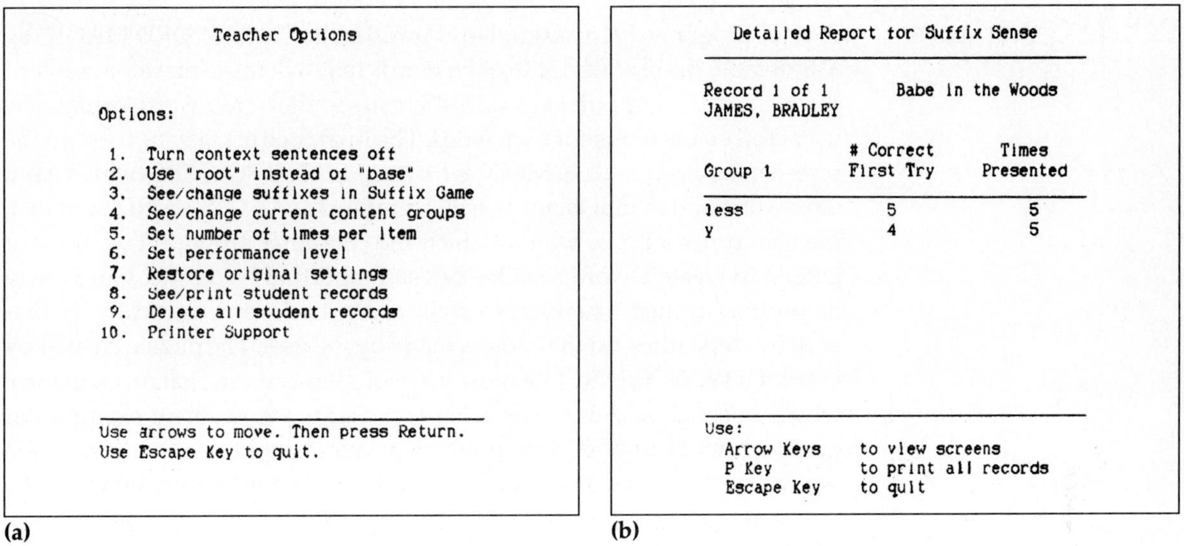

```
           Teacher Options

   Options:

      1.  Turn context sentences off
      2.  Use "root" instead of "base"
      3.  See/change suffixes in Suffix Game
      4.  See/change current content groups
      5.  Set number of times per item
      6.  Set performance level
      7.  Restore original settings
      8.  See/print student records
      9.  Delete all student records
     10.  Printer Support


   ─────────────────────────────────────
   Use arrows to move. Then press Return.
   Use Escape Key to quit.
```
(a)

```
        Detailed Report for Suffix Sense
   ──────────────────────────────────────

   Record 1 of 1          Babe in the Woods
   JAMES, BRADLEY

                        # Correct      Times
   Group 1              First Try    Presented
   ──────────────────────────────────────
   less                     5            5
   y                        4            5




   ──────────────────────────────────────
   Use:
      Arrow Keys      to view screens
      P Key           to print all records
      Escape Key      to quit
```
(b)

Figure 9.7 The student record feature illustrated from MECC's WORDS AT WORK series helps teachers keep track of student performance.

waste of time and funding if teachers are not fully involved in integrating student needs, curriculum, and ILS instruction. ILS companies such as Education Systems Corporation, Prescription Learning, WICAT, Wasatch, and Computer Curriculum Corporation are good resources for additional information on these systems. Addresses for these companies are listed in Appendix D.

TEACHER UTILITIES

Programs that make it possible for teachers to create learning materials are included in the broad category of teacher utilities. The word processing programs described earlier in this chapter could be used to generate tests, design puzzles, and even create computer lessons. However, programs that offer templates and lesson shells have advantages over the same formats created with a word processing package alone. These programs save the teacher time that is normally spent in designing pages, counting spaces, and experimenting with formats—all tasks that the developer of the teacher utility software has already done.

Puzzle Generators

Several programs help design word puzzles. In CROSSWORD MAGIC by Mindscape, the user first enters the words that will make up the crossword puzzle, and the computer arranges them in standard crossword format. The user then enters a clue for each word. The final product may be used on the screen or as a printout. In MECC's PUZZLES AND POSTERS (which has a crossword option that is not as well formatted as CROSSWORD MAGIC), the user types a list of words (which the computer arranges in a block of letters) to create a word search—or "seek and find"—puzzle. Words may be written in their usual left to right order, backward, vertically, or diagonally, depending on the choices made by the user. The puzzle created by Hartley's WORDSEARCH (Figure 9.8) is similar and can contain up to forty words selected by the teacher. These programs are excellent examples of quality teacher utilities that produce a professional product giving the teacher control of the data used. We've come a long way from the age of the purple ditto!

Figure 9.8 Word puzzles can be created easily by students or teachers with programs like WORDSEARCH by Hartley.

```
                 HALLOWEEN WORDSEARCH
                 ---------  ----------

      T G A J G G V H V G X T N N P V K T O R
      W D E O S O H T R I C K C I M Q C X D C
      M X L T Q S C H E X Y R V P P S Q T Z Z
      K G O N D C H A E H R L U C A T Q Y K F
      Y Z H Q Z K M F T W C G V S Q F E R M V
      I P T O I O K F M D B U E J B U Y Z I Z
      R U G I S W F T R E A T Z U Y S N C U W
      J M N T D T K Y W T O D H Y R P Z X B D
      H P K H Q J K K H A U N T E D I T T D T
      H K X U R C V C B J F V O X Y R Q O Z D
      S I A B C P G Y G J R L W L M I Y N X Z
      P N Q W Q H A L L O W E E N O T T T Y B
      O S Q G C D U D Q N F Y E V H D Y B C L
      O G K F C M B S F C C L Q G S Y X N J Q
      K M A S K M N V B Y C V Q H T F C E Z J
      Y V Y N O S B Y B F J R Q R Y X N K W F
      X F N S M X M Q P Y N P E O U C R D B U
      C X T H O D V Z I I A G Q R G W M G Q N
      L X E A I F I G A A H P J I O J N Z O P
      N N C J N B U G R Q N P O V R C Q S J Z


                        WORDS
                        -----

      HALLOWEEN          GHOST           SPIRIT
      HAUNTED            SPOOKY          MASK
      PUMPKIN            TRICK           TREAT
      CAT
```

Test Generators

Although the idea of computerized test generation often appeals to teachers, in practice the currently available test generators are not as useful to the elementary language arts teacher as the puzzle generators described above. In language arts, teachers must use an extensive variety of methods to evaluate listening, oral, and written skills. Especially at the primary level, a written test would be an inappropriate or incomplete method for evaluating student progress. For teachers who would benefit from storing written tests, a word processing program is often helpful. Easy editing allows teachers to add or delete questions with a minimum of effort. To create a file of test questions some teachers prefer using a database management program. This application allows teachers to store questions and categorize them according to topic, curricular objective, and format (Figure 9.9). By using the database's search function, teachers can control the test questions based on the proper search criteria.

Two test generators *are* worth mentioning for teachers of the upper elementary grades. STUDY GUIDE by MECC is easy to use and creates tests based on four question types: multiple choice, true/false, matching, and completion. Questions can be stored by objective, which is helpful when determining the scope of the test. Not only can the test be printed but students can also review questions on the screen. Teachers may add feed-

Figure 9.9 A database program can help create a bank of test questions arranged according to topic, curricular objective, or format.

```
File:    QUESTION BANK                                              Page 1
Report: Question Bank

SUBJECT: Language arts
OBJECTIVE: Identifying antonyms
QUESTION: The opposite of "off" is _____.
ANSWER CHOICES:
ANSWER: on
FORMAT: Fill in the blank




SUBJECT: Language arts
OBJECTIVE: Identifying antonyms
QUESTION: The opposite of "outside" is _____.
ANSWER CHOICES:
ANSWER: inside
FORMAT: Fill in the blank




SUBJECT: Language arts
OBJECTIVE: Identifying antonyms
QUESTION: Which of the following words is the opposite of introvert?
ANSWER CHOICES: a. extravagant    b. extrovert  c. outrovert
ANSWER: b. extrovert
FORMAT: Multiple Choice
```

back and prompts to assist students in choosing the correct answer. TESTWORKS by Milliken provides many of the same options and also permits interactive testing; students take tests at the computer, which analyzes and stores the results for later reference. The strengths and limitations of test generators are discussed in greater detail in *The Computer in the Classroom* (Vockell and Schwartz, 1988).

Interactive Computer Lessons

Just a few years ago creating interactive computer lessons required extensive programming skills. Teachers were entirely at the mercy of software developers. Today software publishers are sensitive to the need for teacher-designed lessons and have provided a method to accomplish this. A lesson template or shell is already stored on the program disk. All the teacher has to do is provide the content. CREATE LESSONS and CREATE LESSONS—ADVANCED by Hartley (Figure 9.10) are examples. More sophisticated authoring systems and languages, such as Hartley's EZ-PILOT II, provide more instructional options, but they are more difficult to learn. These programs allow the teacher to design software that can be used by students for drill, tutorials, or tests. Features that give opportunities for the teacher to provide hints and explanations for incorrect responses reflect the very personal input the teacher has in using such programs. These programs facilitate the creation of several lessons on the same topic to meet individual student needs.

In addition, with a moderate amount of programming knowledge, teachers can often design or modify programs of their own to supplement instruction in language arts. For example, *Model Programs for Instruction* (Vockell, 1987) provides a set of pedagogically sound programs providing drills on various sorts of factual information. The book provides a "cookbook" approach that enables teachers with little or no programming knowledge to modify the programs to suit the needs of their students.

Teachers should *not* be expected to spend vast amounts of time writing computer programs for their students. A comparison to traditional, non-computerized teaching may be useful. Good teachers have traditionally used textbooks, library resources, films, and other published materials to teach their students. But most teachers have also found it necessary to supplement published materials with self-designed materials—often copied in the teacher work area the morning before class. In the same way, teachers who use computers should expect to use published software; the

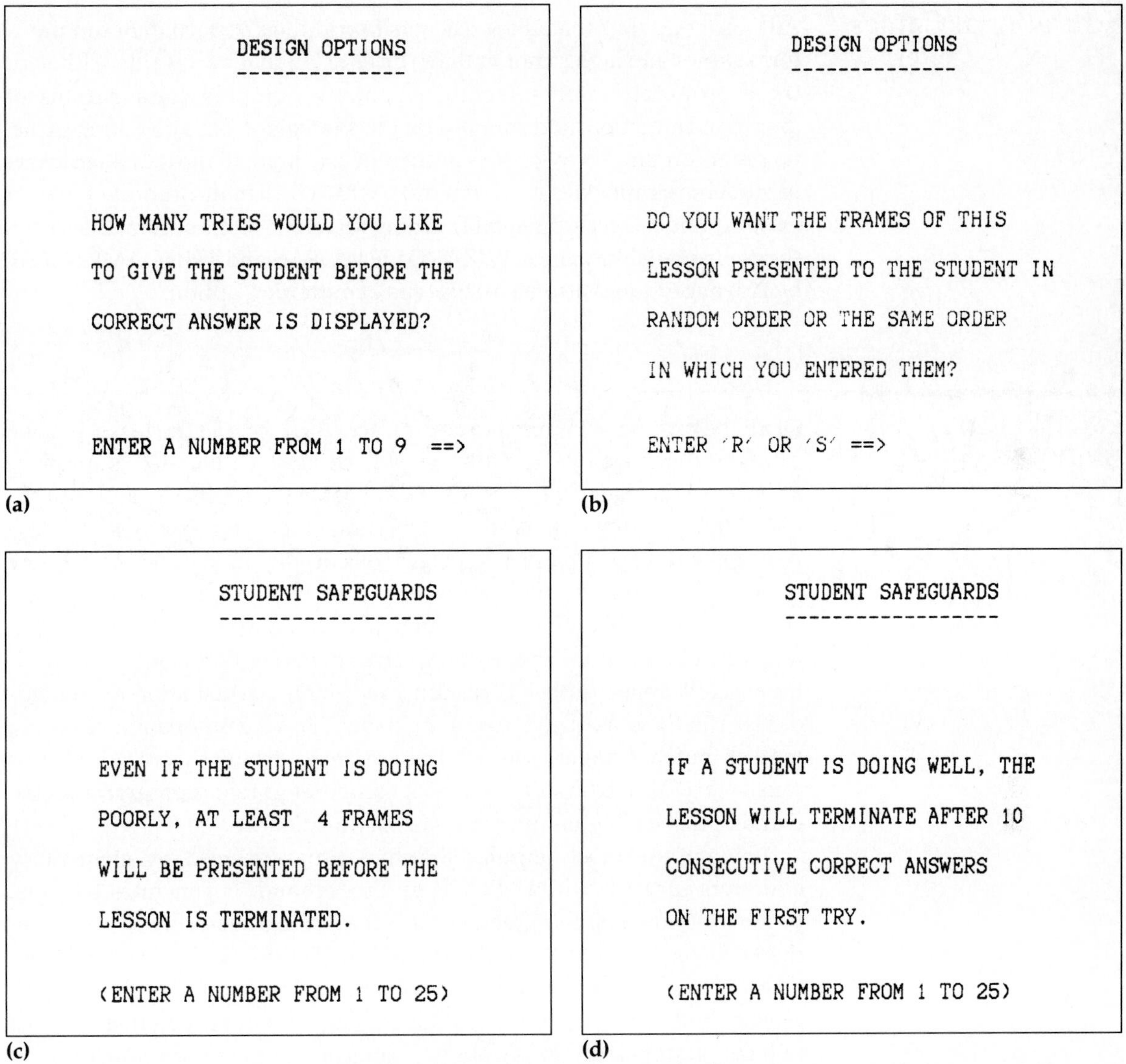

```
        DESIGN OPTIONS
        --------------




HOW MANY TRIES WOULD YOU LIKE

TO GIVE THE STUDENT BEFORE THE

CORRECT ANSWER IS DISPLAYED?



ENTER A NUMBER FROM 1 TO 9  ==>
```
(a)

```
        DESIGN OPTIONS
        --------------




DO YOU WANT THE FRAMES OF THIS

LESSON PRESENTED TO THE STUDENT IN

RANDOM ORDER OR THE SAME ORDER

IN WHICH YOU ENTERED THEM?



ENTER 'R' OR 'S' ==>
```
(b)

```
       STUDENT SAFEGUARDS
       ------------------




EVEN IF THE STUDENT IS DOING

POORLY, AT LEAST  4 FRAMES

WILL BE PRESENTED BEFORE THE

LESSON IS TERMINATED.


(ENTER A NUMBER FROM 1 TO 25)
```
(c)

```
       STUDENT SAFEGUARDS
       ------------------




IF A STUDENT IS DOING WELL, THE

LESSON WILL TERMINATE AFTER 10

CONSECUTIVE CORRECT ANSWERS

ON THE FIRST TRY.


(ENTER A NUMBER FROM 1 TO 25)
```
(d)

Figure 9.10 A shell program provides the format for creating test questions that are reviewed on-screen. Hartley's CREATE LESSONS is shown in this figure.

authoring systems and shell programs described in this section enable them to design computerized materials to suit the needs of their students without requiring the teacher to spend an inordinate amount of time doing so.

Educational Games

Authoring options that allow teachers to add their own content can transform games into highly motivational drills of language arts skills. Although these programs often integrate ingenious, complex combinations of graphics, animation, and sound with the strategies from an exciting game, no programming knowledge is needed to use them. In most cases teachers or students simply add a list of words, which is then incorporated into an existing game. Developmental Learning Materials offers several titles in its series of arcadelike games. WIZARD OF WORDS and THE GAME SHOW by Advanced Ideas also have this type of authoring option.

GRAPHICS PROGRAMS

Of all the programs planned to assist teachers in completing tasks, the one category that seems to excite even the "computer illiterate" is graphics programs. No other type of program can match the feelings of accomplishment (not to say wonder!) that a first-time computer user feels when a personally designed banner or poster rolls off the printer. No matter how poorly the user draws, the appearance of the final product reflects professional design. One of the authors remembers the time involved in creating original bulletin-board and learning center materials that would be appealing visually, relate to the curriculum, and invite participation by her students. The tools used to create such materials were an opaque projector, marker, butcher paper, and a lot of patience. Results were not always satisfactory. Nowadays the variety of computer graphics programs on the market practically guarantees satisfactory results.

By far the most popular graphics program used by elementary educators today is PRINT SHOP by Broderbund. It generates banners, posters, letterheads, and greeting cards that are created primarily by using the keyboard's arrow keys and the Return key to make selections from menus. Nothing could be easier. It even allows those teachers blessed with artistic abilities the option of creating graphics and importing their designs into the products they are creating. Using colored paper or colored ribbon adds to the attractiveness of any product. Other programs have been patterned after PRINT SHOP. Broderbund has produced the GRAPHICS LIBRARY series, offering additional graphics choices, and PRINT SHOP COMPANION, offering additional borders, fonts, and a handy calendar program. Broderbund also provides a teacher's guide with lesson plans and applications in a variety of subjects. Public domain graphics disks to supplement PRINT SHOP are available from companies such as P. D. Software in Houston, Texas. The problem of finding the time and expertise to create materials has been solved. Because of this program the biggest problem now is which graphic or font to choose from all the possibilities. That's the kind of problem teachers like!

What materials can be created with PRINT SHOP that assist in the teaching of language arts? The answer depends on your imagination, because the possibilities are endless. Many teachers begin to use PRINT SHOP as a "cosmetic" tool to brighten their classroom environment. That's a good beginning. Bulletin boards and learning centers can be enhanced with professional graphics, and the variety of fonts prevent all text from looking like it came from a cookie cutter. Teachers may choose to add a graphic to the corner of a worksheet (Figure 9.11) or design a class letterhead to be used in all home-school communication. However, PRINT SHOP is more than a cosmetic tool. It can help create materials for instruction while saving the teacher time and producing a product that is personal and motivational.

Figure 9.11 PRINT SHOP (Broderbund) adds a bit of interest to worksheets.

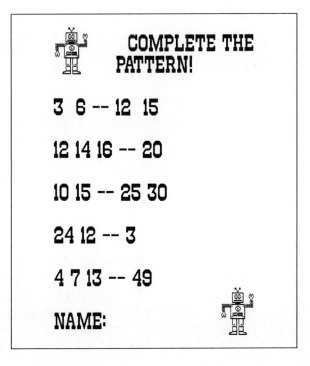

Rather than adding a simple graphic to a worksheet, teachers can create the entire worksheet with the "poster" selection on PRINT SHOP. One drawback must be explained to students, however. Fonts in the program are all uppercase. The PRINT SHOP COMPANION has a lowercase font, but neither program allows the designer to use the Shift key to make a capital letter as word processing programs do. The poster selection can be a basis for creating new vocabulary lists, weekly spelling lists, or any list of words that students could use as a study or reference guide. Teachers in primary grades especially like the large letters that make it easy for their young students to read. Story starters created with the poster selection are great motivators for creative writing. Students enjoy designing their own story starter sheets and sharing them with their peers.

Birthday cards to celebrate that special day with a student and thank-you notes to parents and others who lend classroom support are two possible applications with PRINT SHOP's greeting card selection. By entering a vocabulary word on the front of the card and a definition or graphic inside, teachers can create personalized flash cards, as discussed in Chapter 6.

The calendar option on PRINT SHOP COMPANION is another feature that teachers can use to create materials. Sending home a weekly or monthly calendar of assignments, activities, or extracurricular plans is an excellent way to communicate with parents. With children of our own, the authors know that the standard question asked by parents at the end of the school day is "What happened at school?" The standard reply is usually "Nothing!" With a calendar to inform them of school activities, parents feel more connected to what is happening in their children's school day.

Teachers give feedback to students in many ways: a verbal compliment, a pat on the back, or a printed award are all part of communicating satisfaction. Although commercially printed awards are available, PRINT SHOP's poster selection can be used to design awards that say exactly what the teacher wishes to communicate. The personal input on every option in this versatile program is what makes PRINT SHOP a good choice in the area of graphics programs.

Other graphics programs make this computer application a popular one as well. CERTIFICATE MAKER by Springboard (Figure 9.12) and AWARD MAKER PLUS by Baudville are excellent programs for generating awards. Each offers two hundred templates from which to choose and choices of borders and font styles. The ease of creating awards means that teachers can quickly respond to their students with a positive form of reinforcement. In addition, parents are informed of their child's progress when awards are sent home.

Desktop publishing has made its way out of the business world and into elementary classrooms. The sophisticated graphics and word processing available with these programs are used to generate newsletters and newspapers. Although desktop publishing programs are successfully applied in the writing curriculum, they should also be considered for teacher tasks. Because of the combination of graphics and text, these programs can create masters for overhead transparencies and printed worksheets and could be used in place of a regular word processing program for any task that requires the addition of graphics. PUBLISH IT! (Timeworks Platinum), THE CHILDREN'S WRITING AND PUBLISHING CENTER (The Learning Company), PAGEMAKER (Aldus), and SPRINGBOARD PUBLISHER

Figure 9.12 CERTIFICATE MAKER (Springboard) creates professional looking awards in a matter of keystrokes.

Figure 9.13 PUBLISH IT! (Timeworks Platinum), CHILDREN'S WRITING AND PUBLISHING CENTER (The Learning Company), PAGEMAKER (Aldus; shown here), or SPRING-BOARD PUBLISHER (Springboard) have text and graphic capabilities that make designing handouts or transparencies easy.

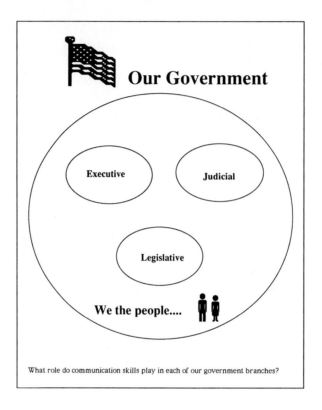

(Springboard) are used successfully by elementary teachers for such tasks (see Figure 9.13).

SUMMARY

Many professionals, including teachers, rely on tools to complete tasks. Educators wisely surround themselves with tools to assist them in instructional management, presentation techniques, and materials generation. Choosing the suitable tool often leads the teacher to the computer. With the help of peripherals like the LCD projection system, presentations reach more students. With the variety of teacher utility software available, teachers can create attractive printed materials that contain the content needed to reach their goals without wasting valuable time. The computer can assist in everything from grade management to creating rewards for student progress. The computer *is* the ultimate tool for teachers!

REFERENCES

Vockell, E. L. *Model Programs for Instruction*. Englewood Cliffs, N.J.: Prentice-Hall, 1987.

Vockell, E. L., and D. Kopenec. "Record Keeping Without Tears." *Clearing House* 62 (1989): 355–359.

Vockell, E. L., and E. Schwartz. *The Computer in the Classroom*. Watsonville, Calif.: Mitchell, 1988.

CHAPTER 10

KEYBOARDING SKILLS

IN PREVIOUS CHAPTERS WE have shown how the computer can support language arts instruction. Ironically, the appearance of the computer in the classroom has created the need to add a new "communication" skill—keyboarding—to the curriculum. However, this particular skill's place in the curriculum is still being debated in the education community. Many legitimate questions are being asked by teachers and administrators.

> What is "keyboarding"?
> Should it be taught at the elementary level?
> Who needs to learn keyboarding and who should have the responsibility to teach it?
> When should it appear in the curriculum?
> How should it be taught?
> Can you effectively teach keyboarding with one computer and twenty-five students?
> How do you select software?

Educators are struggling with these questions. This chapter deals with some possible answers.

WHAT IS KEYBOARDING?

We define keyboarding as a psychomotor skill that involves the proper touching of keys with the appropriate fingers, an established rhythm, keeping eyes on copy, and using correct posture (Kisner, 1984). In educational journals you may find that *keyboarding*, *touch typing*, and *typewriting* refer to the same skills. In this sense, "typewriting" includes keyboarding skills *plus* the use of proper formats for letters, memos, and the like.

Traditionally typewriting has been taught at the high school level exclusively in business education classes. However, researchers have long indicated that elementary students *can* learn keyboarding skills. Until recently this skill was ignored at the elementary level for the following reasons (Sormunen, 1984):

1. Lack of accessibility to equipment
2. Lack of teacher preparation in keyboarding methods
3. Lack of time in the elementary school day
4. Lack of opportunity to apply the skill

In view of these problems, there was simply no perceived urgency for elementary students to learn keyboarding.

That perception has changed dramatically in the last five years. With thousands of computers now available, the first problem—lack of equipment—is no longer as pressing. Many elementary schools have a lab available in addition to computers in individual classrooms. In other schools innovative scheduling of multiple computers provides a minilab of four to eight stations that can be wheeled from classroom to classroom. Some rural campuses house the elementary, middle, and high schools in adjoining buildings, which often allows the high school lab to be shared with elementary students. Given these innovations, it is still often the case that a class may have only one computer available at a time. In this situation teaching keyboarding to a classroom of students would at best be difficult and would take time away from using the computer for other applications.

The fourth problem has largely been solved by the many uses for the computer in the curriculum, giving students ample opportunity and motivation—indeed, the *need*—to develop keyboarding skills.

With opportunity to apply the skill, and if access to computers can be achieved, perhaps it is time to deal with the two remaining problems—training teachers and finding time for students to develop keyboarding skills. We can approach solutions to these problems by first addressing the question of whether keyboarding *should* be taught at the elementary level.

SHOULD KEYBOARDING BE TAUGHT TO ELEMENTARY STUDENTS?

The real question is more appropriately stated by Wetzel (1985): "What experiences do students need to learn to enjoy and to improve their writing?" In Chapter 7 we addressed this issue in terms of how the computer can contribute to the writing curriculum. Now—assuming that the computer is part of the writing process—we must consider the possible effect that the lack of keyboarding skills may have on the overall process.

Have you observed students who lack keyboarding skills as they compose writing assignments at the keyboard? They often interrupt their flow of creative thought to search for the proper keys. If this interruption is a source of frustration, then we are allowing the lack of keyboarding skills to interfere with the writing process. We are not following Wetzel's suggestion of providing experiences that enable our students to both enjoy and improve their writing.

With proper keyboarding skills, students gain several advantages (Wetzel, 1985). First, they use computer time more efficiently. Second, they focus on the task, not the location of keys on the keyboard. And finally, they acquire a lifelong skill.

Students "learn" keyboarding skills each time they use the computer. Each interaction requires pressing a key with a finger. Each move sets a pattern for future moves. By ignoring the skill, teachers may encourage students to establish bad habits that can become obstacles to learning proper keyboarding technique. In keyboarding, as in the acquisition of other psychomotor skills, it is easier to learn correct technique from the start than to unlearn habits that have been acquired through negligence (Graham, 1986).

Researchers have discovered additional reasons for introducing keyboard instruction in the elementary grades. They have found that keyboarding skills can improve children's reading and writing ability. To achieve improvement, two principles must be followed: keyboarding lessons must not replace the usual reading and writing instruction, and integration in meaningful language arts activities is essential (Balajthy, 1987).

Integrating keyboard instruction with language arts activities is one way to address the lack of time for this skill in an already-overcrowded elementary curriculum. By using software such as TYPE TO LEARN by Sunburst (Figure 10.1), the integration is simplified. Additional activities that incorporate spelling, grammar, reading, and composition can be designed by the teacher to solidify the connection between keyboarding and language arts.

The most natural connection between keyboarding and language arts is through word processing. Students need keyboarding skills before they can efficiently use a word processor for a writing tool. Most fourth, fifth, and sixth graders can copy by hand seven to ten gross words per minute (gwpm). To make adequate use of the computer, students of this age need to type only ten gwpm (Wetzel, 1985). South-Western's MICROTYPE: THE WONDERFUL WORLD OF PAWS is one program that records wpm (Figure 10.2). The ten gwpm goal is often reached with as little as eight hours of instruction (Wetzel, 1985). Unfortunately, without instruction, students typically type approximately half that fast, wasting valuable learning time. If a student uses the computer two hours or more weekly, then the invest-

Figure 10.1 Language arts exercises that incorporate keyboarding practice prevent teachers from attempting to add to an already full elementary day. TYPE TO LEARN (Sunburst) is one program that achieves this connection by providing meaningful text with controlled vocabulary for students to use while practicing their typing skills.

ment in instruction is worth the time involved (Wetzel, 1987). Without continued application of keyboarding skills, students regress. Therefore, the school system must be committed to continued application.

Another way to examine this question is in terms of academic learning time (discussed in Chapter 1). The purpose of developing keyboarding skills should be to help students use their time more effectively at the computer. A student who spends ten hours developing keyboarding skills can regain all this time by using twenty subsequent hours twice as effec-

Figure 10.2 MICROTYPE: THE WONDERFUL WORLD OF PAWS (South-Western) combines a structured introduction, practice, and games into its program.

tively as would otherwise be possible. (If during these ten hours the student uses content related to existing curriculum objectives, then the cost is proportionately lower and the gain proportionately higher.) If such paybacks are available, then a strong case can be made to allocate curriculum time for keyboarding instruction. If such paybacks are not available, then it may be best to delay keyboarding instruction until a better opportunity arises.

WHEN SHOULD KEYBOARDING BE TAUGHT?

So when is the appropriate time to teach keyboarding? When the skill is needed! That answer may sound oversimplified, but it *is* the proper response. Not all computer applications require complete keyboarding skills. The need for keyboarding skills depends on four factors (Wetzel, 1987), which we examine on the next page.

Important Note

This chapter argues persuasively that keyboarding skills are important and should be developed early, as the need arises. Students can use computers for instruction most effectively if they possess fairly sophisticated keyboarding skills.

But remember, students *can* use computers effectively even if they possess only very limited keyboarding skills. For 95 percent of the programs discussed in this book, keyboarding is a secondary skill—students use their brains, not their typing skills. And even if students are only 10 percent as efficient as they could be at the keyboard, they still gain substantially by using these programs.

Although messages must be typed in when using, say, PRINT SHOP, variations in typing skills do not really affect the usefulness of the program. Likewise, students running a spelling program must find the keys to spell words correctly; but students who use a rapid hunt-and-peck approach benefit from running these programs as much as touch typists do.

The point is that you should not let keyboarding skills interfere with education in your school or classroom. If students *can* develop keyboarding skills, that is wonderful and should be encouraged. However, if for any reason teaching keyboarding becomes a problem in the curriculum, realize that the computer can *still* help students attain many signifcant goals, even without specific attention to keyboarding.

Even students with *no* formal training in keyboarding can participate in significant and exciting applications of the computer.

An academic area needs improvement.

Keyboarding for the sake of keyboarding is a waste of valuable instructional time. An academic area that could be improved by the use of computers should be identified before the development of a keyboarding curriculum is begun. Language arts is often identified as such an area, specifically the writing process and the skills involved in written communication. Once an area is identified, then the second factor should be considered.

Improvement can be achieved using the computer.

If the area that needs improvement is language arts, and specifically written communication, then addressing keyboarding issues may be helpful. Creative writing and the use of word processing software add a new dimension to student productivity and motivation. As stated earlier in this chapter, a lack of keyboarding skills may prevent students from achieving improvement, as well as possibly depriving them of enjoyment in the writing process.

The computer application requires repeated and frequent use of most keys.

If students are only required to type *Y* or *N*, their name, a number, and the Return key, then there is no need to teach extensive keyboarding skills. In the primary grades (K–2), simply locating the few frequently used keys is an appropriate goal of keyboarding instruction (Jackson and Berg, 1986). At the intermediate level, keyboarding could be a prerequisite for text entry on a word processor. In addition, students need more advanced keyboarding skills to accurately type word lists, phrases, and sentences in computer-assisted instruction (CAI) programs. Formal instruction in using the entire keyboard can begin in third grade, although some researchers suggest that fourth grade is better for the earliest successful implementation of such a program (Jostad and Madian, 1987).

Enough computers are available to achieve the goals of a keyboarding program.

If students are expected to type at least as fast as they write and to learn the proper keyboarding techniques, extended computer time is required. Eight to thirty hours (Wetzel, 1987; Jackson and Berg, 1986) are required to achieve these goals. One computer in the classroom is not sufficient to accomplish this. Access to a lab where students can work one-to-one at the computer is ideal. Minilabs of four to six computers on movable carts can also provide accessibility.

WHO SHOULD TEACH KEYBOARDING?

Although it is often expected that business education teachers teach keyboarding to elementary students, it is impractical (and in many states illegal, because of certification requirements). Nevertheless, it is also unfair to place another burden on the shoulders of elementary teachers, who may not even be trained to teach these skills. One way to deal with the situation is to involve both business education and elementary teachers in a compromise.

Business teachers can provide the expertise in planning and presenting in-service programs to elementary teachers, and under the supervision of keyboarding experts, elementary teachers can learn or strengthen their own skills as well as acquire an understanding of keyboarding methodology (Jackson and Berg, 1986; Sormunen, 1984). For those elementary teachers who do not have keyboarding skills, a complete course in keyboarding, offered as part of the district's staff development program, may be necessary. A flexible program such as MAVIS BEACON TEACHES TYPING by Electronic Arts (Figure 10.3) is a good program to use as a refresher or as a tutorial. (One of the authors found it necessary to enroll in a continuing education course at the local high school to learn keyboarding skills!) In most instances, teachers who can type need only a day of instruction to be able to work effectively with students (Wetzel, 1987).

Teacher training is the foundation of a well-structured keyboarding curriculum (Wetzel, 1987; Sormunen, 1984). Teachers involved in the program must be made aware of several pivotal factors in the teaching of keyboarding skills. First, they must understand that keyboarding is a kinesthetic skill that can be developed only through a hands-on approach at the keyboard.

Second, teachers should establish their role immediately. Although the computer may provide the drill and practice needed, teachers must facilitate by encouraging students to practice, observing their technique, and offering assistance when necessary.

Third, teachers must prioritize technique, speed, and accuracy in beginning skill development. Last and most important, they need to be

Figure 10.3 MAVIS
BEACON TEACHES
TYPING (Electronic Arts) has
several levels of instruction,
so that students of any age
can benefit.

aware of the components of a successful keyboarding program and know
the teaching methods suitable for the identified grade levels.

WHAT MAKES A SUCCESSFUL KEYBOARDING PROGRAM?

Teacher competence and computer accessibility are the prerequisites for a
successful program. Realistic goal setting, controlled presentation rate,
variety of activities, suitable time for practice, and immediate feedback
complete the criteria for a successful program. The approaches taken to
include these components in the primary and intermediate grades differ
greatly.

The Primary Keyboarding Program

At the primary level a realistic keyboarding goal may simply be familiarity
with the keyboard. A large keyboard used as a visual on a classroom wall
can be the focus of keyboard discussions as well as other letter-related talks.
That same keyboard can be used on the floor for a "twister" activity, which
allows the children to place a foot or hand on the key called out by the
teacher (this activity is excellent reinforcement for letter recognition in
general). Software programs such as THE FRIENDLY COMPUTER by
MECC (Figure 10.4) and WELCOME ABOARD by Broderbund deal with
keyboard familiarity. Either would provide suitable activities for primary
students. It should also be pointed out that alternate keyboards (such as the
Muppet Learning Keys described earlier in this book) may help very young

Figure 10.4 Keyboard familiarity instead of actual keyboarding skill is the goal of THE FRIENDLY COMPUTER by MECC.

learners; and there is no reason to believe that familiarity with an alternate keyboard will interfere with subsequent attempts to use the standard one.

Beyond familiarity, primary students do need to use several keys efficiently for the CAI programs appropriate for them. Software used in K–2 often requires little more than a *Y* or *N* and the Return key to respond to questions on the screen. At the beginning of a program students are also often asked to type in their name. In addition, some programs require students to press the Caps-Lock key before the program will function correctly.

These simple keyboard requirements are realistic goals for a primary program and do not indicate the need for complete keyboarding skills. Nevertheless, beginning with a student's first time at the computer, teachers can encourage the use of two hands at the keyboard. Many ingenious ideas have been used to stress the two-hands approach. The keyboard can be color coded with small, colored dot stickers to divide the keys into left- and right-hand use. Teachers can further enhance this by giving the student colored wristbands for left and right. In addition, the keyboard can be physically divided with a small strip of colored paper wedged between the left and right side of the keyboard.

Young students can easily be taught to use the proper finger positions for the keys mentioned. The *Y* and *N* are both reached with the right index finger. Again, a small sticker placed on the key as well as on the finger is a gentle reminder to use the correct finger. We have even seen a smiley face

Alternate Keyboards

Alternate keyboards, such as the Muppet Learning Keys shown here, make it possible for young learners with very limited typing abilities to use the computer to enter fairly complex information quickly and easily. The letters are arranged in a simple alphabetical format, and additional keys (such as the green "go" key) have meanings that children easily understand.

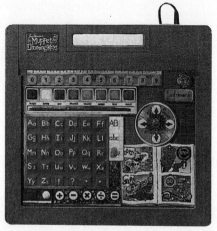

The logic behind such keyboards is that children who are just beginning to learn the alphabet do not need to be confused by an arrangement of letters on the keyboard that seems irrational. Very young children have no need yet for touch typing, so it makes sense to present the letters to them in alphabetical order. When children outgrow the need for the simplified keyboard, they progress to the traditional format.

on the space bar that corresponds with a small sticker placed on the student's thumb! Another sticker could be used to indicate the little finger and the Return key. Young students need to *see* the proper finger placement and such color matches are helpful reminders. (Don't be concerned with damage to the keyboard. The stickers can be removed by gently rubbing them with alcohol and a soft cloth.)

To teach students to enter their names takes a little more ingenuity, but primary students respond positively. They realize that touching the keys with the correct finger is the way adults use the keyboard and are eager to acquire this skill in even a small way. Teaching the correct technique to enter personal names prevents children from using the hunt-and-peck approach. A keyboard worksheet that identifies the keys and finger placement can introduce the correct positions (Figure 10.5).

The Intermediate Keyboarding Program

The keyboarding needs of intermediate students (grades 3–6) encompass much more than single-key entry. At this level, CAI packages require students to type words and phrases. If word processing is a part of their weekly activities, knowledge of the entire keyboard is necessary for the most efficient use of academic learning time. A unit of instruction that addresses the entire keyboard can effectively fulfill these needs. The unit should focus on proper technique, speed, and accuracy. At the end of the unit, students should be able to type at least as fast as they write by hand. With this goal in mind, let's look at some guidelines (Wetzel, 1985; Carney, 1986) and a sample lesson plan.

Student Involvement

Intermediate students gain ownership in keyboard instruction if they first examine *why* they need the skill. If students are allowed to brainstorm the need for keyboarding skills at the beginning of the keyboarding unit, they become much more committed to the task. As the unit proceeds, students

Figure 10.5 A keyboard worksheet that identifies keys and finger placement.

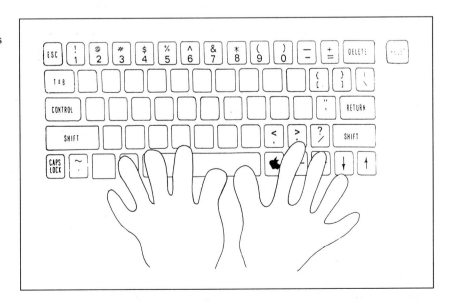

should be given charge of their own learning by being responsible for recording personal progress and identifying their own goals.

Time

Keyboarding is a kinesthetic skill, and kinesthetic skills require repeated practice for their proper development. Therefore, students need ample time at the computer keyboard for practice and feedback. The ideal amount is thirty minutes per session. In general, research suggests two or three sessions per week to maintain skills.

Rate of Presentation

Since home-row orientation is also critical (Jackson and Berg, 1986), two or three sessions devoted to the home row create a solid foundation for proper technique. Thereafter, two new keys can be introduced each session.

Monitoring

Although a good software package provides constant feedback, it can only suggest—not supervise—proper finger placement. Teachers should monitor finger placement and reaches carefully, especially in the early stages, when habits are formed. During this time, some students find watching fingers and keys to be helpful. If eyes on copy is the eventual goal, do not let students rely on visual location of keys for an extended time.

Speed Versus Accuracy

The consensus of the experts in the business field is that speed over accuracy should be the focus for early instruction. Considering the easy editing features of word processing packages, this is a sensible approach.

Language-based Approach

The keyboarding unit should be connected to language skills. Good typists type in phrases, not letters. As soon as possible, students should move from letter entry to words and phrases, based on patterns used in spelling and reading.

Competition

Ideally students should compete against their own best score or speed and not against each other. As we stated in Chapter 2, although the very fastest students in a class actually benefit from competing with others, such competition is often a huge turnoff to the children who know they cannot win. By using a gamelike atmosphere, however, teachers can sometimes combine competition with others and competition with self to get the benefits of both. But remember: students who lose competitions with others often lose more than the winners gain; and the winners can often be equally well motivated by competing with their own scores.

Student Interaction

Even though keyboarding is an individual skill, student interaction can provide positive reinforcement. Students can evaluate each other at the end of a lesson, or help while the lesson is taking place. For instance, one student can use a piece of paper to cover the hands and keyboard while another student types a passage. The "evaluator" can then check the text on the monitor and verify the test on the student chart.

Variety

Elementary students require a variety of activities to encourage the practice necessary to improve their keyboard skills. Activities based on an appropriate software package, a keyboarding textbook plus a word processing package, or teacher-designed games and worksheets add to the enjoyment of the sessions.

A Sample Lesson Plan

A session should consist of at least thirty minutes of hands-on practice. As the basis of instruction some teachers simply choose a good keyboarding software package. Their role becomes one of supervisor or monitor in each session. Later in this chapter we shall discuss how to evaluate such keyboarding software.

The other format for instruction uses a textbook and word processing program. In this method the teacher presents the lesson and uses the text and visuals for each session. *Elementary Keyboarding* (Graham, 1986) is an excellent resource for this approach. Any word processing package that allows quick access to a "blank page" would be acceptable. A sample lesson plan for the latter approach is shown in Figure 10.6.

Variety Encourages Practice

With either a teacher- or software-directed approach, elementary students require a variety of motivational activities to encourage them to practice.

Figure 10.6 Sample lesson plan for a keyboarding unit.

- **Warm-up (three to five minutes)**
  Review learned keys by typing an exercise used in a previous lesson or one of the motivational activities described under the heading "Variety Encourages Practice."

- **Introduce First New Key (five to eight minutes)**
  Find the new key on a wall keyboard chart and demonstrate the appropriate finger placement and reach. Begin student practice with a "letter call." This is a technique in which the teacher says the letter or letter combination aloud and the students type it. Further practice from the text can follow.

- **Introduce Second New Key (five to eight minutes)**
  Repeat sequence above.

- **Extended Practice (ten minutes)**
  Allow students time for extended practice from text or worksheets. The teacher observes finger placement and reach.

Even the most engaging software package becomes boring with overuse. Fortunately, variety can come from simple changes in session format. Let students "call" letters or phrases to be typed by the class (as discussed in Figure 10.6) or let students choose favorite passages from books for their practice. As long as all letters in the passage have been introduced, students can choose text from anywhere—from favorite books, poems, songs, and so on.

Speed drills are popular as long as the teacher does not stress competition among classmates. A thirty-second drill is appropriate for intermediate students and can be a part of the extended practice time in the session. In addition, some arcadelike typing programs such as STICKYBEAR TYPING by Weekly Reader Software provide useful practice (see Figure 10.7). Students who spend their money at the local arcade are often tremendously motivated by such programs. However, be wary of programs that emphasize an arcade-game format unless students have achieved a skill level that allows them to benefit from this type of practice. Such games sometimes sacrifice technique for speed by encouraging fast, single strokes instead of fluency (Jostad and Madian, 1987). Therefore, introducing arcade games too soon may undermine the very skills you wish to encourage.

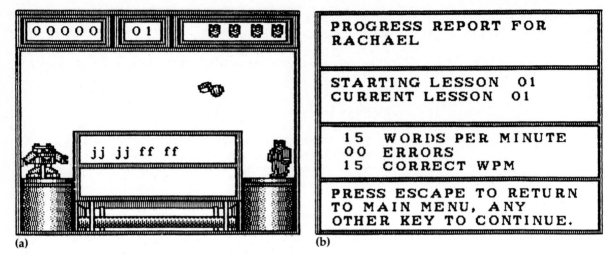

(a)   (b)

Figure 10.7 Arcade-game formats such as that found in STICKYBEAR TYPING (Weekly Reader) motivate students. In this example, the faster the student types, the faster the Stickybear throws balls at the robot, thereby increasing the chances that the Stickybear will "thump" the robot before getting "thumped" himself.

Blind typing encourages students to keep their eyes on the text they are typing, and students usually enjoy it. This can be accomplished in several ways. Have students turn off their monitors and type a passage. Verbally reinforce the eyes-on-copy skill while students are typing. Then have them turn on the monitors and check the passage. This activity is usually accompanied by lots of smiles and giggles! To make it more fun, have the students wear a real mask or blindfold while they type instead of turning off the monitor.

Typing instructions that create mystery shapes can enhance practice (see Figure 10.8). The mystery shape can be used to practice any key or combination of keys. Once students understand the activity, they are very willing to create mystery shapes for the class to "solve."

Contests in which students compete against themselves add variety to mundane drills. Awards given at the end of each lesson or when a particular skill is exhibited encourage the student to continue practice. In fact, any activity that motivates students to use proper technique could be added to the list of practice activities.

Figure 10.8 A "mystery figure" that can be used to help teach keyboarding skills to intermediate students.

```
    m
     m
   m
mmmmmmmmmmmmmmmm
   m
     m
      m
```

The figure above was created by following these steps. Press the Return key at the end of each line.

1. 3 spaces 1 m
2. 2 spaces 1 m
3. 1 space 1 m
4. 15 m
5. 1 space 1 m
6. 2 spaces 1 m
7. 3 spaces 1 m

SELECTING KEYBOARDING SOFTWARE

The lesson plan and motivational practice activities described above are intended for an approach that uses a word processing package to teach keyboarding skills. The teacher delivers instruction (demonstrates key location, finger placement, reach, etc.) and students use a word processor to practice the skills. The other approach to keyboard instruction focuses on a software program to deliver the lesson content. The criteria for choosing software to teach keyboarding skills extend beyond the criteria for general evaluation discussed in Chapter 3 (Balajthy, 1987; Ramondetta, 1987). Good keyboarding software should include:

- Well-structured tutorials
- Realistic graphics illustrating finger placement
- Integration of language arts activities
- A variety of motivational practice activities
- A built-in student record system
- A manual with additional activity suggestions

Many keyboarding programs on the market today include these criteria. Below are several programs that meet most or all of the criteria (check Appendix B for a more detailed description):

Touch Typing

To his eternal embarrassment, one of the authors of the textbook you are now reading cannot type. He uses a very rapid hunt-and-peck method that he taught himself back in high school, when typing was not considered a suitable subject for "college prep" students.

This person, who prefers to remain anonymous, sees no point in learning to type the "right" way. He is over thirty-nine years old, and he finds it very irritating to try to break the old habits.

Does this person possess keyboarding skills? He certainly does. He just doesn't type as quickly as someone else in most cases. However, this person uses the computer with extreme proficiency. He knows all the tricks to make his work easier—ranging from using word processing and database management programs to the special keys that generate "macros" (which type several commands with a single keystroke). In fact, the computer saves more time for this slow typist than it would for a fast typist using a typewriter on the same task.

Would this person be able to use the computer more efficiently if his repertoire of keyboarding skills included touch typing? Certainly. Should this person stop what he is doing and learn how to touch type? Probably not.

Should young people who plan to use computers be taught *all* the keyboarding skills, including touch typing? Certainly—as long as it doesn't cause a problem, say, by taking valuable learning time away from something else. Do young people *need* keyboarding skills in order to use computers effectively? Certainly. Does touch typing have to be one of these skills? No, it does not. But children who learn faulty typing habits are likely to be in the same position as our anonymous author—at a time when they need to develop typing skills, it's going to be more difficult to unlearn any bad habits. The best way to learn to type is to develop correct habits from the start.

ALPHABETIC KEYBOARDING (South-Western)
TYPING FOR NEW TYPISTS (Grolier)
TYPE TO LEARN (Sunburst)
MICROTYPE: THE WONDERFUL WORLD OF PAWS (South-Western)
KEY WORDS (Humanities Software)
MECC KEYBOARDING (MECC)
MAVIS BEACON TEACHES TYPING (Electronic Arts)

In addition, it is possible to combine both approaches. For example, a teacher using the word processing approach could integrate parts of the above programs that focus on specific skills.

SUMMARY

Keyboarding at the elementary level may soon become a necessity for effective use of computers in the language arts curriculum. Students who do not have a high level of keyboarding skills certainly can and do use the computer effectively. However, students who spend two hours or more a week at the keyboard or who enter text regularly may need to learn the skills that will make their time on task more productive. Keyboarding instruction will give them a lifelong skill, one that they will need to communicate their thoughts and feelings as adults in the twenty-first century. This chapter has provided guidelines for addressing keyboarding skills at the elementary level.

REFERENCES

Balajthy, E. "Keyboarding and the Language Arts." *Reading Teacher* 41 (1987): 86–87.

Carney, C. C. "Teacher + Computer = More Learning." *The Computing Teacher* 13 (1986): 12–15.

Graham, D. *Elementary Keyboarding*. New York: McGraw-Hill, 1986.

Jackson, T. H., and D. Berg. "Elementary Keyboarding—Is It Important?" *The Computing Teacher* 13 (1986): 10–11.

Jostad, K., and J. Madian. "Keyboarding Issues and Concerns." In J. Madian (Ed.). *Making the Literature, Writing, Word Processing Connection: The Best of the Writing Notebook*. Mendocino, Calif.: Creative Word Processing in the Classroom, 1987.

Kisner, E. "Keyboarding—A Must in Tomorrow's World." *The Computing Teacher* 11 (February 1984): 24–26.

Ramondetta, J. "But Can They Type? Keyboarding Software." *Learning* 16 (1987): 71.

Sormunen, C. "Inservice Workshops: One Answer to the Issue of Elementary School Keyboarding." *Journal of Business Education* 60 (1984): 14–17.

Wetzel, K. "An Interview with Keith Wetzel." In J. Madian (Ed.). *Making the Literature, Writing, Word Processing Connection: The Best of the Writing Notebook*. Mendocino, Calif.: Creative Word Processing in the Classroom, 1987.

Wetzel, K. "Keyboarding Skills: Elementary, My Dear Teacher?" *The Computing Teacher* 12 (1985): 15–19.

CHAPTER 11

WHAT THE FUTURE OFFERS

THE TEACHING AND LEARNING of language arts has changed drastically during the last decade. Ten years ago few elementary students had access to computers; on-line searches were limited to university libraries. What a difference a decade makes! No longer are teachers and their students limited to the information in a textbook. They are free to explore the world beyond the walls of the classroom without ever leaving their computer workstation. The resources discussed in this book have changed the way we teach the skills of speaking, listening, writing, and reading. Technological advances will make possible even more new applications to language arts instruction. The following sections will describe some of these possibilities.

HYPERTEXT

Occasionally a new medium encourages entirely new ways of thinking. Hypertext is likely to have this kind of impact on communication processes. Hypertext is exemplified by a program called HYPERCARD (Apple Computer) (see Figure 11.1). The basic idea behind hypertext is that readers are presented with a segment of text from which they can branch to any other segment as needed. For example, people usually read an instruction book, say, on how to use a computer, from beginning to end. With hypertext, however, users might read the first screen and then go wherever their interests or needs suggested. This might mean going to the second screen, or it might mean going into a more detailed explanation of a term mentioned on the first screen. Readers branching to a screen providing a

Figure 11.1 The branching choices illustrated in HYPER-CARD allow users to choose the learning path they wish to pursue.

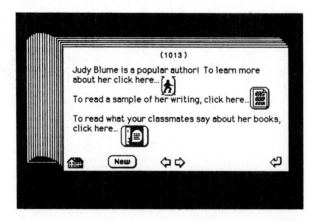

detailed explanation might go to yet another screen that furthers this explanation, then to a screen that defines or diagrams a term used in the explanation, and then back to the first screen of the original text.

It may have occurred to you by now that hypertext, when used in this way, is really nothing more than sophisticated branching programmed instruction, which enables learners to move through text in exactly the order that is appropriate to their needs. What is unique about programs like HYPERCARD is that they provide an *interface* that makes it *easy* for designers to program this degree of branching and *easy* for users to move through the text. The same branching strategy used for an instruction manual could be applied to a novel, to a computerized poem, to a database, to an art collection, or to almost any topic imaginable.

As hypertext becomes more common, it is likely that readers will become accustomed to the idea of nonlinear thinking. However, the nonlinear structure of hypertext is by no means haphazard. Since hypertext requires careful planning and complete sets of information, hypertext programmers and users will learn to incorporate and expect these characteristics in their thinking and presentations.

Currently HYPERCARD is available only for the Macintosh computer. Before its use becomes widespread in schools, either its makers will have to convert it to the Apple II or schools will have to acquire more Macintoshes. However, there are similar programs for other computers.

Programs with hypertext features available for the Apple II series of computers include HYPERSTUDIO (Roger Wagner Publishing), TUTOR-TECH (Techware), and HYPERSCREEN (Scholastic). SUPER STORY TREE (Scholastic) enables students and teachers to write and illustrate stories that incorporate hypertext strategies to branch based on reader decisions. These provide an interesting approach to reading and storytelling. STORYWORKS (Teacher Idea and Information Exchange), which offers similar branching opportunities, has the advantage of being based on APPLEWORKS, with which many teachers and students are already familiar. However, a disadvantage of STORYWORKS is that it requires considerable off-computer planning to develop stories rather than the simple menu prompting offered by the other hypertext programs.

Applied to language arts instruction, hypertext will make possible the incorporation of dictionaries directly into reading lessons. As we pointed out in Chapter 6, although dictionaries are very useful for learning words in context, few readers actually look up words when they need to because

---

Common Hypertext Terms and Resources

A *stack* refers to a typical hypertext program, which consists of a collection of index cards, each containing systematic information, including words, pictures, animated sequences, and sound, or a combination of these. These cards are imagined to be arranged in a stack, and the hypertext program enables the user to go almost instantly from any point on one card to a related point on another card in the stack. Synonyms for *stack* include *file, story,* and *set.*

A *card* usually refers to a single screen in the stack. These are sometimes referred to as *pages* or *segments.*

The *home card* is the starting point in the stack. From this point the user can most efficiently branch to any other point in the stack.

Links among cards are referred to as *buttons.* Selecting a button enables the user to branch to another card. Some buttons go forward to new text, others go backward to previous text, some ask questions, others play music, and so on. Sometimes the buttons look like actual buttons. Other times the buttons are covered by icons that identify functions (e.g., a right arrow to go to the next page). Sometimes the buttons are invisible; for example, a screen may include a Halloween picture, with invisible buttons hidden inside a ghost, a witch, a pumpkin, and so on. When the user selects a button, the program branches according to programmed instructions.

Clicking refers to the act of selecting a button and thereby telling the computer where to branch. Clicking usually involves moving the cursor to the button's location and then pressing a key on the keyboard or pressing a button on a mouse.

The term *hypermedia* usually refers to the process of integrating several different media with a hypertext program. For example, a good hypertext program can present text, sound, pictures, and animation—all accessible at the push of a button. Compton's MULTIMEDIA ENCYCLOPEDIA is a good example of such a program.

Interest in hypermedia is expanding rapidly, and new developments and peripherals constantly improve its flexibility. For example, the Apple II Video Overlay Card is a useful circuit board that permits a single video monitor to show both the computer text and the visual presentation from a VCR or videodisc player.

The *HyperStudio Forum* newsletter from the HyperStudio Network, *Stack Central* from A2-Central, and *The Stack Exchange* from Techware offer information about existing stacks for teachers and students. Hypermedia stacks will undoubtedly proliferate in coming years.

---

doing so disrupts their thought. Hypertext programs make it possible for readers to obtain definitions easily, at the moment when these definitions are most valuable—when the reader is reading the words in context.

Teachers can learn to use Apple's HYPERCARD as an authoring system to design instructional packages for a wide variety of topics. Various vendors have produced supplementary software to make HYPERCARD more easily adaptable to specific subject areas. For example, HYPERCALL (Kinko's Service Corporation) offers easy access to specific options not generally automatically available with HYPERCARD, including pop-up menus, help cards, notes, interface with digitized sound and laserdisc, access to a dictionary stack, and a link between graphics cards and review questions. Future versions of HYPERCALL will include "buttons" to provide animation, a student activity log, and access to a VCR tape drive. These options can make HYPERCARD more useful for language arts instruction.

INTERACTIVE VIDEO TECHNOLOGY

With present technology, teachers often enhance reading and writing lessons with films or videotapes. Interactive video technology—the combination of a laser videodisc (laserdisc) and a computer—is likely to make these enhancements even more effective. This technology, which is still in its developmental stages, makes it possible to access various combinations of moving pictures, still pictures, text, and sound almost instantaneously. For example, a student might be reading a passage on the computer screen about a large collie, who seems almost human and is stranded away from home in Scotland. While reading, the child might call up the map of Scotland. After finishing the passage, the child might request a video presentation of the same story, with the written text appearing on-screen. In addition, the child might be able to stop the video presentation at any time to receive a menu of choices—whether to move back to an earlier part, skip ahead, provide a definition, simply pause, or exercise some other option. This is just one example of what can be done with interactive video. Numerous applications are likely to become available as the technology develops, becoming less expensive and more common.

A further advantage of laserdiscs is that they store large amounts of information and are virtually indestructible. As we pointed out in Chapter 8, CD-ROM disks can also store huge amounts of information, at a slightly lower expense. In addition, by interfacing laserdisc and CD-ROM technology with a program like HYPERCARD, it may soon become conveniently possible to develop and use really first-class databases that include still and moving pictures as well as written text. For example, students will be able to browse through a well-prepared and interesting laserdisc devoted to a specific topic to answer questions and solve problems posed by their teachers or by themselves. They might watch a video segment that introduces a topic; quickly move back to a combination of several still diagrams with accompanying text specifically related to that topic; develop a rough draft; move to another segment of the laserdisc that examines the topic from another perspective; go back for another look at the original segment; go to slow motion or stop action to examine certain aspects more closely; look for additional information on another laserdisc; state a new topic . . . and continue this process until they have satisfactorily answered whatever questions are on their minds. During this process, of course, students would not be obligated to work solely or even predominantly with the interactive laserdisc. Rather, like other good resources, the laserdisc material simply serves as a vital resource, providing useful information to individuals, small groups, or entire classes.

Interactive video technology is currently available even without HYPERCARD. However, it is expensive and somewhat difficult to program for specific applications. In addition, at present there are relatively few good laserdiscs for educational topics. Within the past year, good disks have become more common, and prices have begun to drop. Our prediction is that programs like HYPERCARD will help solve the programming problem. This is because HYPERCARD programmers will simply concentrate on organizing the laserdisc into a useful database from which information can be easily accessed, without consideration for the specific questions users will want to answer. Teachers and students can use the resulting flexible, first-class series of databases to answer questions and solve problems they consider to be important.

In Chapter 8 we described Compton's MULTIMEDIA ENCYCLOPEDIA, which takes advantage of CD-ROM technology to offer rapid access to information via a computerized encyclopedia. Persons who see this product are usually impressed and initially assume that such electronic encyclopedias will render traditional reference books extinct. This will not necessarily happen. As the popularity of electronic encyclopedias expands, students will certainly learn to use them efficiently; but it is unlikely that many schools will want to devote a large number of computers to encyclopedia searches. Eventually, students will probably begin their searches on the electronic encyclopedia, move to the traditional book version after they have identified sources, and then return when necessary to the electronic version. It is actually likely that use of traditional encyclopedias will increase rather than decrease with the introduction of their electronic counterpart.

INTELLIGENT COMPUTER-ASSISTED INSTRUCTION (ICAI)

Chapter 1 of *The Computer in the Classroom* (Vockell and Schwartz, 1988) thoroughly covers tutorials that provide branching programmed discussion as a form of computer-assisted instruction. It is possible to combine branching tutorials with artificial intelligence to provide a strategy called intelligent computer-assisted instruction (ICAI). Like a good human tutor, an ICAI program monitors student responses and tries to determine reasons behind student errors. The computer then provides tutorial or remedial information specifically designed to overcome these errors.

A program called MENDEL, which tutors high school and college students on various aspects of genetics, is a good example of this strategy. MENDEL is both a problem-solving simulation and an intelligent tutorial. In its first role MENDEL presents problems for the student to solve; the student uses the computer to conduct experiments and collect or interpret data. In its second role MENDEL assumes the role of a human tutor. This program is described in detail in Vockell and Schwartz (1988) and in Streibel et al. (1987).

Applied to language arts, such a program could perform the following tasks for a student studying a passage of text:

1. It could make inferences about a student's answers, drawing conclusions about the skills he or she possesses or still needs to develop.
2. It could maintain a history of a student's actions (including the strategies the student tried and the results of these strategies).
3. It could make inferences about the reasons for the student's problem-solving actions. These are drawn from a combination of what the student has done and said. (Human tutors do this as well—building a model or representation of each student's or group of students' comprehension abilities based on what the tutors have observed.)
4. It could compare a model of a student's knowledge with the tutor's understanding of the problem.
5. It could make a decision on the type of tutorial advice and the timing of this advice.
6. It could evaluate whether the student has benefitted from the advice.

Students running such a program would have an experience similar to reading and thinking about a passage with a human tutor seated beside them who possesses broad knowledge of comprehension skills and a willingness to help whenever needed. The development of this program is described in greater detail in Streibel et al. (1987). A program like this does not yet exist for language arts but the technology is available. Similar programs could be developed in other areas as well.

Within the next few years we expect to see software and book publishers expand their offerings in language arts, taking advantage of the full strengths of the computer. Specifically, we expect to see more programs that (1) make better use of speech synthesis, (2) help develop writing skills, (3) facilitate the overall implementation of the language-rich environment and the Language Experience Approach to reading, and (4) provide management systems for keeping track of individual progress.

SUMMARY

The future of language arts instruction is likely to see expanded computer applications and innovations resulting from technological advances. Hypertext will make it possible to provide information (such as definitions of words) at the time and in the order it is really needed. Interactive video will make it possible to integrate textual and visual presentations and allow learners to move easily backward and forward within a software package. Intelligent computer-assisted instruction will make it possible for the computer to respond more precisely to the specific needs of individual learners during computerized language arts instruction.

Publishers are also likely to expand their efforts in producing good materials for developing writing skills and for promoting the language-rich environment. Since computer technology is still in a stage of rapid development, it is likely that other innovations will lead to instructional developments that cannot be predicted at the present time.

REFERENCES

Streibel, M. J., J. Stewart, K. Koedinger, A. Collins, and J. R. Jungck. "MENDEL: An Intelligent Tutoring System for Genetics Problem-Solving, Conjecturing, and Understanding." *Machine-Mediated Learning* 2 (1987): 129–159.

Vockell, E. L., and E. Schwartz. *The Computer in the Classroom*. Watsonville, Calif.: Mitchell, 1988.

CHAPTER 12

SOFTWARE REVIEWS

THIS CHAPTER PROVIDES FAIRLY detailed reviews of twenty software packages available for the language arts curriculum (see Appendix B for less detailed summaries of a much larger number of programs). The goal of this chapter is to describe programs that typify the kinds of help teachers can expect from the computer in their language arts classrooms. Many of the programs discussed here have been mentioned elsewhere in this book, and cross references can be found in the book's index.

TITLE: APPLEWORKS

Publisher: Claris
Hardware: Apple II
Type: Utility
Grade Level: 4–adult
Topics: Word processor, database, spreadsheet

DESCRIPTION

APPLEWORKS is an integrated program that includes a word processor, database, and spreadsheet. Two disks that provide the new user with background information (APPLE PRESENTS APPLEWORKS) and practice (APPLEWORKS TUTORIAL) are enclosed in the package. The word processor is an easy-to-use eighty-column program with both basic and fairly advanced editing features. The database allows a maximum of 1,350 records with a maximum of 1,024 characters per record. The spreadsheet provides room for 6,000 filled cells with a maximum of 127 columns and 999 rows. The beauty of APPLEWORKS is its ease of use and the integration of information among the three applications. The copy and move options make it simple to use information from the spreadsheet or database in a word processing document. Keystroke cues are common to all three applications, which makes switching from one function to another easy. In addition to student tasks, this program can support teacher tasks such as grade and student information management and test design. Supplementary programs from the TIMEOUT series by Beagle Brothers offer additional options such as spelling correction and an on-line thesaurus.

Other word processors are available for young learners, including BANK STREET WRITER, MAGIC SLATE, and FREDWRITER, but these are not as easily integrated with the database and spreadsheet as is APPLEWORKS. Teachers who themselves were educated without the use of an integrated program like APPLEWORKS are sometimes unaware of the tremendous advantages such a program has for gathering, organizing, and presenting information.

TITLE: THE CHILDREN'S WRITING AND PUBLISHING CENTER

Publisher: The Learning Company
Hardware: Apple II
Type: Utility
Grade Level: 2–adult
Topics: Desktop publishing

DESCRIPTION

THE CHILDREN'S WRITING AND PUBLISHING CENTER is an entry-level desktop publishing program. It combines a word processor with graphics and layout design. The student can select from one- or two-column layout, eight font styles, and 140 graphics. The teacher's guide contains lesson ideas and activities. A data disk of templates is included. This desktop publishing program introduces primary students to the skills involved in creating and printing a newsletter. While this is a truly impressive program, teachers should also consider the possibility of using a more sophisticated desktop publishing program, such as PUBLISH IT! Although the more advanced programs are probably prohibitively complex for young children to use without adult guidance, teachers often discover that they themselves benefit from using them. If a teacher becomes adept at using PUBLISH IT! or a similar program, it is relatively easy to introduce the desktop publishing process to students and to guide young learners in its use.

TITLE: CROSSWORD MAGIC

Publisher: Mindscape
Hardware: Apple II, MS-DOS, Commodore, Macintosh
Type: Utility, drill, game
Grade Level: 3–adult
Topics: Vocabulary development

DESCRIPTION

CROSSWORD MAGIC allows teachers and students to easily create crossword puzzles that are professionally formatted. The teacher or student enters words, which the program arranges on the screen in a crossword design. Then the user enters definitions (clues). Once again, the computer handles the formatting. After the puzzle is complete, it may be printed out and filled in traditionally or saved to disk and filled in on-screen. In either case, original puzzles can be designed to meet individual or group needs. Other companies also publish programs that generate crossword puzzles, but we have seen none as easy to use and with output as attractive as CROSSWORD MAGIC. However, MECC's PUZZLES AND POSTERS has the advantage of generating "word search" activities from the words used in a crossword puzzle, without requiring the teacher to enter the words a second time to generate the word search.

TITLE: FIRST LETTER FUN

Publisher: MECC
Hardware: Apple II
Type: Drill, game
Grade Level: P–K
Topics: Letter recognition, initial sounds

DESCRIPTION

This program provides practice in matching pictures with the beginning sound of the word. Four backgrounds are used for the scenes: a farm, a circus, a magician, and a park. Students choose the appropriate letter from the four given. If the correct selection is made, the word appears underneath the picture. After two incorrect responses, the correct letter flashes. Teachers have the option of using upper or lowercase letters and can choose to have the sound on or off. FIRST LETTER FUN can initiate dialogue among students that could lead to dictation stories or storytelling. Several of the Sunburst programs associated with the Muppet Learning Keys offer similar learning opportunities.

TITLE: GRAMMAR GREMLINS

Publisher: Davidson
Hardware: Apple II, MS-DOS, Commodore
Type: Drill, tutorial, game
Grade Level: 4–adult
Topics: Abbreviations, verb tense, verb agreement, capitalization, contractions, parts of speech, plurals, punctuation, sentence structure

DESCRIPTION

GRAMMAR GREMLINS contains over six hundred practice sentences to reinforce learning of the grammar rules it covers. Each of four levels begins with a pretest that assesses skills in which additional practice is needed. Practice takes two forms. In "Build Your Skill" a grammar rule is presented, followed by twenty applications. The student can review the rule at any time. "The Grammar Gremlins Game" presents questions and several choices for answers with the help of "gremlins" who appear in the windows of the haunted house. After completing all lessons, the student may take the review test consisting of twenty questions that cover the content at that level. An editor allows the teacher to create lessons with an originally stated rule and multiple-choice questions for review. There is also a record-keeping option in which student scores can be viewed on the screen or printed.

TITLE: LOGOWRITER

Publisher: Logo Computer Systems
Hardware: Apple II
Type: Utility
Grade Level: K–8
Topics: Logo programming language with word processor

DESCRIPTION

LOGOWRITER combines the Logo language and its graphic applications with the composing and editing features of word processing. The result is a program that encourages learner exploration on many levels. LOGOWRITER features twenty-five turtle shapes plus a shape editor that allows students to create their own turtles. The graphics, animation, word processing, and music capabilities of LOGOWRITER offer students and their teachers unlimited possibilities in all curriculum areas. One difficulty with LOGOWRITER is that teachers must spend some time (at least ten to thirty hours) learning how to use it themselves and additional time to teach it to their students, whereas most word processing and graphics programs (like APPLEWORKS and PRINT SHOP) can be learned much more quickly. However, teachers who take the time to learn LOGOWRITER and to teach it to their students often report dramatic and interesting results.

TITLE: MAGIC SLATE II

Publisher: Sunburst
Hardware: Apple II
Type: Utility
Grade Level: 2–adult
Topics: Word processor

DESCRIPTION

MAGIC SLATE II is a word processing program available in twenty-, forty-, and eighty-column versions. Each version includes the standard editing features of most word processors plus an interesting assortment of type styles and custom print options. The large letters on the twenty-column version make it especially suitable to primary students. The forty- and eighty-column versions include a student planner, which guides the student in the planning and revising stages of the writing process. Teacher-only options provide several ways for teachers to customize student activities. A "fill-in" option allows the teacher to create fill-in-the-blank exercises in which the students are locked out of making changes in the file except for the actual answer. A teacher planner option provides a prompted writing format so that teachers can write directions, questions, or comments that cannot be edited by the student using the exercise. The teacher's guide includes a handbook that could be copied for student use; lesson plans for language arts; and a troubleshooting section that provides answers to common problems. Additional type styles are available for MAGIC SLATE II, and the SCHOOL SPELLER is a companion program for the forty- and eighty-column versions.

TITLE: MUPPET SLATE

Publisher: Sunburst
Hardware: Apple II
Type: Utility
Grade Level: K–2
Topics: Word and graphics processor

DESCRIPTION

MUPPET SLATE is a word and picture processor designed for use with young children. Its large letters and easy-to-use features allow the child to independently create and print original stories. A clip art library includes 126 graphics that can be incorporated into the stories to substitute for words or illustrate ideas. Borders enhance the printed product. The program also contains twenty-four detailed language arts lessons to extend the learning experience. Teacher options include prompted writing formats, a utilities section for handling student disks, customization for individualizing lessons, and printing.

TITLE: ONCE UPON A TIME

Publisher: Compu-Teach
Hardware: Apple II
Type: Utility
Grade Level: K–6
Topics: Word processor, graphics generator

DESCRIPTION

With ONCE UPON A TIME students can design and publish original books. They may choose a farm, jungle, or city setting. Students then choose from a variety of graphics in the picture section to illustrate their story. They can move or erase the graphic chosen, print the picture, or write their story. The Explore-A-Story programs from D. C. Heath, such as ROSIE THE COUNTING RABBIT, offer similar creative opportunities; these programs offer effective animation as well. CARTOONER by Electronic Arts permits students to draw their own animated cartoons, but this program has the disadvantage of working very slowly unless you use an accelerator card.

TITLE: PAINT WITH WORDS

Publisher: MECC
Hardware: Apple II
Type: Utility, game
Grade Level: K–2
Topics: Picture processor

DESCRIPTION

Presented with a list of words, students choose those they want to illustrate and place them on the screen. When the student presses the space bar the word transforms into a picture. Pictures can be moved or erased from the screen as students experiment with the picture they wish to create. The teacher can use the management options menu to create up to twelve word lists from 124 primary-level pictures/words. Although words can be deleted or changed, the graphics remain. Backgrounds can be selected from twelve scenes (lake, street, rooms, farm, hills, school, river, castle, picnic, winter, forest, and zoo). This program can promote dialogue among students that can then become dictated stories.

TITLE: PRINT SHOP

Publisher: Broderbund
Hardware: Apple II, Apple IIGS, MS-DOS
Type: Utility
Grade Level: P–adult
Topics: Graphics and text generator

DESCRIPTION

The PRINT SHOP is a popular graphics and text generator that can be used to design posters, banners, greeting cards, and letterheads. Choices for borders, fonts, and graphics are made with simple key strokes using the arrow keys and the Return key. A preview option allows the user to see the final product before it is printed. The popularity of this program has spawned many companion programs and imitators. The color version of PRINT SHOP takes advantage of three- and four-color ribbons to generate colorful posters, banners, and the like. PRINT SHOP COMPANION, GRAPHICS LIBRARY (I, II, and III), HOLIDAYS AND FESTIVALS, PARTY EDITION, and SAMPLER EDITION provide additional graphics, fonts, and borders to complement those on the original disk. The PRINT SHOP's teacher's guide shares ideas to expand the use of the program beyond merely "decorating" the classroom. In the hands of a creative teacher the PRINT SHOP and its companion programs can be used instructionally as well! Similar programs include the GARFIELD series by Random House, SIGN DESIGNER by Sunburst, PROFESSIONAL SIGN MAKER and SUPER SIGN MAKER by Sunburst, STICKYBEAR PRINTER by Weekly Reader Software, and the WALT DISNEY series by Walt Disney.

TITLE: READER RABBIT

Publisher: The Learning Company
Hardware: Apple II, Apple IIGS, MS-DOS, Commodore
Type: Drill, game
Grade Level: K–2
Topics: Vocabulary development, spelling, letter/pattern recognition, decoding, comprehension

DESCRIPTION

Students can choose one of four games to practice a variety of reading skills. By pressing the space bar in "The Sorter," students identify three-letter words that have the same letter pattern as the target word. In "Labeler" three pictures of animals are shown; the student must choose the letters that spell the animal's name. "Word Train" is more complex. In this game students must choose words that differ by one letter from the previous choice. "Matchup" provides several formats for matching pictures and words in a "concentration" card game. Students can match picture to picture, picture to the whole or partial word, or word to word. The graphics used for feedback are delightful and give the student a lot of motivation. As with all Learning Company materials, the teacher's guide provides lesson plans and off-line activities to extend the instruction. WORD-A-MATION from Sunburst provides similar opportunities for older students to play with and see relationships among words.

TITLE: SENTENCE STARTERS

Publisher: Teacher Support Software
Hardware: Apple II (Slotbuster speech card)
Type: Drill, utility
Grade Level: K–3
Topics: Writing, sentence completion

DESCRIPTION

SENTENCE STARTERS is part of the software publisher's Language Experience series, which uses writing, reading, and listening activities based on the students' experiences. This program contains five disks: a program disk and four data disks. Each data disk holds ten story starters. The topics are Animals and Nature, Seasons and Holidays, Things I Like and Do, and People and Places. Once the student decides on a topic and title, a "sticker book" screen appears with space for five "stickers" or graphics and five sentence starters. After creating the sentences and selecting graphics, the student can choose to have the sentences read aloud or printed. The manual includes off-line activities that can lead up to the actual computer activity.

TITLE: STICKYBEAR ABC

Publisher: Weekly Reader
Hardware: Apple II, Commodore
Type: Drill, game
Grade Level: P–1
Topics: Letter recognition

DESCRIPTION

By touching any letter on the keyboard children are rewarded with an animated picture and melody. The picture has an object that begins with the letter pressed. This program is a perfect initial-letter computer activity for young children. There is just enough activity to keep them interested and no teacher management is necessary. Children are free to explore and enjoy the graphics and letters that appear on the screen. Several of the Sunburst programs associated with the Muppet Learning Keys offer similar learning opportunities.

TITLE: TALKING TEXT WRITER

Publisher: Scholastic

Hardware: Apple II, MS-DOS, (Echo, Cricket, or PC2 speech synthesizer board)

Type: Utility

Grade Level: P–6

Topics: Word processor with speech capabilities

DESCRIPTION

With the help of a speech synthesizer and TALKING TEXT WRITER, students can have letters, words, sentences, or pages of typed text "read" back to them. In addition to the common editing features available, this program allows the user to change the pronunciation of a word if it is mispronounced. A feature called "Comment Box" allows the teacher to add instructions and comments to encourage the student. The "Dictionary Box" reads a word and its definition when activated. The program includes a tutorial to guide the setup that will best benefit the class. TALKING TEXT WRITER is more advanced than Hartley's DR. PEET and MY WORDS, but teachers sometimes find that by the time students are ready for the more advanced features, they do not need a "talking" computer anyway.

TITLE: THOSE AMAZING READING MACHINES I–IV

Publisher: MECC
Hardware: Apple II
Type: Drill, game
Grade Level: 3–6
Topics: Comprehension, sequencing, reading for details

DESCRIPTION

In THOSE AMAZING READING MACHINES students may choose from three activities. In the "Graphics Room" they are asked to read the description of an amazing machine and then decide which of three machines illustrated match it. The description may be reread and the machines can be animated to determine how they work. Another approach to comprehension is used in the "Editing Room." Students read a description, in which one paragraph has a mistake, and observe the machine in action. They then must identify and correct the mistake. "Cut and Paste" presents several paragraphs that describe a machine—but the order is scrambled. Students must reorder the paragraphs so that the machine is properly described. Teacher options include customizing the lesson by determining how many parts a machine has, the number of problems presented, the mastery level, and the difficulty level (in "Cut and Paste").

TITLE: VERB USAGE 1–4

Publisher: Hartley
Hardware: Apple II, MS-DOS
Type: Drill, tutorial
Grade Level: 3–5
Topics: Verb tense

DESCRIPTION

VERB USAGE is a four-disk package containing ten lessons on each disk. Each lesson reviews one verb. The student is asked to choose whether the present, past, past participle, or infinitive form of the verb correctly completes the sentence given. Students may try out different forms to view how each fits in the sentence before making a final choice. Errors are recorded for later viewing by the teacher. After an incorrect answer, a hint may be given to guide students to the correct choice. The number of chances is controlled by the teacher. The teacher can also modify a lesson's vocabulary, add hints or explanations, print out students' progress reports, and set a student safeguard that ends the lesson if the student has reached frustration level. Pretests and post-tests on each disk can be used for placement or mastery.

TITLE: WHERE IN THE WORLD IS CARMEN SANDIEGO?

Publisher: Broderbund
Hardware: Apple II, MS-DOS, Commodore
Type: Drill, game
Grade Level: 4–12
Topics: World geography, problem solving, note taking, vocabulary
    development

DESCRIPTION

WHERE IN THE WORLD IS CARMEN SANDIEGO? is an adventure game that places the user in the role of detective. The mission is to follow, identify, and capture Carmen Sandiego or one of her gang of thieves who has stolen a national treasure. Clues are given to help the user obtain the thief's whereabouts and his or her identity. A world atlas is enclosed for reference. The crime computer at Interpol, one of the options offered in the program, assists in issuing a warrant for the thief's arrest. As cases are successfully solved, the user is promoted from Rookie through various levels to Master Sleuth. Other Carmen Sandiego capers are produced by Broderbund with a similar format: WHERE IN THE USA IS CARMEN SANDIEGO?, WHERE IN EUROPE IS CARMEN SANDIEGO?, and WHERE IN TIME IS CARMEN SANDIEGO? These adventures appeal to children of all ages. Since players soon discover that reference books greatly expedite the crime-solving process, the programs provide meaningful practice in reference skills, map decoding, and problem solving.

TITLE: WIZARD OF WORDS

Publisher: Advanced Ideas
Hardware: Apple II, MS-DOS, Commodore
Type: Drill, game
Grade Level: K–adult
Topics: Spelling, vocabulary development, problem solving

DESCRIPTION

WIZARD OF WORDS consists of five motivational games based on either the built-in registry of words (thirty-eight thousand words) or an original list entered by the user. Before each game the user determines the level of difficulty and selects the word list to be used. "Jester's Jumble" presents a scrambled word and challenges the user to unscramble it. After each incorrect guess the Jester rescrambles the word in an order that is easier to interpret. "Castle Capers" is played in the hangman format. Banners hang from the castle wall; the user must guess which letters should appear on each banner. Incorrect responses cause the gate to descend. The object is to guess the correct word before the gate closes. In "Dragon's Spell" the dragon's breath contains a large word from which smaller words can be made. After the learner enters a word it is matched to the dictionary and points are awarded. "Word Spinning" is a word game played on a grid. The object is to create more words than your opponent. In "Herald's Hark" the heralds choose a secret word and the user makes guesses. Each guess is matched to the secret word by the number of letters they have in common. Teachers or students can create original word lists to use with "Jester's Jumble" or "Castle Capers" by following the easy-to-use directions in the program "King Author." The variety offered by programs like WIZARD OF WORDS will keep the attention of students and challenge them to practice their spelling skills.

TITLE: WRITER RABBIT

Publisher: The Learning Company
Hardware: Apple II, MS-DOS
Type: Utility, game
Grade Level: 2–4
Topics: Sentence parts, writing

DESCRIPTION

Students who first use WRITER RABBIT can begin with a tutorial that provides practice in recognizing the function of sentence parts. Six engaging games provide practice in recognizing sentence parts and sequencing. A cloze activity asks students to choose from optional sentence parts or write their own part of the story on the line provided. Stories can then be printed out to enjoy over and over. The game options selection allows the teacher to set reading level, time, speed, sound, and the type of sentence parts to be used in the first five games. As with all Learning Company materials the teacher's guide provides lesson plans and off-line activities to extend the instruction.

GLOSSARY OF IMPORTANT TERMS

Academic Learning Time (ALT). The amount of time a student spends attending to relevant academic tasks while performing those tasks at a high rate of success.

ALT. See *Academic Learning Time.*

Artificial Intelligence. The use of computers to imitate or expand human intelligence. Computers that play chess usually employ artificial intelligence. Another example is found in the "expert systems" being developed to offer doctors "second opinions" on their diagnoses of patients.

Authoring Language. A computer program that enables the user to enter commands that instruct the computer to carry out various tasks, such as the presentation of a *drill* or *tutorial.* An authoring language is usually easier to learn but less flexible than a *programming language.*

Automaticity. See *Overlearning.*

Auxiliary Storage Device. Any device (such as a tape or a *floppy disk*) on which programs and other computer data can be stored in order to be transferred into the computer's memory.

BASIC. One of the most commonly used *programming languages* for *microcomputers.*

Branching Programmed Instruction. A form of programmed instruction in which the nature of each step in a learning sequence is determined by the student's response at the previous step.

Byte. A single character stored in the computer's memory.

CAI. See *Computer-assisted Instruction.*

Cathode Ray Tube (CRT). The televisionlike screen that displays output from the computer.

CBE. See *Computer-based Education.*

CD-ROM Disk. A laser-optical disk closely resembling a compact music disk and holding much more information than an ordinary floppy disk can. Currently users can read data from these disks but cannot store information on them.

Cloze Strategy. A type of reading comprehension test or exercise in which words or letters have been omitted according to some prescribed pattern (e.g., every fifth word). Students fill in the blanks to complete the passage.

CMI. See *Computer-managed Instruction.*

Competencies Model. A model for the language arts curriculum based on the behavioral studies that have found children to mature in predictable, recognizable stages; it assumes that language arts skills can be broken down into increments that lead to the defined skill or concept.

Competitive Learning. A learning atmosphere in which the success or failure of learners is based on the comparative performance of other learners.

Computer-assisted Instruction (CAI). The use of the computer to provide instruction directly to the learner. When students run a *drill, tutorial,* or *simulation,* they are engaged in CAI.

Computer-based Education (CBE). See *Computer-managed Instruction.*

Computer-managed Instruction (CMI). The use of the computer to coordinate instructional activities. Although CMI is often used in conjunction with *CAI,* it can also be used to coordinate noncomputerized instruction.

Computer Program. A set of instructions that makes the computer carry out specified operations.

Cooperative Learning. A learning atmosphere in which students are encouraged to cooperate with other learners rather than compete with them. Important features of cooperative learning include individual responsibility and positive interdependence.

Corrective Feedback. Information that explains to the learner the nature of a mistake or suggests ways to move from an incorrect answer to a correct answer.

Courseware. Computer *software* designed for instructional purposes.

CRT. See *Cathode Ray Tube.*

Cursor. The *prompt* (often a flashing box or a flashing line) that indicates where the next entry will take place on-screen.

Database. An organized set of information.

Database Management Program. Provides electronic access to a set of information by permitting entry, storage, sorting, and retrieval of data.

Desktop Publishing. The production on a personal computer of professional-appearing materials, such as newsletters, course guides, and bulletins, using a combination of *word processing* and *graphics* strategies.

Direct Instruction. Academically focused, teacher-directed strategies using logically sequenced instructional materials or teacher guidance to see that students stay on task effectively.

Disk. See *Floppy Disk.*

Disk Drive. A mechanism into which *floppy disks* are inserted in order to transfer information to and from the computer's *random access memory.*

Documentation. *Hardcopy* or electronic information that describes how to use a piece of *hardware* or *software.*

Drill. A program that provides repeated practice and feedback regarding a skill or concept.

Electronic Bulletin Board. An electronic communications system, usually accessed via *modem,* that enables users to share information about topics of common interest.

Feedback. Information indicating that a response is right or wrong. Feedback may be either *positive* or *negative.*

File Server. A computer dedicated to storing and sharing files with other computers linked to a network.

Floppy Disk. A small and compact *auxiliary storage device* on which information can be kept for subsequent transfer to the computer's *random access memory.*

Generalization. The application to a new situation of a skill or concept learned in an earlier instructional setting.

Gradebook. A program designed to keep records and generate reports regarding student performance.

Grade Management Program. See *Gradebook.*

Graphics. Diagrams and pictures drawn with the aid of the computer.

Hardcopy. Output that is printed on a permanent surface (such as paper) instead of merely appearing on a temporary surface (such as a *CRT* screen).

Hardware. The physical equipment that comprises a computer system. It is differentiated from the *software,* which runs on this physical equipment.

Help Screen. A screenful of information that provides instructions on a specific topic or gives answers to the user's questions. Help screens usually appear in response to a request initiated by the user.

Hypermedia. A programming strategy that permits a user to examine a segment of text or graphic information and then branch immediately to any other segment as needed.

Hypertext. See *Hypermedia.*

ICAI. See *Intelligent Computer-assisted Instruction.*

Individualistic Instruction. The classroom environment in which students pursue their own instructional objectives without concern for the needs or interests of their classmates.

Individualized Instruction. The strategy that suits instruction to the specific needs of individual students.

Input. Information that is sent to the computer's memory, usually from a *keyboard*, from an *auxiliary storage device*, or through a *modem*.

Integrated Learning System (ILS). A comprehensive package of computer-based instruction in basic skills that diagnoses students' needs, prescribes lessons, tracks progress, and provides information to the teacher.

Intelligent Computer-assisted Instruction (ICAI). The application of principles of *artificial intelligence* to *computer-assisted instruction* that enables the computer to analyze learner characteristics and to adjust its presentation of information in response to these characteristics.

Interactive Videodisc System. A combination of a computer with a *videodisc* that displays visual and auditory sequences in response to a user's *input*.

Joystick. An instrument that permits the user to move the *cursor* or in some other way control movement on the *CRT* screen.

Keyboard. The typewriterlike portion of the computer that allows users to enter characters (*input*) into the computer's memory.

Keyboarding. A psychomotor skill that involves the proper touching of keys with the appropriate fingers, an established rhythm, keeping eyes on copy, and using correct posture to input information or responses into the computer via the keyboard.

Kilobyte. One thousand *bytes*. The computer's *memory size* is normally indicated in kilobytes.

Laserdisc. See *Videodisc*.

Learning Center. A broad term applied to any area in the classroom where related materials are collected for individual or group exploration.

Learning Phase. The period of instruction during which students who have not yet mastered knowledge or skills need feedback to focus attention correctly, to detect and clarify misconceptions, and to come to a relatively clear understanding of the concepts or principles under consideration.

Light Pen. A device, similar to a pen, that permits *input* to the computer when the user holds the pen near the *CRT* screen and pushes the pen's button.

Linear Programmed Instruction. A form of programmed teaching in which all learners go through the lesson from beginning to end, in exactly the same sequence.

Logo. A computer programming language that is particularly easy to teach to young children. It is especially useful for programming the computer to draw pictures, and a version called LOGOWRITER is easily integrated into written text.

Mastery Learning. This instructional principle holds that, given enough time and help, about 95 percent of the learners in any group can come to a complete mastery of the designated instructional objectives.

Memory Expansion Card. A device inserted into the computer that contains memory chips and increases the computer's *random access memory*.

Memory Size. The number of *bytes* of *random access memory* that the computer makes available to the user. In general, computers with greater memory sizes can run more complex programs and store larger amounts of data than those with smaller memories.

Menu. A screenful of information and *prompts* that enable the learner to choose from a list of activities that the computer can perform.

Microcomputer. A relatively small computer that employs a microprocessor. Microcomputers are also referred to as *personal computers*. They are smaller than minicomputers, which in turn are smaller than mainframe computers.

Modeling. The process by which an observer learns by watching someone else (such as a teacher, peer, or cartoon character) perform an activity. The observer derives vicarious benefit from seeing the other person (the model) receive feedback for performing the task.

Modem. A device for transferring information from one computer to another, usually across telephone lines.

Monitor. A *CRT* screen that is connected to a computer system and displays the *input* being placed into the system and the *output* coming from it.

Monochrome Monitor. A monitor that displays *output* in a single color on a background of another single color (e.g., black on white). It is distinguished from a color monitor, which can generate a wide variety of background and foreground colors.

Mouse. A device for moving the *cursor* or in some other way controlling movement on the *CRT* screen. A mouse differs from a *joystick* in that it controls movement more precisely but is less suited to many gamelike activities.

Negative Feedback. Information indicating that the learner's response was incorrect. If negative feedback also explains to the learner the nature of the mistake, it becomes *corrective feedback*.

Network. A series of computers that are interconnected. Some networks are permanent (the computers remain connected and work together), whereas others are temporary (the computers are only joined for particular operations).

New Heritage Model. A model for the language arts curriculum based on the history, values, and skills that have made it possible for our generation to learn about our culture and to continue to share that knowledge with our descendants.

Output. The information provided by the computer in response to instructions or *input* from a user. The output usually appears on the *CRT* screen or on a sheet of paper; however, it could be sent directly to an *auxiliary storage device* or to another computer.

Overlearning. The strategy of continuing to study and practice skills or concepts well beyond the point of initial mastery, in order to make them automatic for the learner.

Paddles. Tools for moving the *cursor* or for producing some other kind of movement on the *CRT* screen. Like the *joystick*, paddles are used mostly in gamelike applications.

Peer Tutoring. An instructional approach in which students help teach other students. Both the student doing the teaching (the tutor) and the student being taught (the tutee) benefit from the interaction.

Peripheral Devices. Any of the devices that are added on to the main computer system. Peripherals include *disk drives, printers, joysticks, modems*, and the like.

Personal Computer. See *Microcomputer*.

Port. An external point of connection for the *peripheral devices* associated with a computer system, such as a *printer* or *modem*. Ports are often built into the computer and serve the same functions as *interface cards*, which usually must be added to the system.

Positive Feedback. Information indicating that the learner gave the correct response. Positive feedback is usually considered to be a form of *reinforcement*.

Practice Phase. The period of instruction during which external feedback from a skilled teacher is less important, because the student—exercising skills previously learned—gets feedback automatically from the situation or from the student's own insights.

Printer. A mechanism for generating *hardcopy* (the printed *output* from a computer).

Process Model. A model for the language arts curriculum based on the belief that the curriculum should guide learners to use language for effective communication, primarily by using learner-generated processes rather than teacher-directed approaches.

Programming Language. A set of rules and commands that instructs the computer to carry out various tasks. A programming language is usually more difficult to learn but also more flexible than an *authoring language*.

Prompt. This term has two separate meanings. First, it referes to the *cursor* or some other symbol that indicates the computer is waiting for the user to make a response. Second, in instructional computing it refers to a clue that stimulates the learner to give a correct answer. The latter kind of prompt usually appears when the learner has made a mistake or requested help.

Public Domain Software. Software that is not protected by copyright restrictions. It is legal to make copies of public domain software.

RAM. See *Random Access Memory*.

Random Access Memory (RAM). The temporary portion of the computer's memory. All information in RAM is erased the moment the computer is turned off. Information is loaded into RAM through the *keyboard*, from a *floppy disk* or another *auxiliary storage device*, or through some other *input* device.

Read Only Memory (ROM). The permanent portion of the computer's memory. ROM is not erased when the computer is turned off. Part of the ROM includes instructions to automatically transfer information into *RAM*. Although ROM information is immediately available as soon as the computer is turned on, it cannot be easily modified.

Reinforcement. The strengthening of a behavior by providing pleasant consequences. In *computer-assisted instruction*, reinforcement usually consists of either *positive feedback*, some sort of pleasant visual or auditory display, or the opportunity to engage in a pleasant activity (such as an electronic game).

Resolution. The degree of precision or clarity produced in *graphics* displays. High-resolution graphics are created with a large number of tiny dots on the screen. Low-resolution graphics are created with small squares. Pictures drawn with higher resolution look much more realistic.

ROM. See *Read Only Memory.*

Shell Program. A computerized drill program into which users can easily insert their own instructional material. For example, a vocabulary shell program might permit the teacher or student to insert words or definitions; the computer then would provide a drill on those terms.

Simulation. A program that imitates realistic events that would otherwise be difficult or impossible to incorporate into the classroom—because such a presentation would be expensive, dangerous, time-consuming, unethical, or otherwise impractical.

Software. The instructions and information (program and data) given to the computer to make it perform designated activities. The software is the set of instructions that makes the *hardware* carry out its appropriate functions.

Speech Synthesis. See *Voice Synthesizer.*

Spreadsheet. A program that permits the organized entry and tabulation of numerical data in such a way as to provide automatic recalculation of formulas programmed by the user.

Telecommunications. For computers, refers to the process of communicating between computers via a *modem.*

Template. A predesigned document that the user alters in some way to perform a specific task, as with a *word processor* or *database management program.*

Test Generator. A program that automatically generates tests or quizzes, using items and guidelines entered by the instructor.

Transfer. The generalization of a concept or skill learned in one environment to a new environment.

Tutorial. A program that provides instruction on a topic. A tutorial is usually a computerized presentation of *branching programmed instruction.*

User-Friendliness. The ability of a program to accept and respond to *input* in such a way that the user can easily interpret and make use of the computer's response.

Videodisc. An *auxiliary storage device* that employs laser technology to present audio and video displays. Videodiscs can be used in combination with a *microcomputer* for interactive instruction.

Voice Synthesizer. *Software* or a *peripheral device* that permits the computer to communicate with the user in a human-sounding voice. Some speech synthesizers, for example, can read aloud text that users have created on a *word processor*.

Whole Language Model. A model for teaching language arts that builds around whole learners learning whole language in whole situations. The whole language approach is best implemented in a language-rich learning environment, like that described in Chapter 3 of this book.

Word Processor. A computer program that allows users to create, save, and edit documents.

SOFTWARE SUMMARIES

The following table contains information pertaining to the software programs mentioned in this book. Each entry begins with the **Title** column followed by the **Publisher**. Addresses for publishers may be found in Appendix D.

Hardware describes computer brands for which the software is available. Abbreviations are as follows: *II* stands for the Apple II series and compatibles. *IIGS* means that the program is designed especially for the Apple IIGS. (Nearly all programs labeled for the Apple II will also run on the IIGS; several programs designated for the Apple II have a separate version that takes advantage of the full capabilities of the IIGS.) *Mac* is for the Macintosh. *MS-DOS* refers to IBM and compatibles (e.g., the Tandy 1000). *Co* stands for the Commodore line, and *Echo* refers to the Echo speech synthesizer. *TW* stands for touch window, and *CD-ROM* is self-explanatory.

In the **Type** column the abbreviations are as follows: *D* for drill and practice; *T* for tutorial; *S* for simulation; *G* for educational game; and *U* for utility. The last term, *utility*, is a broad category that encompasses most of the tool applications of the computer.

Grade refers to grade level based on the publisher's identification. *P* is preschool and *K* is kindergarten; the numbers 1 through 12 correspond to grade levels, and *A* stands for adult.

Finally, the **Content** column briefly describes the topics covered in the program. Many of these programs are described in greater detail elsewhere in this book, and cross references can easily be found in the book's index.

TITLE	PUBLISHER	HARDWARE
ADJECTIVES	Hartley	II, MS-DOS
ADVERBS	Hartley	II, MS-DOS
ALPHABET ZOO	Spinnaker	II
ALPHABETIC KEYBOARDING	South-Western	II, MS-DOS
ANTONYMS/SYNONYMS	Hartley	II, MS-DOS
APPLEWORKS	Claris	II
AWARD MAKER PLUS	Baudville	II, Mac, Co
BANK STREET FILER	Scholastic	II, MS-DOS
BANK STREET WRITER III	Scholastic	II, MS-DOS
BE A WRITER	Sunburst	II
BLACKOUT: A CAPITALIZATION GAME	Gamco	II, Co
BOOK BRAIN	Oryx	II, MS-DOS
BOOKMATE	Sunburst	II
BOOKSHELF	JMH Software of Minnesota	Co
BOOKWORM	MECC	II
BOPPIE'S GREAT WORD CHASE	DLM	II
CALENDAR CRAFTER	MECC	IIGS
CALENDAR SKILLS	Harley	II

TYPE	GRADE	CONTENT
D	4–6	Identification of adjectives, possessive nouns, and pronouns
D	4–6	Identification and use of adverbs
G	K–2	Games for letter recognition and simple spelling practice
T, D	7–A	Teaches proper keyboarding method
D	4–6	Antonym and synonym identification and use
T	4–A	Integrated program with word processing, spreadsheet, and database
U	4–A	Creates certificates with choice of fonts, borders, and message
U	4–12	Simple database management program
U	2–12	Word processor with on-line dictionary, thesaurus, and tutorial
U, T	3	Companion disk to MAGIC SLATE; guides student to write a book
G, T	1–6	Practices capitalization applications in a game format
U	1–9	Recommends books for the user to read based on answers to questions
U	4–6	Four activities that assist students in finding books of interest
D	4–12	Practice on principles of correctly shelving library books
U	3–5	Database for compiling book information
G	1–8	Arcadelike game offering practice in spelling and word recognition
U	K–A	Creates calendars for week, month, or year
D	2–5	Practice on common calendar facts

TITLE	PUBLISHER	HARDWARE
CAPITALIZATION	Hartley	II
CAPITALIZATION PLUS	Mindscape	II
CERTIFICATE MAKER	Springboard	II, MS-DOS, Mac
CHILDREN'S WRITING AND PUBLISHING CENTER	Learning Company	II, MS-DOS
CLOZE-PLUS	Milliken	II, MS-DOS
COMPOUND WORDS AND CONTRACTIONS	Hartley	II
COMPUPOEM	Stephen Marcus	II
CREATE LESSONS	Hartley	II, MS-DOS
CREATE LESSONS—ADVANCED	Hartley	II
CREATE SPELL-IT	Hartley	II
CREATE WITH GARFIELD	DLM	II
CROSSWORD MAGIC	Mindscape	II, MS-DOS, Co
DAZZLE DRAW	Broderbund	II
DECISIONS, DECISIONS Series	Tom Snyder	II, MS-DOS
DESERT, THE	D. C. Heath	II, IIGS
DIALOG ON DISK	Dialog Information Retrieval Services	MS-DOS, II
DINOSAUR DAYS	Teach Yourself by Computer	II

TYPE	GRADE	CONTENT
D	3–6	Capitalization rules and their application
D, T	4–9	Covers capitalization rules; includes diagnostic test, error analysis
U	4–A	Creates certificates from 200 predesigned choices
U	2–A	Desktop publishing program especially designed for children
D, T	3–6	Reading comprehension, vocabulary development
D	1–3	Building compound words and contractions; modifiable; record keeping
D, T	4–A	Guides writing process, practice in identifying parts of speech
U	K–4	Format for creating lessons, tests, and tutorials on-screen
U	4–12	Creates and prints worksheets and tests
U, D	K–7	Spelling tests with CCD (cassette control device)
U	2–8	Creates original cartoons in strip or poster format
U	3–12	Produces original crossword puzzles on screen or hardcopy
U	3–A	Graphics program provides 16 colors, cut-and-paste, and zoom
S	5–12	Creatively involves entire classroom in the decision process
S	K–5	Interactive program in which students create model of desert environment
U	5–A	On-line database
T	3–6	Basic information on dinosaurs

TITLE	PUBLISHER	HARDWARE
DINOSAUR DISCOVERY	Omega Star	II
DR. PEET'S TALK/WRITER	Hartley	II, Echo
EASY GRAPH	Grolier	II, MS-DOS
ELECTRONIC ENCYCLOPEDIA	Grolier	MS-DOS, CD-ROM
EXPLORE-A-STORY Series	D. C. Heath	II, IIGS
EZ-PILOT II	Hartley	II
FACT OR OPINION	Hartley	II, MS-DOS
FACTORY	Sunburst	II, MS-DOS, Co
FANTAVISION	Broderbund	II, IIGS, MS-DOS
FAY'S WORD RALLY	Didatech	II
FIRST DRAFT	Scholastic	II, IIGS, MS-DOS
FIRST LETTER FUN	MECC	II
FLODD, THE BAD GUY	Tom Snyder	II
FOCUSING ON LANGUAGE ARTS: DICTIONARY I–II	Random House	II
FOCUSING ON LANGUAGE ARTS: PREFIXES/SUFFIXES	Random House	II
FOCUSING ON LANGUAGE ARTS: USAGE I–II	Random House	II
FOCUSING ON PUNCTUATION	Random House	II

TYPE	GRADE	CONTENT
T	6–12	Factual description of history of the dinosaur
D, U	K–2	Letter and word exploration, simplified word processing with speech
U, T	7–12	Teaches graphing and generates graphs
U	6–A	Electronic encyclopedia on a compact disk
U, T	K–3	Provides story starters or editing options based on printed story
U	7–12	Introduction to computer programming, encourages use of text and sound
D	3–6	Fact and opinion; modifiable; record keeping
S	4–8	Visual discrimination, problem solving, sequencing
U	4–A	Animation, special-effects program
D, G	2–6	Maze game based on clues to mystery words; authoring option
U	6–A	Outlining and organizing documents
D	K–1	Matching initial letters with pictures
S, G	3–8	Interactive story with branching capabilities
D, T	3–6	Verb tense, subject-verb agreement, pronouns, adjectives, adverbs
T, D	3–6	Lessons focus on alphabetizing and using guide words
T, D	3–6	Practice in the identification and use of prefixes and suffixes
D, T	3–6	Proofreading exercises with punctuation mistakes

TITLE	PUBLISHER	HARDWARE
FREDWRITER	CUE	II
FRIENDLY COMPUTER	MECC	II, MS-DOS
FRIENDLY FILER	Grolier	II
GAME SHOW	Advanced Ideas	II, MS-DOS, Co
GARFIELD DOUBLE DARES	Random House	II
GARFIELD, EAT YOUR WORDS	Random House	II
GETTING READY TO READ AND ADD	Sunburst	II, MS-DOS
GRADE MANAGER	MECC	II
GRAMMAR EXAMINER	DesignWare	II, MS-DOS
GRAMMAR GREMLINS	Davidson	II, MS-DOS
GRAPHICS EXHIBITOR	Koala Technologies	II
GREAT BEGINNINGS	Teacher Support Software	II
HINKY PINKY GAME	Learning Well	II
HOLIDAYS AND FESTIVALS	Right On	II
HOMEWORD PLUS	Sierra On-Line	II
HOW CAN I FIND IT IF I DON'T KNOW WHAT I'M LOOKING FOR	Sunburst	II
HYPERCARD	Claris	Mac
HYPERSTUDIO	Roger Wagner Publishing	IIGS

TYPE	GRADE	CONTENT
U	4–A	Word processing program provides easy-to-use editing features
G, D	P–3	Keyboard introduction
U, D	3–A	Introduction to database features
G	3–9	Based on a TV game show, allows input of word lists and definitions
D	K–4	Garfield lets students guess words with rhyming clues
D	K–3	Garfield lets children guess words through clues
D	P–1	Matching letters, numbers, and shapes
U	K–A	Records grades, computes percentages, and prints grades
G, D, T	4–12	Proofreading skills highlighted in a journalism setting
T, D	3–6	Focuses on grammar basics: punctuation, parts of speech, verb tense
U	4–A	Creates slide show using original pictures
U	K–3	Illustrated word processor
D	4–12	Students use clues to guess pairs of rhyming words
T	1–3	Introduction to U.S. national holidays
U	3–A	Word processing program with on-line spelling checker
U, T	4–9	Functions of resource books
U	4–A	Hypertext applications
U	6–A	Authoring system combining text, sound, and graphics

TITLE	PUBLISHER	HARDWARE
I CAN WRITE!	Sunburst	II
INFORMATION CONNECTION	Grolier	II, Co, MS-DOS
JACK AND THE BEANSTALK	Tom Snyder	II, MS-DOS
JUNGLE RESCUE—SPELLING	Learning Well	II
KIDS ON KEYS	Spinnaker	II
KIDWRITER	Gessler	II
KINDERKONCEPTS	Midwest	II
KITTENS, KIDS, AND A FROG	Hartley	II, MS-DOS
KOALA PAINTER	Koala Technologies	II
LANGUAGE EXPERIENCE RECORDER	Teacher Support Software	II
LET'S LEARN ABOUT THE LIBRARY	Troll	II
LETTER RECOGNITION	Hartley	II
LINKWAY	IBM	MS-DOS
LISTEN TO LEARN	IBM	MS-DOS
LOGOWRITER	LCSI	II, MS-DOS
MACDRAW	Claris	Mac
MACPAINT	Claris	Mac

TYPE	GRADE	CONTENT
U	2	Creative writing companion to MAGIC SLATE
T, D	6–A	Teaches telecommunications skills
S	P–2	Interactive storybook designed to read aloud to children
D	5–8	Lessons emphasize specific skills such as word structure and letter pattern
G	K–4	Introduces young children to the keyboard
U	5–12	Allows students to create stories with pictures
D, G	K–1	Reading readiness skills: shapes, alphabet, sequencing, discrimination
D	1–2	Inferential and factual comprehension
U	3–A	Generates drawings using the Koala pad Touch Tablet
U	K–A	Word processor provides readability analyses
T	4–8	Introduces card catalog, Dewey decimal system, and book categories
D	K–1	Match letter to keyboard
U	4–A	Hypertext applications
T, D	K–3	Voice synthesis for reading and language arts
U	K–12	Integrates a word processing program with Logo options
U	3–A	Drawing program offers a variety of drawing tools and patterns
U	3–A	Painting program allows multiple screens and special effects

TITLE	PUBLISHER	HARDWARE
MAGIC CASTLE	Learning Well	II
MAGIC SLATE I–II	Sunburst	II
MAGIC SPELLS	Learning Company	II, MS-DOS, Co
MAKE-A-FLASH	Teacher Support Software	II
MASTER SPELL	MECC	II
MASTERTYPE	Mindscape	II, MS-DOS, Mac
MASTERTYPE'S FILER	Scarborough Systems	II, MS-DOS, Co
MASTERTYPE'S WRITER	Mindscape	II
MAVIS BEACON TEACHES TYPING	Electronic Arts	II, MS-DOS, Mac, Co
MECC GRAPH	MECC	II
MECC KEYBOARDING	MECC	II
MECC SPELLER	MECC	II
MECC WRITER	MECC	II
MICROSOFT WORD	Microsoft	MS-DOS, Mac
MICROTYPE:THE WONDERFUL WORLD OF PAWS	South-Western	II, MS-DOS
MONSTERS AND MAKE BELIEVE	Schoolhouse Software	II
M-SS-NG L-NKS	Sunburst	II, MS-DOS
MULTIMEDIA ENCYCLOPEDIA	Compton	MS-DOS, CD-ROM

TYPE	GRADE	CONTENT
D	2–4	Vocabulary practice in gamelike atmosphere
U	K–A	Word processor with editing features plus print options
G	1–5	Spelling games created from 14 word lists or original lists
U	7–A	Creates flash cards from basal list or original list
U	1–A	Uses original word lists to design games and word practice
D, T	2–A	Develops keyboarding skills
U	2–A	A versatile database management program
U, T	3–12	Word processor designed for children
T, D	4–A	Teaches the fundamentals of typing
U	7–9	Creates graphs based on data entered
D	5–9	Drill on basic keyboarding skills
U	6–A	Spelling checker to use with MECC WRITER
U	6–A	Word processing program with 80-column display only
U	6–A	Sophisticated word processing program
T, D	3–9	Introduces typing skills through a variety of games and drills
U	6–A	Word processor and graphics generator
D	5–8	Reading activities based on context clues
U	4–A	An on-line encyclopedia with graphics and effective search strategies

TITLE	PUBLISHER	HARDWARE
MULTIPLE MEANINGS	Hartley	II
MULTISCRIBE	Styleware	II, IIGS
MUPPET SLATE	Sunburst	II
MUPPET WORD BOOK	Sunburst	II
MY WORDS	Hartley	II, Echo
NEWBERY ADVENTURES: CALL IT COURAGE	Sunburst	II
NEWBERY ADVENTURES: CHARLOTTE'S WEB	Sunburst	II
NEWBERY ADVENTURES: CRICKET IN TIMES SQUARE	Sunburst	II
NEWBERY ADVENTURES: ISLAND OF THE BLUE DOLPHINS	Sunburst	II
NEWBERY ADVENTURES: MR. POPPER'S PENGUINS	Sunburst	II
NEWBERY ADVENTURES: MRS. FRISBY AND THE RATS OF NIMH	Sunburst	II
NEWBERY ADVENTURES: WRINKLE IN TIME	Sunburst	II
ONCE UPON A TIME	Compu-Teach	II
OPPOSITES	Hartley	II, MS-DOS
OREGON TRAIL	MECC	II, MS-DOS

TYPE	GRADE	CONTENT
D	4–6	Words with multiple meanings; modifiable; record keeping
U	4–A	Word processor with pull-down menu
U	K–2	Beginning word processing program with 126 graphics
D, G, T	P–1	Beginning language concepts: upper/lowercase letters, consonants, vowels
U	K–4	Word processor with speech capabilities
D, T, G	3–6	Vocabulary, sequence, and comprehension practice based on Newbery winning book
D	4–8	Comprehension and vocabulary development based on Newbery winning book
D, T, G	5–8	Vocabulary development and comprehension practice based on Newbery winning book
D, G	3–7	Vocabulary development with adventure-game format based on Newbery winning book
D, T, G	4–8	Vocabulary development, comprehension practice based on Newbery winning book
D, G	4–8	Comprehension and vocabulary development based on Newbery winning book
D	4–8	Comprehension and vocabulary development based on Newbery winning book
U	K–6	Word processor with graphics choices to illustrate text
D	2–6	Vocabulary development, antonyms
S	5–A	User encounters problems faced by pioneers as they traveled west

TITLE	PUBLISHER	HARDWARE
PAGEMAKER	Aldus	Mac, MS-DOS
PAINT WITH WORDS	MECC	II
PAINTWORKS PLUS	Mediagenic	IIGS
PFS: FILE	Software Publishers Corporation	II, MS-DOS
PHONICS PRIME TIME: BLENDS AND DIGRAPHS	MECC	II
PHONICS PRIME TIME: FINAL CONSONANTS	MECC	II
PHONICS PRIME TIME: INITIAL CONSONANTS	MECC	II
PHONICS PRIME TIME: VOWELS I	MECC	II
PHONICS PRIME TIME: VOWELS II	MECC	II
PLAYWRITER'S THEATER	Prescription Learning	II
POP R SPELL	Milliken	II
PRINT SHOP	Broderbund	II, IIGS, MS-DOS
PRINT SHOP COMPANION	Broderbund	II, IIGS, MS-DOS
PRINT SHOP GRAPHICS LIBRARY I–III	Broderbund	II, IIGS, MS-DOS
PRINT YOUR OWN BINGO	Hartley	II
PROFESSIONAL SIGN MAKER	Sunburst	II, MS-DOS

TYPE	GRADE	CONTENT
U	5–A	Desktop publishing software
U	K–2	Vocabulary builder with voice option
U	3–A	Paint, animation, and graphics program with 4,000 colors and clip art
U	5–A	Easy-to-use database
D	1–3	Practice recognizing 34 different blends and digraphs
D	K–2	Final consonant practice exercises
D	K–1	Matching beginning consonants with pictures
D	1–2	Long and short vowel sounds
D	1–3	Vowel practice with emphasis on diphthongs and r-controlled vowels
U, S	4–8	Creates a play with choices of scenery, characters, dialogue, and music
D	3–6	Three letters pop onto screen and students guess which belongs in word
U	K–A	Creates posters, banners, greeting cards, and letterheads
U	K–A	Used with the PRINT SHOP for calendars, additional fonts and borders
U	K–A	Clip art collections of additional graphics to use with PRINT SHOP
U	3–A	Creates and prints individual bingo cards
U	3–A	Creates graphics and letters for signs and overhead transparencies

TITLE	PUBLISHER	HARDWARE
PRO GRAMMAR	South-Western	II
PRO-SENTENCE	South-Western	II
PUBLISH IT!	Timeworks Platinum	II, MS-DOS, Mac
PUNCTUATION-PUT-ON	Sunburst	II, MS-DOS
PUZZLER	Sunburst	II, MS-DOS, Co
PUZZLES AND POSTERS	MECC	II
QUICK FLASH	MECC	II
READ-A-LOGO, LEVELS I–II	Teacher Support Software	II
READER RABBIT	Learning Company	II, MS-DOS
REBUS WRITER	Mindscape	II
REPORT CARD	Sensible Software	II, MS-DOS
RIPLEY'S BELIEVE IT OR NOT	SVE	II
ROOTS AND AFFIXES	Hartley	II, MS-DOS
SAMPLER EDITION (PRINT SHOP IIGS GRAPHICS LIBRARY)	Broderbund	IIGS
SCHOLASTIC MULTISCRIBE	Scholastic	II
SCHOLASTIC PFS:FILE/REPORT	Scholastic	II, MS-DOS
SCHOOL SPELLER	Sunburst	II

TYPE	GRADE	CONTENT
G, D	6–9	Sentence building, grammar skills
G	6–9	Supplement to workbook exercises focusing on grammar, sentence building
U	4–A	Desktop publishing program
D, G	3–8	Punctuation practice emphasizing ending and internal marks
D	3–6	Predicting, comparison, drawing conclusions, context clues
U	1–A	Creates banners, posters, crosswords
D, U	P–A	Creates on-screen flash cards
D, T, G	P–3	Reading, writing, speaking, and listening activities based on logos
D, T, G	K–2	A game approach to developing reading and spelling skills
U, D	3–A	Vocabulary development by interpreting and creating rebus puzzles
U	A	Grade manager with various individual and class reporting options
D	6–10	Practice library skills by looking up interesting facts
D	4–6	Root words, prefixes and suffixes, Greek and Latin roots
U	3–A	Companion to the PRINT SHOP IIGS, contains 190 graphics, 30 backgrounds, 15 fonts
U	7–A	Word processor with graphics and multiple font features
U	7–A	Filing and reporting system
U	4–A	Spelling checker for MAGIC SLATE II

TITLE	PUBLISHER	HARDWARE
SCIENCE TOOL KIT, MASTER MODULE	Broderbund	II
SEMANTIC MAPPER	Teacher Support Software	II
SENSIBLE SPELLER	Sensible Software	II
SENTENCE COMBINING	Milliken	II
SENTENCE STARTERS	Teacher Support Software	II
SEQUENCER	Teacher Support Software	II
SHOWOFF	Broderbund	IIGS
SKILLS MAKER	Follett	II
SLIDE SHOP	Scholastic	II, MS-DOS
SOUND IDEAS: CONSONANTS	Houghton Mifflin	II, Echo
SOUND IDEAS: VOWELS	Houghton Mifflin	II, Echo
SOUND IDEAS: WORD ATTACK	Houghton Mifflin	II, Echo
S-P-E-L-L	Sunburst	II, MS-DOS
SPELLAGRAPH	DesignWare	II, MS-DOS
SPELLAKAZAM	DesignWare	II, MS-DOS
SPELLER BEE	First Byte	IIGS, Mac, MS-DOS
SPELLEVATOR	MECC	II
SPELLING ATTACK	Educational Technology	II

TYPE	GRADE	CONTENT
U	3–12	Computer becomes a lab instrument with light and temperature sensors
U	3–A	Vocabulary and concept development using webbing, clustering, mapping
U	6–A	Spelling checker companion to word processing programs
D, T	4–9	Activities to strengthen grammar and word usage
U, T	K–3	Provides sentence starters to initiate the writing process
U	2–A	Sequencing a story, directions, main ideas, and details
U	6–12	Creates transparencies, slide shows, posters, handouts
U	4–9	Generates worksheets based on the library's collection
U	4–A	Creates interactive, multimedia presentations
T, D	K–1	Matching consonant sounds with pictures and words; speech synthesis
T, D	K–1	Uses synthesized speech to practice vowel sounds
T, D	K–1	Practice in word attack using speech synthesis
D, T, G	4	Complete spelling curriculum, tests, games
D	2–9	Spelling words and guess pictures hidden behind squares
D, G	2–8	Spelling game with authoring option
D, G	2–6	Talking spelling game with built-in word lists and authoring options
D, G	1–12	Practice spelling words in a game format
G, D	1–6	Spelling practice using the Ufonic speech synthesizer

TITLE	PUBLISHER	HARDWARE
SPELLING SYSTEM	Milliken	II
SPELL IT	Davidson	II, Mac, MS-DOS, Co
SPELL IT PLUS	Davidson	II, MS-DOS
SPIDER HUNT SPELLING	Gamco	II, Co
SPRINGBOARD PUBLISHER	Springboard	II, MS-DOS
STICKYBEAR ABC	Weekly Reader	II, Co
STICKYBEAR TYPING	Weekly Reader	II
STORY MACHINE	Spinnaker	II
STORY TREE	Scholastic	II, MS-DOS
STUDY GUIDE	MECC	II
STUDY SKILLS	Houghton Mifflin	II
SURVEY TAKER	Scholastic	II, MS-DOS, Co
TALES OF ADVENTURE	Scholastic	II, MS-DOS, Co
TALES OF DISCOVERY	Scholastic	II, MS-DOS, Co
TALKING TEXT WRITER	Scholastic	II, MS-DOS, Echo
TESTWORKS	Milliken	II
THOSE AMAZING READING MACHINES	MECC	II
TIGER'S TALES	Sunburst	II
TIMEOUT	Beagle Brothers	II

TYPE	GRADE	CONTENT
D, T	3–8	Reviews spelling rules and provides guided practice
D, G	4–8	Spelling games based on rules with proofreading format
T, G, D	4–A	Reinforces spelling rules and patterns
D, G	3–9	Timed spelling game with built-in word lists and authoring option
U	4–A	Desktop publishing program
G	P–1	Animated scenes correspond to letters pressed
D	4–12	Practice on basic typing and keyboarding skills
U	K–4	Creates animated sequences from stories typed by students
U	4–8	Story writer with built-in branching capabilities
U	3–A	Design multiple choice, true/false, completion, or matching questions
D, T	3–8	Contains 61 lessons on reference materials and organizing information
U	4–8	Interprets data entered into bar graphs and tables
S, G	4–8	Part of the Twistaplot series; branching stories
S, G	4–8	Part of the Twistaplot series; branching stories
U	P–6	Word processing program with built-in speech synthesis
U	A	Test construction
D, G	3–6	Comprehension practice with crazy machines described and animated
T, D, G	K–2	Vocabulary development and reading comprehension
U	4–A	A series of companion tools to APPLEWORKS

TITLE	PUBLISHER	HARDWARE
TOUCH 'N WRITE	Sunburst	II, TW
TYPE TO LEARN	Sunburst	II, MS-DOS
VCR COMPANION	Broderbund	II, IIGS, MS-DOS
VERB USAGE 1–4	Hartley	II, MS-DOS
VERBS	Hartley	II
WALLY'S WORD WORKS: ELEMENTARY	Sunburst	II
WALT DISNEY Series	Walt Disney	II, Co
WELCOME ABOARD	Broderbund	II
WHERE IN THE WORLD IS CARMEN SANDIEGO?	Broderbund	II, MS-DOS, Co
WIZARD OF WORDS	Advanced Ideas	II, MS-DOS, Co
WORD-A-MATION	Sunburst	II
WORD ATTACK PLUS	Davidson	II, MS-DOS
WORD BLASTER	Random House	II, MS-DOS
WORD CRUNCH	Teacher Support Software	II
WORD DETECTIVE	Sunburst	II, MS-DOS, Co
WORD HERD: LOOK-ALIKES	MECC	II
WORD HERD: SOUND-ALIKES	MECC	II

TYPE	GRADE	CONTENT
U, D, T	K–2	Manuscript handwriting curriculum
T, D	2–8	Keyboarding skills in a language arts context
U	4–A	Adds titles, transitions, credits, closings to videotapes
D, T, U	3–5	Four programs of verb usage practice; tracks student progress
D, T	3–8	Verb tense, subject-verb agreement
D, G, T	4–6	Parts of speech, context clues
D, G	P–2	Reading games
T	3–6	Introduction to keyboard and computer terms
D, G	4–12	Explores cities of the world as user hunts for thief
D, G	1–12	Five game formats provide spelling practice
D, T, G	4–8	Vocabulary development: synonyms, antonyms, verb tense, homonyms
D, T, U	4–A	Activities for vocabulary development; authoring; record keeping
T, D, G	3–6	Vocabulary development
D, G	K–6	Spelling skills game
G, D	3-12	Word game encourages correct spelling and vocabulary development
D, T	5–9	Look-alike words have different meanings, spellings, and pronunciations
D, T	5–9	Meanings and usage of 12 sets of homophones

TITLE	PUBLISHER	HARDWARE
WORD LAUNCH	Teacher Support Software	II, Co
WORD MUNCHERS	MECC	II
WORD ORDER	Teacher Support Software	II, Co
WORD QUEST	Sunburst	II
WORD SPINNER	Learning Company	II
WORD WIZARD	MECC	II
WORDS AT WORK: CONTRACTION ACTION	MECC	II
WORDS AT WORK: PREFIX POWER	MECC	II
WORDS AT WORK: SUFFIX SENSE	MECC	II
WORDSEARCH	Hartley	II
WRITE A STORY!	Sunburst	II
WRITER RABBIT	Learning Company	II, MS-DOS
WRITER'S HELPER	Conduit	MS-DOS
WRITE WITH ME!	Sunburst	II
WRITING ACTIVITY FILES FOR THE BANK STREET WRITER	Scholastic	II, MS-DOS
WRITING A NARRATIVE	MECC	II
WRITING TO READ	IBM	MS-DOS

TYPE	GRADE	CONTENT
G, D	K–10	Vocabulary development and spelling practice
G, D	1–5	Practice in identifying vowel sounds; includes teacher management
D, G	K–6	Game format for alphabetizing drill, based on basal series
D, G	3–9	Alphabetizing and search strategies
D, G	K–5	Practice provided in identifying word families, letter patterns
D	3–8	Students guess words based on clues
D	2–4	Match correct spelling of contractions and corresponding words
D, G	3–6	Practice identifying 16 common prefixes
D	3–5	Suffixes and their meaning
U	3–A	Creates a word puzzle from original word lists
U	5–7	Creative writing; companion to MAGIC SLATE
D, T, G	2–4	Sentence construction and vocabulary development
U	9–A	Collection of programs to prompt writing skills
U	4	Creative writing; companion to MAGIC SLATE
U, D	2–9	Three separate programs of writing activities to use with BANK STREET WRITER III
U	5–9	Elements of narrative writing
T, D, G	K–1	An integrated learning system utilizing a station approach

TITLE	PUBLISHER	HARDWARE
WRITING WORKSHOP: ACTIVITY FILES	Milliken	II
WRITING WORKSHOP: POSTWRITING	Milliken	II
WRITING WORKSHOP: PREWRITING	Milliken	II
ZANDER	SVE	II

TYPE	GRADE	CONTENT
U	3–10	Guided writing activities include brainstorming, composing, editing
U	3–10	Revision activities for the postwriting stage of process writing
U	3–10	Three programs that emphasize the prewriting stage
G, S	6–10	Allows students to create own culture and explore "realities"

APPENDIX *C*

ANNOTATED BIBLIOGRAPHY

- Ainsa, Trisha. "The Writing Center." *Teaching and Computers* 6 (September 1988): 67–69.

  The computer as a tool in the writing center is the main topic of this article, which includes management tips, software resources, and sample lesson plans for primary teachers. The author incorporates ideas for introducing word processing to young students through message board activities and journal writing.

- Anderson-Inman, Lynne. "Teaching for Transfer: Integrating Language Arts Software into the Curriculum." *The Computing Teacher* 15 (August 1987): 24–29.

  This article describes a four-step strategy for selecting software and integrating it into the language arts curriculum.

- Anderson-Inman, Lynne, William Adler, Mary Cron, Michael Hillinger, Richard Olson, and Bonnie Proshaska. "Speech: The Third Dimension." *The Computing Teacher* 17 (April 1990): 35–39.

  This article provides an overview of speech-enhanced technology in the language arts classroom. It presents a concise description of the technology required, applications, research findings, and software selection.

- Blanchard, Jay S., and George E. Mason. *The Computer in Reading and the Language Arts.* New York: Haworth Press, 1987.

  A collection of essays on a large number of topics about using the computer to teach language arts. The essays focus on both practical and theoretical issues.

- Blankenbaker, Ruth, and Diane Hamstra. "Over the Hurdle: Writers, Word Processors, and Prewriting Strategies." *Journal of Reading, Writing, and Learning Disabilities International* 5 (1989): 43–59.

  Brainstorming, clustering, and chunk writing are some of the prewriting strategies suggested for word processing activities. These approaches are designed to encourage the reluctant, learning-disabled writer. However, the strategies described are effective with any writer who needs to generate, organize, and compose ideas in the writing process.

- Dauite, Collette. "Play and Learning to Write." *Language Arts* 66 (1989): 656–664.

  This article connects the conversations of children at play to the process of writing. It stresses the need for "talk" as children develop the ideas they wish to share in writing. In collaborative writing the importance of dialogue is stressed.

- D'Ignazio, Fred. "The Multimedia Classroom: Making It Work." *Classroom Computer Learning* 10 (November/December 1989): 36–39.

  The author describes the endless possibilities for integrating technology in a multimedia center. He focuses on hardware, software, and connections—both technology based and people based. This is the second article in a two-part series on multimedia in the classroom (the first part is "The Multimedia Sandbox," see below).

- D'Ignazio, Fred. "The Multimedia Sandbox: Creating a Publishing Center for Students." *Classroom Computer Learning* 10 (October 1989): 22–29.

  According to this article, multimedia doesn't have to be highly expensive to be highly productive. The author takes a very positive approach to creating a multimedia publishing center from available resources. His suggestions are upbeat and practical.

- Dockterman, David. *Teaching in the One-Computer Classroom*. Cambridge, Mass.: Tom Snyder Productions, 1989.

  The author views the computer in the classroom from several perspectives: as a tool for professional teacher tasks, such as grade and information management, home-school communication, and generating instructional materials; as a "smart" chalkboard consisting of computer and projection system; as a discussion generator; and as a group activator. This book offers practical suggestions for making the best use of one computer in a classroom setting.

- Goodman, Kenneth S. *What's Whole in Whole Language?* Portsmouth, N.H.: Heinemann Educational Books, 1986.

  While describing the whole language movement, the author of this book presents a background of language development and the case for whole language in literacy development. He describes whole language programs currently in progress and suggests ways to begin a program based on the whole language philosophy.

- Goodman, Kenneth S. "Whole Language Research: Foundations and Development." *Elementary School Journal* 90 (1989): 207–221.

  This article concisely summarizes the characteristics of whole language education. It provides a theoretical basis as well as a discussion of research on whole language. This entire issue of the *Elementary School*

Journal is devoted to the whole language approach to language arts education.

- Goodman, Yetta M. "Roots of the Whole Language Movement." *Elementary School Journal* 90 (1989): 113–127.

  This article gives a history of the whole language movement and discusses its current status in language arts education.

- Hanson-Smith, Elizabeth. "Cooperative Learning and CALL." *The Computing Teacher* 15 (February 1988): insertion pages 1–8.

  This insert to *The Computing Teacher* is actually an issue of the newsletter *C.A.L.L. (Computers and Language Learning)*, the entire issue of which focuses on cooperative learning applications of the computer to language learning.

- Henney, Maribeth. "Reading and Writing Interactive Stories." *The Computing Teacher* 15 (May 1988): 45–47, 60–61.

  Interactive stories written by older students for younger students can promote skill development in oral communication, listening, reading, and writing. The project described in this article is a good example of how skills can be integrated when the computer and appropriate software are used by creative teachers.

- Hohmann, Charles. *Young Children and Computers.* Yspilanti, Mich.: High/Scope Press, 1990.

  After several years of working with young children and computers within the framework of the High/Scope curriculum, the author has compiled a valuable resource. This book answers questions that concern teachers of young children who would like to incorporate computer activities into their program. It offers practical suggestions that cover every imaginable topic from room arrangement to hardware/software decisions. The book describes developmentally appropriate computer activities for young children. It describes the role of the teacher in providing the young child with a balance of direction and freedom to explore.

- Kasnic, Michael, and Sally Stefano. "More Than a Spelling Checker." *The Computing Teacher* Conference Issue (1988–1989): 30–32.

  The authors share ideas and activities to illustrate the instructional potential of spelling checkers. Activities focus on exploring rules and exceptions, generating individual spelling lists, and making the connection between spelling and sound.

- Kostner, Linda. "Computers in the Early Childhood Classroom." *The Computing Teacher* 16 (May 1989): 54–55.

  Computers have a valid place in early childhood programs. This article suggests appropriate methods for using the computer as a stimulus for social interaction and exploration of the child's world. It includes the criteria for choosing developmentally appropriate software and ideas for learning centers that incorporate computer technology.

- McClurg, Patricia, and Nancy Kasakow. "Word Processors, Spelling Checkers, and Drill and Practice Programs: Effective Tools for Spelling Instruction?" *Journal of Educational Computing Research* 5 (1989): 187–198.

  Fifth- and sixth-grade students benefited in this study conducted to explore the effects of word processors, spelling checkers, and drill-and-practice programs on spelling skill development. The authors discuss the design of the study and the software and methods used.

- Penso, Rebecca Ann. "No More Scribbles and Hieroglyphics: Computer Composition with Beginners and Slow Learners." *The Computing Teacher* 16 (February 1989): 19–21.

  Using graphics generators is one way to involve slow learners in the writing process. By using programs such as MONSTERS AND MAKE BELIEVE (Schoolhouse Software), PRINT SHOP (Broderbund), and CREATE WITH GARFIELD (DLM), the students in the author's class have become her school's computer experts. The pride and care evident in their work reflects their expanding skills in language arts, particularly in the writing process.

- Solomon, Gwen. "Going On-Line to Expand the Classroom." *Electronic Learning* Special Supplement (1989): 44–47.

  This article describes a telecommunications project in Ramapo Central School District in New York. The project was designed to expand the students' audience for writing and to extend the scope of their research skills. The author shares the success of the project by relating its "humble beginnings" through the successful application of a $100,000 grant to expand the initial project. She discusses the telecommunications, research, and collaborative publishing activities that connected students within the school district and eventually around the world.

- Vockell, Edward L., and Robert van Deusen. *The Computer and Higher-Order Thinking Skills.* Watsonville, Calif.: Mitchell, 1989.

This book gives detailed descriptions of strategies for using the computer to help students develop their higher-order thinking skills. Students must often integrate language skills with other skills in order to think and solve problems effectively.

- Whitaker, Barbara, Eileen Schwartz, and Edward L. Vockell. *The Computer in the Reading Curriculum.* Watsonville, Calif.: Mitchell, 1989.

  A companion to the present volume, this book goes into specific detail on strategies for using the computer to help students develop reading skills.

A P P E N D I X *D*

SOURCES FOR SOFTWARE

The following are the addresses of the vendors whose software has been cited throughout this book:

Advanced Ideas
2902 San Pablo Avenue
Berkeley, CA 94702

Aldus Corporation
411 First Avenue South
Seattle, WA 98104

Baudville
1001 Medical Park Drive
Grand Rapids, MI 49506

Beagle Brothers
6215 Ferris Square,
Suite 100C
San Diego, CA 92121

Broderbund Software
17 Paul Drive
San Rafael, CA 94903

CE Software
P. O. Box 65580
West Des Moines, IA 50265

Claris
440 Clyde Avenue
Mountain View, CA 94043

Compu-Teach
78 Olive Street
New Haven, CT 06511

Conduit
University of Iowa
Oakdale Campus
Iowa City, IA 52242

CUE Softswap
P. O. Box 271704
Concord, CA 94527-1704

D. C. Heath
125 Spring Street
Lexington, MA 02173

Davidson & Associates
3135 Kashiwa Street
Torrance, CA 90505

DesignWare
185 Berry Street
San Francisco, CA 94114

Dialog Information Retrieval
Services
3460 Hillview Avenue
Palo Alto, CA 94304

Didatech Software Limited
810 Broadway, Suite 549
Vancouver, BC, Canada V5Z 4C9

DLM: Developmental Learning
Materials
One DLM Park
Allen, TX 75002

Education Systems Corporation
P. O. Box 7210
Mountain View, CA 94039

Educational Technology
6150 N. 16th Street
Phoenix, AZ 85016

Electronic Arts
2755 Campus Drive
San Mateo, CA 94403

Encyclopedia Britannica
425 N. Michigan Avenue
Chicago, IL 60611

EPIE Institute
Box 839
Water Mill, NY 11976

First Byte
2845 Temple Avenue
Long Beach, CA 98006

Follett Software Company
4506 N.W. Highway
Crystal Lake, IL 60014

Gamco Industries
Box 1911
Big Spring, TX 79720

Grolier Electronic Publishing
95 Madison Avenue
New York, NY 10016

Hartley Courseware
123 Bridge
Dimondale, MI 48821

Houghton Mifflin Educational
Software Division
One Beacon Street
Boston, MA 02107

IBM
P. O. Box 1329
Boca Raton, FL 33432

JMH Software of Minnesota, Inc.
P. O. Box 41308
Minneapolis, MN 55441

Kinko's Service Corporation
Academic Courseware Exchange
255 W. Stanley Avenue
P. O. Box 8000
Ventura, CA 93002-8000

Koala Technologies
70 N. Second Street
San Jose, CA 95113

LCSI
1000 Roche Boulevard
Vaudreuil, Quebec
Canada J7V 6B3

Learning Company
545 Middlefield Road, Suite 170
Menlo Park, CA 94025

Learning Lab Software Publishing
Company
8883 Reseda Boulevard
Northridge, CA 91325

Learning Well
200 S. Service Road
Roslyn Heights, NY 11577

MECC: Minnesota Educational
Computing Consortium
3490 Lexington Avenue North
St. Paul, MN 55126

Mediagenic
3885 Bohannon Drive
Menlo Park, CA 94025

Midwest Software
Box 214
Farmington, MI 48024

Milliken Publishing Company
P. O. Box 21579
St. Louis, MO 63132

Mindscape
3444 Dundee Road
Northbrook, IL 60062

Omega Star, Inc.
Box 87413
Houston, TX 77287

Oryx Press
2214 North Central at Encanto
Phoenix, AZ 85004

Prescription Learning (Jostens)
6170 Cornerstone Court, E,
Suite 300
San Diego, CA 92121

Random House School Division
201 E. 50th Street
New York, NY 10022

Right On Programs
1737 Veteran's Memorial Drive
Cental Islip, NY 11722

Roger Wagner Publishing
1050 Pioneer Way, Suite P
El Cajon, CA 92020

Scarborough Systems
55 S. Broadway
Tarytown, NY 10591

Scholastic
730 Broadway
New York, NY 10003

Schoolhouse Software
290 Brighton
Elk Grove, IL 60007

Sensible Software
335 E. Big Beaver, Suite 207
Troy, MI 48083

Sierra On-Line
36575 Mudge Ranch Road
Coarsegold, CA 93614

South-Western Publishing
Company
5101 Madison Road
Cincinnati, OH 45227

Spinnaker Software Corporation
One Kendall Square
Cambridge, MA 02139

Springboard Software
7807 Crekridge Circle
Minneapolis, MN 55435

Stephen Marcus
SCWriP, University of California
Santa Barbara, CA 93106

Styleware
5250 Gulstone, Suite 2E
Houston, TX 77081

Sunburst Communications
39 Washington Avenue
Pleasantville, NY 10570

SVE: Society for Visual Education
1345 Diversey Parkway
Chicago, IL 60614

Teacher Support Software
502 N.W. 75th Street, Suite 380
Gainesville, FL 32601

Teach Yourself by Computer
Software
2128 W. Jefferson Road
Pittsford, NY 14534

Techware
P. O. Box 151085
Altamonte Springs, FL 32715

Timeworks Platinum
444 Lake Cook Road
Deerfield, IL 60015

Tom Snyder Productions
123 Mt. Auburn Street
Cambridge, MA 02138

Troll Associates
100 Corporate Drive
Mohawk, NJ 07430

Walt Disney Personal Computer
Software
500 S. Buena Vista
Burbank, CA 91521

Wasatch Micro Systems
7630 Twin Lake Circle
Salt Lake City, UT 84121

Weekly Reader Family Software
245 Long Hill
Middletown, CT 06457

WICAT
1875 South State Street, Box 539
Orem, UT 84058

INDEX